With Wings As Eagles

William B. Oglesby, Jr.

Toward Personal Christian Maturity

Abingdon/Nashville

WITH WINGS AS EAGLES

Library of Congress Cataloging in Publication Data

OGLESBY, WILLIAM B
  With wings as eagles.
  1. Christian life—1960-   I. Title.
BV4501.2.035 1980 248′.4   79-18717

ISBN 0-687-45880-3

Scripture quotations are chiefly from the Revised Standard Version of
the Bible, copyright 1946 and 1952 by the Division of Christian
Education of the National Council of Churches, and are used by
permission. However, the Scripture quotations quoted by characters
in the narrative are from the King James Version because that is the
version most people grew up with and would most easily recall as
adults.

MANUFACTURED BY THE PARTHENON PRESS AT
NASHVILLE, TENNESSEE, UNITED STATES OF AMERICA

Preface to the Second Edition

It has been more than a dozen years since *With Wings As Eagles* first appeared as a study book in the then Covenant Life Curriculum. I had been asked to write a book on personal Christian maturity, and after several unsuccessful starts decided to abandon an essay format and write a narrative of human pilgrimage.

So it is, that this is essentially a fictionalized account using the biblical model of the Elder Brother and the Prodigal (Luke 15) to tell the story in which all of us participate in one sense or other. In this story we come to know Frank and William, and in so doing find ourselves caught up in the lives of Mary, of George and Grace, of John and Martha, of Miss Morrison, Dr. Watson, Harold, and a host of others whose pilgrimage helps us in understanding our own.

All the people in this story are real people, although the data have been altered enough so that their true identity cannot be detected. They are people I knew many years ago when I was a parish pastor, people who were willing for me to become a part of their lives in a very significant fashion. We laughed together, we cried together, we wrestled together with the tearing issues that emerge in human relationships. There were times of great triumph, and there were times of agonizing failure. And through it all they became my greatest teachers, the "living human documents" to use Anton Boisen's phrase.

It was in the 1940s that I first became associated with Alcoholics Anonymous. As I listened to the stories of bitter tragedy and was privileged to participate in the liberation experienced by so many men and women, the concluding verses of Isaiah 40 continually came to mind. "Hast thou not known? hast thou not heard, that the everlasting God, the Lord, the Creator of the ends of the earth, fainteth not, neither is weary? there is no searching of his understanding. He giveth power to the faint; and to them that have no might he increaseth strength. Even the youths shall faint and be weary, and the young men shall utter fall: But they that wait upon the Lord shall renew their strength; they shall mount up with wings as eagles; they shall run and not be weary; and they shall walk, and not faint" (Isaiah 40:28-31). Slowly, the conviction formed that one day I would attempt to tell their story, which is the story of all of us whatever our "presenting symptom." Today, most of those I knew in AA over thirty years ago are no longer living, but my memory of them is as vivid as if it were yesterday. I continue to be grateful to them for the ways they opened for me the doors of understanding by allowing me to be a part of their struggle.

This, then, is their story, and the story of countless others whose lives enriched my own. For that reason I am pleased that *With Wings As Eagles,* having gone out of print, is now available again for reading and study. I must say, in all candor, that reading it now, I am amazed at the way the issue of masculine/feminine language was not a part of our thinking in the 1960s. We were caught in the civil rights struggle, the tragedy of Viet Nam, and the pressures of dealing with the violence epitomized in the assassination of the President. These seemed to have crowded out matters that now catch our attention, such as world hunger, nuclear rearmament, and the sense in which our use of language obscures the appropriate awareness of women as persons. I decided to leave the text as it was written since it represents in and of itself part and parcel of the continuing human struggle. We have come a long way since the mid-sixties, and still have a long way to go. But the fact that we can no longer settle for "sexist" language is gratifying. I trust that you, the reader, will rejoice with me that we have come so far in so short a time, and allow the evidence of progress here to be an encouragement for us all that we can move forward on other fronts as well.

And so, I invite you to enter into the lives of these people, and let them enter yours. It is my hope and expectation that they will mean as much to you as they have to me. As noted above, they are all persons I have known, living in a city in the southern United States. Because that is so, the cultural and sociological factors of that region naturally permeate the narrative. Even so, the unity of human nature transcends regional practice, and I believe you can readily translate these experiences into your own idiom.

At the end of the text there is an Index of Scripture References signifying the ways the biblical material is an informing factor in understanding the human pilgrimage.

Following the Index there are suggestions for the ways this book may be used which have been relayed to me by individuals and groups across the country. I would be happy to hear from any of you in regard to other fashions you have discovered useful in making the content of this story of value in your own pilgrimage toward personal Christian maturity.

Wm. B. Oglesby, Jr.
Richmond, Virginia
Summer, 1979

They that wait upon the Lord

shall renew their strength;

they shall mount up with wings as eagles;

they shall run,

and not be weary;

and they shall walk,

and not faint.

ISAIAH 40:31 K.J.V.

Contents

1. THE BEGINNING   11
Grow up in every way

2. CONSCIENCE   25
Keep your conscience clear

3. ANXIETY   43
Wretched man that I am

4. HOSTILITY   59
Be angry but do not sin

5. DECISION   75
Therefore choose life

6. FREEDOM   93
The law of the Spirit of life in Christ Jesus has set me free

7. FAITH   111
This is the victory . . . even our faith

8. HOPE   129
Hope does not disappoint us

9. LOVE   147
The greatest of these is love

10. JOY   163
That your joy may be full

11. PEACE   181
Peace . . . which passes all understanding

12. GRATITUDE   197
In everything . . . with thanksgiving

13. THE GOAL   215
I can do all things in him who strengthens me

NOTES   235

SCRIPTURE INDEX   237

SUGGESTIONS FOR USE BY INDIVIDUALS AND GROUPS   238

Grow up in every way
EPHESIANS 4:15

1
The Beginning

FRANK MASON sat staring vacantly into the dying coals of the fire. This would probably be the last fire of the year, and he hated to see it go out. The room had gradually become chilled, but somehow he hadn't noticed. He was vaguely conscious that it had grown late, very late. Is it too late? Is it too late? The question kept coming back, and he didn't know the answer. He closed his eyes as if to shut out the memory of what had happened, but how could you forget the biting words?

"Bill! Watch out, Bill! For heaven's sake, why do you have to be so clumsy!"

"But, Dad, I was only . . ."

"Don't 'But, Dad' me, young man! You know better than to play with the bookends, and especially on the coffee table."

Bill burst into tears and buried his face in his mother's lap.

"Frank, I'm ashamed of you! I asked Bill to bring me that bookend. Don't be so childish! He didn't mean to drop it."

"Now don't you start in on me. Isn't it enough for him to break the glass without you putting in your two cents' worth?"

"I don't know what's the matter with you, Frank, but whatever it is, I don't have to sit here and listen to that!" Mary slammed the hall door as she took Bill back to the bedroom.

For awhile Frank thought she might come back, but she didn't. What is the matter with me? Why do my nerves seem so frayed? Of course he knew it was childish to fly off the handle; but it hurt when she said so, and it hurt not to know why, and it hurt not to know what to do. Guess there's nothing to do about it tonight. Anyhow, he knew he had to get to bed and get some sleep. Or try to. Tomorrow was another day, and maybe it'd be different then. Maybe it would. He rose slowly and threw his cigarette into the fire. Tomorrow will be different. It has to be. It has to be.

MARY could not get to sleep. She'd heard the clock strike eleven. Then twelve. Frank must still be in the living room. What is happening to us? We seem to quarrel more and more these days. This can't go on, it just can't. But Frank ought to realize that Bill is only four years old and you can't expect him to do everything just right. And yet it doesn't help to fly into a rage and yell at Frank. I know that. But he ought not to hop on Bill all the time. Twelve-thirty. She'd have to take another one of those tablets Dr. Harris had given her. Would the time ever come when she could get to sleep without them? Wonder when Frank's coming back.

BILL had long since fallen into deep sleep. He was tired. The big boys who go to school had let him play ball with them when they came home. Actually, his job was to stand behind the catcher and chase any balls that got away. There weren't too many, but it was an important thing to do. One of them had said "Nice going" when he kept the ball from rolling into a mud puddle. He couldn't throw it very far or very straight, but he was learning.

It'd be nice if Dad had time to teach him just a little. It was hard to figure Dad out. Hard to figure any grown-ups out, but particularly Dad. They told you not to fuss and fight, but they fussed and fought. Maybe the rules were different for older people. He'd sure like to be an older people. It must be wonderful, getting to do just as you pleased. You could stay up as late as you wanted, and when you dropped something it would be just an accident—not clumsy at all. And you could fuss at people whenever you wanted to. Well, maybe he wouldn't do that. But when he got older, he'd show them.

FRANK stopped by Bill's room on his way to bed. For a moment he stood silent. He could see the tousled head resting on the little pillow, and by the dim light from the hall he could recognize the outline of a baseball glove clutched in his hand. For a moment he was still and everything was quiet. He could hear the regular breathing of deep sleep. How could you turn back the clock? How could you be young again? Could you start over? It really *would* be different, then. Maybe.

He found himself remembering the words of a poem he hadn't thought of for years. Must have been in Miss Morrison's class that he'd learned it. She was always teaching them poetry and things like that.

> I remember, I remember The house where I was born,
> The little window where the sun Came peeping in at morn;

How did it go? The words wouldn't come. Something about fir trees. Oh yes, now I have it.

> I remember, I remember The fir-trees dark and high;
> I used to think their slender tops Were close against the sky:
> It was a childish ignorance, But now 'tis little joy
> To know I'm farther off from heaven Than when I was a boy.[1]

He had wondered what it meant when he had learned it. Strange that he should think of it now. It'd be nice to be back in Miss Morrison's class again, learning poetry and hearing her say, "That was just splendid, Frank." Sometimes it'd been real hard to learn, but it was worth it when she said you had done a good job. I'd like to do good now, but it's harder. Lots harder. You could memorize a poem, then, or work a problem in arithmetic or go to Sunday school every Sunday and get a pin. But it's not like that now.

IT IS NOT EASY to define maturity. This is not to say that no one knows what it means. We speak of grain or fruit as being mature when it is ripe; we speak of judgments or decisions as being mature when they are sound; we speak of plans and programs as being mature when they are completely worked out. We also speak of persons as being mature, but here the meaning becomes more complex. It is evident that maturity is not the same thing as growth, although we speak of growing into maturity. Rather, maturity implies a quality of growth different from growth which is simply the addition of more of the same.

From one point of view, we think of maturity as being a goal toward which we strive, an ideal we hope to attain. From another point of view, we think of maturity as being a state or condition, a quality which can be possessed and which can be demonstrated. The meaning is complicated by the fact that in certain instances the lack of maturity is considered appropriate, but in other instances it is inappropriate. We judge Bill's behavior differently from that of Frank or Mary. We can understand Bill's immaturity; but we react differently when we encounter it in his parents.

Is it completely accurate to say that Frank is immature? It is evident that he lost his temper, that he spoke sharply to his wife and son. In practically any definition of personal maturity one would expect to find the ability to deal with tension, to behave responsibly in time of crisis, to sustain pressure, to manifest a genuine understanding of and concern for others. In this sense, therefore, we would have to say that Frank's behavior was immature. But is this the same as saying that Frank is immature? There is, of course, much more to the story. If we look more closely, we will note that Frank is a person of genuine responsibility in the world of finance and is an executive in an important business firm. He has not attained this position overnight. Following graduation from college, he continued his business education even after he became employed as a junior executive, and gradually worked his way up through the organization. If we were to raise the question of his maturity at the office, we would probably receive an affirmative answer. Does this mean that he is mature in one situation and immature in another? If maturity is a quality of growth, does it apply equally to all areas of the person's life, or is it more evident in some areas than in others?

FRANK is a member of the church. He can remember when he and some of his friends attended a communicants' class that met on Saturday mornings from ten o'clock until eleven o'clock, and subsequently "joined" the church one Sunday morning. The minister had asked them several questions which he had already explained to them in the six sessions of the class. Frank had been to all but one, and that Saturday he had gone with his family to visit his grandmother. The questions were hard, but the answers were not too hard. At the right time, the minister concluded with the words, "Do you?" and everyone was supposed to answer, "I do." He could do that, all right. He didn't seem to feel much different after that Sunday, but he knew that he could take Communion when the trays were passed around. When he stopped to think about it now, he realized that it really hadn't meant much to him at the time. But it was certainly a good thing to do. Everybody agreed about that. He could still remember them saying that they were so proud of him and wasn't it nice that he was a member of the church now, and didn't he look fine standing up there with the others and wouldn't his Uncle Frank have been proud of him today.

If you'd asked Frank whether he considered himself mature, in all likelihood he would have said, "Of course." This wouldn't have meant that he was not troubled by his own behavior; but a person just doesn't come right out and say he is immature. You can't say that, even if you feel it. Why, what would they think if you ever said a thing like that?

But what *do* you say, and how do you say it? How do you say, for example, that you wish you could pray? He had known how to pray ever since he was a little boy. It had seemed so easy to pray then. "Now I lay me down to sleep, I pray Thee, Lord, my soul to keep." For a long time he had thought it was "I pray *the* Lord my soul to keep. If I should die before I wake, I pray the Lord, my soul to take." He hadn't wanted to die before he waked, and he had wished that part wasn't in the prayer. But it was there, and you said it just like they taught it to you. And of course you didn't let them know that you didn't like that part. There were other things, too, that you weren't very sure about. How did God take your soul if you did die before you waked? But that was in the prayer, and it was better to go on and say it. It was easy to pray when somebody gave you the words, even if you didn't know what they meant. They all said that Frank had learned to say his prayers so well. "God bless Papa and Mama and Frank, and help Frank to be a good boy and help him mind his Mama." You could pray, then. How do you find the words now? Who tells you the right words to say? O, God, help Frank to be a good boy. Amen.

IT IS EASIER to define maturity than to attain it. It didn't always seem so. There was a time when it seemed that maturity would come with the passing years. This was the way Bill thought of it, when he thought of it at all. People were always asking him, "What are you going to be when you grow up?" He wished they wouldn't ask him things like that. He never knew what to answer, although it was clear that some answer was expected. Gradually he had learned that if you told them "a cowboy" or "an astronaut" everybody would laugh and be pleased with you, and look at each other and make comments about you. What he really guessed he would be when he grew up was *grown*. It would be good to be grown up. Then maybe people wouldn't ask questions you couldn't answer, or make you do things you didn't want to do. Yes, it would be wonderful to be grown up. You could reach things that were too high now, and you'd know everything. You'd be able to throw a ball as far as anybody, and the big boys would let you play ball with them right out on the diamond and not just back behind the catcher. And when you said something people would listen to you, really listen, and they would believe you. Yes, it would be wonderful all right.

WHEN FRANK thought about maturity he realized it was not quite that simple. The years had passed, all right, and in one sense he couldn't complain. He remembered how he had felt during those early days in the office when he was just starting out. He'd make it. He knew he would. He would have to work hard, but he was willing to do that. He used to think that it would be different if he could just get past thirty. No one really paid much attention to you while you were still in your twenties. But after you were thirty, then they would recognize that what you had to say amounted to something. Well, in one sense, it had happened just like that. But somehow, everything hadn't been solved on the day following his thirtieth birthday. True, he had been moved into an office by himself, and had his own secretary, and his name was on the door. And yet the freedom hadn't come. His time seemed less and less his own. And he still wasn't sure they listened to him. Oh, they were respectful and nodded their heads when he talked. But did they really listen? He could remember when he used to pass the door of this office and dream of the time when he'd be in it with his name on the frosted glass.

Well, here he was. He couldn't have known there was a kind

of loneliness in here. People didn't drop by like they used to when his desk was in the big office pool. Oh, they came in all right, but it wasn't the same. He could hear them now, laughing around the water cooler. That was Charlie telling one he'd heard in Detroit last week. They listened to Charlie, that was for sure. Maybe it would be better to be like Charlie. He sure took things as they came. Nothing ever fazed him, nothing.

They've moved back to their desks now. Got to get these reports finished. Wonder if the estimates on the Willis contract will stand up? This is a rough way to have to do it, but we really need that one. We've got to have it. It was a tough break missing the Baxter deal. How was he to know that old man Baxter was a sucker for a lot of smooth talk and personal flattery? You couldn't keep up with everything. Charlie could have told him that, but didn't. Things were sure a lot simpler before he moved into this place. Before, you could slip out and go to the ball game and no one would ever know. But you couldn't do that now. What are you going to be when you grow up? He shook his head as he pressed the button for his secretary to come in. What indeed?

THE DAY BEGAN soon enough for Mary. Too soon, as a matter of fact. When you can't get to sleep, you just aren't ready to face the endless round of cooking, dishes, washing, ironing, PTA, bridge lessons, and no telling what else. It was good to have something to do, however. It sort of kept you from thinking, and she'd been doing entirely too much thinking recently.

They ate breakfast in silence. That is, as far as conversation was concerned. There was plenty of noise. Frank always rattled the paper as he tried to get it propped up against the toaster. This morning it got on her nerves. When Bill spilled some of his milk she snapped at him and then scolded Betty.

"Can't you be more careful? Hold your glass with both hands, and stop drinking when you've got your mouth full of food."

"Yes 'um."

"Now drink your orange juice, Betty. Swallow, Betty. Betty, for goodness' sake stop dropping your spoon on the floor!"

Frank slammed his paper on the table. "Do you have to start off the day jawing at the children?"

Betty started to cry. Mary picked her up and walked to the window. Just at that moment she didn't trust herself to say anything. She heard the door slam as he stormed out of the house and got into the car.

Well, things were quiet now, on the surface, that is. Bill was outside riding his tricycle and Betty had had her bath and her bottle and would soon be asleep. The sink was still full of breakfast dishes, but they would have to wait, for a little while anyhow. The same old questions came but there were no answers. What is happening to us? We fuss and fight like children, but what can you do? Is everybody like this? How do they stand it? No, not everybody. Grace Nelson always seems to have everything under control. Whenever you go into her house you find things neat as a pin. And Grace has four children, the oldest only eight. Maybe George helps her some. It would be nice if Frank were a little more help. They hadn't talked in so long, she wondered what he was thinking about these days. Well, maybe they'd get to take that trip this summer. And besides, the dishes couldn't wait any longer.

It will be nice when Betty is a little older and I can teach her to cook and sew. They'd probably be great pals just as she and her mother had been. She thought about those days often. It would be nice to be able to turn back the clock. Sometimes I'd like to climb up in her lap and let her rock me and sing to me the way she used to do. She would kiss me, and everything would be all right then. Yes, everything was all right then. Not like now. I used to think it would be wonderful to grow up, and to have a house of my own, and children of my own, and dishes of my own, and some flowers.

WE HAVE SAID THAT MATURITY can be thought of as the goal of life, that ideal toward which we strive, that fullness which is the mark of the complete man. At the same time, we have also said that maturity is always a process, always a becoming, always an unfolding and an enlarging of the horizons. From a fixed point of view, maturity is that quality of life in which a person has strength and resources sufficient to meet the present situation, has the ability to draw wisdom from the heritage in which he stands without being a slave to the past, has the capacity to re-

spond to the challenge and opportunity of the future without ne-
glecting the tasks at hand. From a process point of view, maturity
is always relative, embracing being and becoming, attainment and
striving, realization and anticipation.

As we look at Frank and Mary, at Bill and Betty, there are certain factors which help us to understand their movement toward
maturity. First, it is clear that all of them have grown, although not
in precisely the same ways. They are not what they once were.
Betty can hold a cup, now, although she does it with some difficulty. Bill can throw a ball; not very well, to be sure, but better
than last year. Mary has learned how to manage her house, although at times she feels that her neighbor, Grace, does the job with
greater efficiency and against greater odds. Frank is certainly successful in the business world from almost any criterion, although he
encounters certain frustrations in the discharge of his responsibili-
ties.

We can also see that their growth has not always been even.
Betty and Bill are often puzzled by the behavior of their parents,
and their behavior tends to reflect the tension which they sense even
when it is not expressed, a tension which becomes terribly threaten-
ing at the times of quarrel. Mary and Frank, on the other hand, are
conscious of the fact that all is not well with them, but they are
puzzled about how to remedy the situation. Both feel caught in the
pressures of daily routine, and find that they are unable to com-
municate with each other.

Moreover, we are aware of the fact that all four are still in the
process of growing, but not in the same way. Betty and Bill are still
growing physically as well as emotionally and spiritually. They are
unable to coordinate their muscular activity, and often find themselves frustrated by tasks that seem so simple for others. Their
mood shifts are quite intense and variable, and they usually reflect
the changing circumstances of their surroundings. Mary and Frank
have attained their physical growth, although there are still physical
changes occurring in them each day. It is evident, however, that
they have not attained emotional or spiritual maturity. For this reason, they find it more difficult to deal with their own mood shifts
than the children do. They know the kinds of expectations considered appropriate to their adult status, and recognize the validity of

these expectations. Thus, when they fail to measure up, they must search for some means to justify or to rationalize their own behavior.

Beyond this, it is evident that not one of them is genuinely content to remain as he is. Despite the fact that they find themselves resisting change, they also long for it. Their conception of what is possible and their idea of what is desirable differ from time to time. Yet, at the deepest level, they do not choose to be as they are. Frank does not want to lose his temper; Mary does not deliberately lose patience with the children; Bill would like to be able to throw the ball with more accuracy; and Betty will be glad when she can eat at the table with the other members of the family. There is a kind of discontent within them which presses them forward. Whatever happens, they are unable to remain where they are. However stubbornly they may resist the forces of growth within them, they will move in some direction.

Finally, it is evident that each of them will need some help if he is to grow qualitatively. That help will not be the same for all, nor will it be the same at all times for any one of them. Nevertheless, they are not completely self-sufficient and never will be.

MARY had pondered the matter of help a great deal lately. It was not the kind of thing you could bring up with just anyone. She could have talked it over with her mother, but now that was no longer possible. She still remembered the day of the funeral. Dr. Watson had been a real comfort to her. She could recall the words he spoke to begin the service: "Our help is in the name of the LORD, who made heaven and earth." She hadn't really heard a great deal of what he had said, but she was grateful to him for his kindness. Particularly since they really hadn't been too regular in their church attendance these past few years. She hadn't, anyway. Since Bill was born, she supposed. Before the time came when she could have gone with him to Sunday school she was expecting Betty. Besides, going to church was sort of a matter of habit. But in one sense it was strange not to go regularly—not at all like it used to be when she was younger. It wasn't that she didn't pray. She'd said her prayers since she was too little to remember. But now as she thought about it, it struck her for the first time what a strange phrase that was, "say your prayers." Were prayers supposed to be merely words to be said? Did she really know how to pray? When Dr. Watson said, "Our help is in the name of the Lord," you got the feeling that it really meant something to him. Which was only natural, when you stopped to think about it. He was the minister, and if it didn't mean something to him, then who could be expected to find meaning in it? Maybe she could talk to him about Frank. But what could you say? Besides, he was terribly busy and Frank would probably be furious. "Our help is in the name of the Lord." It certainly sounded comforting, but when she said it, the words seemed rather hollow.

In any event, she was glad that Bill had already learned to say his prayers each night. "Now I lay me down to sleep . . . God bless Daddy, Mama, Betty, and help Bill to be a good boy . . ." It was so easy for a child, not so easy when you grow up. She could still remember those days in college when she had suddenly come up against the fact that there were many people who didn't even believe in God. Or said they didn't. When they discussed it she always seemed to end rather lamely. It was hard to say *why* you believed in God, but you just knew you did, or at least felt as if you did. That was probably when she first began to miss church services, she supposed. It isn't easy to get up on Sunday morning when you are on your own and have been out late on Saturday night.

In her Junior year she'd met Frank. He was already out of college, but was taking some courses in business administration. After a while she'd started going to church with him, and had joined after they were married. It seemed strange to her now as she looked back on it that they had talked very little about their faith. Frank seemed to take it for granted that going to church was what you did. She'd wondered even then what it really meant to him. He certainly was faithful enough as far as attending was concerned, yet she'd never been really sure just what he honestly felt about it. Things might have been a lot different if they had started having family prayer when they were first married. She'd thought about suggesting it on several occasions, but never could find just the right words or the right time. After all, Frank was much more religious than she was, and it seemed strange for her to be the one to bring it up. It was too late, now, of course. After a while you really couldn't say anything like that. Anyhow, now they couldn't even talk to each other, let alone pray together.

FRANK bowed his head at the Civic Club Luncheon while someone gave the invocation. Rather long, he thought. Some people must think they'll be heard for their much speaking. Suddenly it struck him that he really had no reason to be in such a hurry. How strange it was that he was pressing all the time! Hurry up and finish this in order to get on to the next thing, and the next, and the next. "Help us to be still and know that Thou art God." Wonder why he put that in the blessing? The words seemed to echo in his ears. Hard to find time to be still for any purpose these days. The memory of the dying fire came back to him. "Tomorrow will be different." Well, if things were going to be different, you certainly couldn't tell it from what happened at the breakfast table. "In the Master's Name. Amen." Lunch now—the usual meat loaf. No matter, nothing seemed to taste very appetizing these days, anyhow. He found himself drumming on the table with the tips of his fingers. "Be still and know . . ."

"Oh, hello, Craig. Hi, Vince. No, I'm not saving these for anybody. Won't you all sit down?"

WE HAVE SAID THAT MATURITY involves a quality of growth rather than simply the addition of more of the same. As we look at Mary and Frank, we can see that they have within themselves various ideas about God and their relationship to him which never seem to come to focus in any meaningful way. They both grew up with certain religious concepts, and both learned early to say their prayers. They went to church, Frank more regularly than Mary. But they were not able to pray together or even to talk about the things that pertained to their relationship to God. In due time they had sent Bill to Sunday school and Betty would go as soon as she was old enough to behave properly. The paradoxical thing, of course, was that they were themselves "babes in Christ," to use the Apostle Paul's phrase. It is one thing to be a babe in Christ when you are little; but quite another when you are grown. Somehow there is a necessity to keep up appearances, and you hate to admit that there is an emptiness on the inside. Who would understand? Everyone thinks you are getting along just fine. Little by little the gulf widens between what you seem to be and what you actually are. Frank knows that; so does Mary. By now the gulf is quite wide, nor will it be bridged easily. The hopeful fact, of course, is that within they feel a longing for the presence of God, the restlessness "until we rest in thee." The tragic fact is that they can literally see no way to make a start. Thus, to borrow another phrase from the Apostle Paul, they are like "children, tossed to and fro and carried about with every wind of doctrine."

In his Letter to the Ephesians, Paul speaks of the gifts of Christ to the church as being for the explicit purpose that "we all attain to the unity of the faith and of the knowledge of the Son of God, to mature manhood, to the measure of the stature of the fulness of Christ." And then he says, "we are to grow up in every way into him who is the head, into Christ . . ." There are several things in this letter which attract our attention with regard to the attaining of maturity. In the first place, maturity never occurs in isolation. Fullness of life comes in encounters, in relationships with others, in the give-and-take of everyday experiences. At the same time, however, it is also evident that maturity never comes apart from one's relationship to Christ. Paul is not exhorting the Ephesians to raise themselves by their own bootstraps. Rather, his figure of speech is quite dramatic: "You he made alive when you were dead . . ." In the fourth chapter he reaffirms that it is through the "gifts" of Christ that one finds it possible to attain "mature manhood." Finally, Paul calls attention to the fact that Christ is the model or the goal of maturity. "We are," he says, "to grow up in every way into him who is the head, into Christ."

When we think of these things in relation to Mary and Frank we can sense that they have a long way to go. They did not become who they are overnight. The patterns form slowly and after awhile change becomes difficult. But this does not mean that it cannot come. It does mean that the very factors which have blocked their movement toward maturity will continue to stand in their way. The tragic fact is that the things which hinder come to be perceived as the things which are essential, so that the difficulty arises in having to reject the very thing which has become a way of life.

On the positive side of the ledger Frank and Mary have one tremendous asset just now. Both of them have been jolted out of the seeming complacency which is in itself a kind of cover-up for the inner struggle. That the struggle will break through to the surface is inevitable. But when it does, there is a sense of panic because they do not honestly see any possible way out of the dilemma. For them, this is a time of crisis. For awhile, at least, "the hard metal runs." When it has cooled again it will have assumed another form. At this point, it is not possible to predict what that form will be.

In this book we shall be dealing with maturity from many perspectives, but in each instance we will be concerned about the same central focus. We will draw on the insights of the behavioral sciences which have enabled us to see beneath the obvious to discover the significant. We will note the ways in which man tends to destroy his freedom, and the way in which freedom is recovered. And we will set the whole in the context of the Christian faith, drawing on the resources of him who enables us to "grow up in every way."

In the course of our investigation we shall have an opportunity to stand with Mary and Frank as they wrestle with the crisis in which they find themselves. Inevitably their lives will be bound up with those of Bill and Betty. In addition, we shall come to know Grace and George Nelson, Dr. Watson, Miss Morrison, Charlie, Craig and Vince, William, John and Martha Mason, Harold Clark, Dr. Harris and many others whose experiences will help us probe into the depths of behavior, and in whose lives we may come to see our own. It is a kind of pilgrimage which invites us all to "grow up."

Keep your conscience clear
1 PETER 3:16

2
Conscience

"If you ask me, you are just making a mountain out of a mole-hill! What the Sam Hill gets into you, anyhow, Frank? I never saw anybody take on about things like you do."

"But you have to admit that it was a pretty shabby trick."

"Shabby trick, my Aunt Minnie! We got the contract, didn't we? It was just exactly what they would have done if they'd thought of it first. In a business like this you can't go around with stars in your eyes. Like it or not, it's dog eat dog.

"Well, I don't like it, Charlie. Oh, sure, I know things are rough and you can't let go, even for a minute. But that's not what I'm talking about, and you know it. We were looking right down their throats from the word go. Those guys have to eat, too. They have kids just like you do. How would you like it if you'd been on the losing end? I can hear it now!"

"Don't go preaching to me, old buddy. You are talking like some kind of white-washed angel now, but I don't remember hearing any of these ideas when we were up to our ears getting the specifications together. Why is it that you always get soft in the heart after it's too late to do anything about it?"

"What makes you think I just started feeling this way?"

"Well, I can't read your mind, can I? If you really want to make something out of it, why don't you tell the Chief? Boy, I'd like to have a motion picture of that conference. Simmer down. You make it sound like we'd just robbed some old lady of her last knitting needle. What we did was perfectly legal. The Chief saw to that. Nobody'd have a leg to stand on in court."

"That isn't what I mean, and you know it. It just sorta sticks in my throat that we have to operate like this. Doesn't it bother you at all, even a little? I mean, really?"

"Nah! I got over that a long time ago. You just have to make up your mind that business is business. It doesn't have anything to do with what you think or say outside the office. In here that's the way things are, and the sooner you get this the better."

"Yeah, I guess you're right. But I don't like it. I really don't."

"OK, OK, so you don't like it. It puts groceries on the table and shoes on your kids' feet. It keeps up the payments on your mortgage and lets your wife run up a pretty bill anywhere in town she wants to. You like all that well enough, and as for the rest of it, I guess you'll just have to lump it. I can't stand around here jawing all afternoon. Those specs have to be in the post office by five o'clock. I'll see you tomorrow—if your conscience will let you come back to this 'den of iniquity'!"

Frank was conscious of Charlie's footsteps going down the hall and then he heard the front door close. Charlie was so sure of himself. He even closed doors with a finality. He didn't slam them, but you could tell that they were closed, all right. Wonder what it would be like to be that sure? He began to stuff things into his briefcase. It was late already and he had promised Mary that he would go by the cleaners on the way home.

Funny that Charlie had said, "if your conscience will let you." Hard to tell, now, just what he meant by that. Charlie surely didn't seem to have one, at least not so you could tell it. Frank wondered whether it was a good thing to have a conscience. Maybe it would be better just to go through life with no twinges on the inside. Good or bad, though, this conscience of mine sure does give me a fit. Yet Charlie was right. I wasn't able to say anything while it was still possible to do something about it. Had it always been that way? And why was it that some people didn't seem to think there was anything wrong with these things that proved to be so bothersome to him? Could it be that they were right and he was wrong? He got into his car and turned west on Maple. Traffic seems pretty bad. Probably won't make it home by suppertime. Hope Mary won't be irritable. Shouldn't have talked so long with Charlie, I guess.

LIKE SO MANY WORDS in everyday use, conscience means many things to many people. Probably the most general usage describes an inner perception of right and wrong and a sense of personal responsibility to do the right, together with a sense of uneasiness or guilt about failure to do the right. Such a definition, however, is fraught with many difficulties which become quite apparent as soon as more subtle questions are asked. Is there some kind of universal standard of right and wrong which is valid for all people, or is the distinction between right and wrong a relative matter? Why is it that some persons are filled with remorse over a seeming trifle, whereas others apparently feel no compunction at all in the face of behavior which is generally considered outrageous? What accounts for the fact that different cultures place conflicting values on similar behaviors? In what sense does the conscience change as the person grows up?

ORDINARILY, FRANK didn't think much about the meaning of conscience. He knew he had one, all right, and sometimes he wished he didn't. But it was there, and had been as long as he could remember. He hoped Mary wouldn't ask him about the contract. He'd told her often enough that he didn't like to "bring the office home," that when he got out of that "rat race" the thing he wanted most was to forget it all. Usually she wouldn't bring it up, but he wasn't sure this time. For days they'd been working overtime getting the figures together. It was only natural to expect that she would be interested in how it came out. He dreaded going home since she knew that this was the day they were to get the decision.

Boy! People drive crazy in this town! That fellow cut right in front of a whole line of traffic! It would serve him right if somebody smashed right into him! On such matters as traffic behavior there was no question in Frank's mind about right and wrong. He could spot irresponsibility when he saw it, and found himself wishing to mete out stern justice—"an eye for an eye, a tooth for a tooth." There were no shades of gray here, no mitigating circumstances. If everything hadn't happened so fast he might have seen that the driver of the car was a man he knew quite well. In fact, they had been talking only yesterday about the baby he and his wife were expecting any day. He might have remembered that the street down which the driver turned went to Memorial Hospital. But he didn't think of these things. It is easier to be positive if you do not have to take into account the personal factors. Anyhow, right was right and wrong was wrong no matter what might lie behind it. He wondered what Mary would say when he got home.

He found himself thinking back to a time when he was just a boy. Was he ten? Twelve? Funny how you couldn't remember the exact age. He remembered the occasion, well enough. It was a Sunday afternoon. They'd all been to church that morning just as they were all there every Sunday morning. He was nearly grown before he realized that everybody didn't go to church every Sunday. It just never occurred to him that it could be any different. Anyhow he didn't mind going. It was nice to go to church, even when the sermon was too long. You got to see a lot of people and wear your good suit. It was Sunday afternoons that were bad. You couldn't play baseball or swim or do anything that made noise. You could do quiet things like play "Battleship," or maybe sit on the curb and kick cans.

On this particular Sunday he had been sitting on the curb with some of the other fellows in the neighborhood. They'd kicked a can back and forth across the street for awhile, but they were tired of that. After while somebody said, "Tell you what let's do. Let's go to the movies."

"The what?" He was wide-eyed with amazement.

"The movies. What'd you think I said? There's a real good show at the Gem."

"But this is Sunday!"

"Yeah, I know. What else is there to do on Sunday?"

He could still remember the feeling he had had. He could smile now as he recalled wondering if fire from Heaven would come down and devour a person for such a suggestion. But it didn't.

Suddenly they were all looking at him. "Well, do you want to go, or don't you?"

"Aw, come on, you all. Let's not wait around here all day for old Frank. Gee whiz! He's always bringing up something like this."

Even later, he wasn't sure just how things happened after that, but he could remember the terrible feeling inside. He didn't want them to go off and leave him, but he didn't know whether he could bring himself to go to the movies on Sunday or not. He'd found himself walking along with them, hoping that maybe something would happen on the way that would change the course of things. Actually, he guessed he knew it wouldn't. But he was miserable. He couldn't even remember afterwards what the show had been about.

It was after six when he'd finally gotten home. What would they say? He opened the front door as quietly as possible. Maybe he could come in and they wouldn't notice him.

"Where have you been, Frank?" It was his mother in the kitchen.

"Oh, out."

"Well, it's late. We're getting ready to sit down to supper. You'll just have time to wash your hands and get cleaned up."

"I don't want any supper. I'm not hungry." He started upstairs to his room.

"Of course you want your supper. What do you mean you're not hungry?"

He didn't hear the rest of what she said. He slammed the door to his room and fell across the bed. He remembered wishing that he could die. In just a minute he'd hear his father's steps on the stairs. He'd knock first, and then he'd be standing there beside the bed. "What on earth is the matter with you, Son?"

The light turned green, and the car behind him honked impatiently. "All right!" Frank jammed his foot on the gas pedal.

It was after six when he slipped the key in the front door. "That you, Frank? Where have you been? I was getting worried about you. Supper's ready. Did you get the Willis contract?"

IT IS NOT EASY TO DETERMINE just when the awareness of conscience begins. Long before any critical evaluations emerge, the child understands the kinds of things "we" are for. There is a value system already established in the family, in the neighborhood, in the culture. In this concentric relationship he begins to identify himself. He knows that we are Presbyterians or Baptists or Methodists or whatever. He knows that we are white or black or yellow. He knows that we are Southerners or Northerners or Midwesterners. He knows that we sleep later on Sunday morning and have a different kind of breakfast than we ordinarily have, put on different clothes, do different things. There is no question, really, but that these things are right. He is not actually aware that there is any choice in the matter of value. There is choice only in the matter of personal behavior. He comes to the realization that when he does the kinds of things we are for, things go better, and the big people like him better and say that he is a good boy. At other times, when he is upset by the way things are going, he may do the kinds of things that "we" are not for. This, too, produces a response from the big people. They do not seem to like him as well now, and say that he is a bad boy. In either case, the value system is not in question, but simply his response to it.

FRANK was the first child. It was not difficult for him to perceive that when he was a good boy people said nice things about him. Somewhere deep within he could still remember the words: "Be a good boy and brush your teeth." "Be a good boy and pick up your clothes." "Be a good boy and mind your manners." "Be a good boy and say your prayers." It was usually not too hard to be a good boy. All you had to do was be careful. Sometimes you weren't quite sure what was expected, but not often. Most of the time when you weren't a good boy it was because you had not remembered, or you had thought they weren't around. Like the day he had pulled the leaves off the shrubs. He hadn't meant to do it when he started. Almost by accident he had run his hand down the stem with his thumb and forefinger wrapped around it. The leaves came off in a pretty rosette form. Incredible. Would it happen again? You could try. It did. And another. And another. And another. He was standing in a shambles of leaves when his mother drove up. "Frank!" she had cried. "What on earth possessed you to strip the leaves off the hedge! You can just march yourself right upstairs! And don't you ever let me catch you doing that again!"

He could remember thinking, "OK, from now on I'll make sure not to let you catch me." That part had turned out to be not quite as easy as being a good boy. You had to be careful about what you let them see. Sometimes you'd just forget, but less and less. After awhile it was just easier to be a good boy all the time, or at least as much as you could. Before long they didn't even have to be there. If you did something they weren't for, you got to worrying about what would happen if they knew. It was as if something within you said, "Better not." Or at other times, when you had already done it, the "something" said, "You're going to catch it now." Better to be a good boy. They loved you better then. Only trouble was, they were not always clear on what being a good boy meant, or at least it seemed so. Even stranger, it seemed at times that they did just as nice things for your younger brother, who certainly wasn't a very good boy. He tore up books and drove nails in the back porch. Not that he didn't get his share of switchings, but somehow they didn't seem to faze him.

Frank could remember his mother saying she just didn't know what in the world they would do with William, and why on earth couldn't he be good like Frank, and what did they suppose would happen to him. He wondered where William was now. They didn't hear from him any more. He had left home when he was only nineteen after only one semester in college. The general word was that he was "out West," but that could mean anything. It was better to be a good boy.

DR. WATSON sat in his study and pondered the strange twists and turns a person's life could take. Just that day, two things had happened which illustrated again the wide variety of meanings that exists in the matter of conscience. For one person the slightest deviation from a strict moral code could produce an agony of remorse. For another there seemed to be no twinge of any sort, no matter what the deed.

It had baffled him when he first started out in the ministry many years ago. He could remember how some of the members of his church had been so conscientious that they literally would let nothing stand in the way of doing what they saw as their duty. Actually, it had made him just a little uncomfortable to be with these people. Somehow they made him feel that *he* was not doing all he should, and it had been hard to relax around them. He honestly didn't know what he would do without them, but there were times when he just as honestly didn't know what to do with them. Then there were other persons, a much larger number as he recalled it, who had seemed to take so little interest in the work of the church. He sometimes wondered why they even bothered to have their names on the church roll. Somewhere along the line it must have meant something to them or they wouldn't have joined. But nothing much had seemed to make any difference to them. It had been hard to figure out.

The people who had really baffled him where those who made no pretense at all about the church, or anything else that had to do with right and wrong. He had not actually known these people personally, but he had known enough about them. Often they had gotten their names in the paper. Shameless they were, and getting by with it, too. Talk about conscience, they didn't have any. Or if they did, it was so long ago seared over that there was no sensitivity left. Frankly, it had irritated him sometimes.

As he thought over the events of this day, he wondered how he could ever have believed that matters of conscience were quite that simple. He had long since come to see that people who seemed to be the most conscientious might in fact be harried by agonizing feelings of guilt. What had been even more surprising to him was the discovery that those who seemed to feel no compunction whatsoever were nonetheless burdened by a sense of failure and a fear of retribution.

He thought of Charlotte, a young teen-ager and member of the youth group, as she sat twisting her handkerchief in her hands. Several times she had been on the very verge of tears. Bit by bit the story came out. "It's just awful. I don't know if I can tell you or not. Jack took me to the movie, but when it was over we didn't come straight home." There was a long pause while she choked back the tears. "What must you think of me. I don't know what to say."

"Real hard to find the right words when the story itself is what hurts," he said gently.

"Yes. Yes, that's right. But I have to tell somebody. We went by to get a milk shake at the drive-in, and a bunch of kids were there. When I looked at my watch and saw it was after eleven-thirty, we drove home as fast as we could. Jack turned off the engine and the lights and we sat there for just a minute. Then he came around and let me out, and walked with me to the front door. He held my purse while I opened the door with my key, and when I turned around to say 'good night' he . . . he . . ." She sobbed for a moment, and then bit her lips. "He kissed me, and . . . I *let* him! Then I ran into the house and closed the door, and . . . oh, Dr. Watson, how could I have done it!"

There had been a time in his life when Dr. Watson would have sighed in audible relief, and would have had a hard time keeping from laughing, both in the joy that Charlotte had no more serious matter to report and in amusement that she could have taken such a matter so seriously. That was long ago, however. Through the years he had learned that the content of conscience is a complex matter. And he had also learned that when the conscience hurts, something is wrong. It may or may not be the same thing the person feels is wrong, but something is wrong, nonetheless. It was for this reason he had learned to listen to the person as well as to the story, and he knew that something other than a good-night kiss was troubling Charlotte.

Even as he thought of Charlotte he found himself thinking of Mike Jackson. Everyone in town knew Mike, and generally everyone shuddered when they thought of him. He was a straw boss on a plantation south of town. "Rough and tough as they come" was the description heard most often. Mike was married to a woman in town. No one knew whether she was his third or his fourth wife. But everyone knew that he spent very little time with her, and it was more than rumor that his staying on the plantation bespoke not only a rift between them but also his more than passing interest in a young widow whose morals left much to be desired. Saturday night often found Mike in the county jail roaring drunk. Yes, everybody knew Mike Jackson, and most everybody agreed that there wasn't a moral bone in his body.

"Reverend, this is Mike Jackson." The voice on the phone sounded half fearful, half pleading. "Reverend, could I come talk to you? I'd like to come this afternoon, if that's OK with you."

Half an hour later there was a knock on the door. They'd met before, but you couldn't say they knew each other. Less than two weeks ago Dr. Watson had been fishing on a pond near the plantation, and Mike had come by looking for two mules which had gotten out through a break in the fence. Before he could recognize the men in the boat, he yelled out asking if they had seen the mules, all the while cursing at the top of his voice the ineptness of whoever was responsible for the fence being in poor repair. He'd sputtered to an uneasy halt when Dr. Watson's fishing companion had greeted him, said he'd not seen the mules, and then, "You know Preacher Watson, I reckon. Preacher, this is Mike Jackson."

"Hello, Mike. Pretty tough having to chase those ornery mules through this low country, I reckon."

"Yeah, sure is. Well, Reverend, I didn't notice that was you. I guess I'll be going before those mules get plum out of the county. Hope you all catch a good string."

Now they sat facing each other. Mike hitched forward toward the edge of his chair. "There's something wrong, Reverend, and I want to get it straightened out. I really don't know what it is, and that's the thing that's got me. You see, I haven't ever done anything real bad. Aw, I know I get drunk sometimes, and once or twice I've had to kill a fellow on the plantation who was running wild, but nothing really wrong. But Reverend, there's something awfully wrong with me, and I can't go on like this any longer. Can you help me?"

There had been a time in his life when Dr. Watson would have gasped in amazement, would have found it difficult to keep from voicing a solid rebuttal in regard to what constitutes "bad" behavior, and would have been filled with an almost overwhelming disbelief that such seeming naïveté could be real. That was long ago, however. He had learned that beneath the content of the conscience there is a deeper restlessness that cannot be stilled. Sometimes, as in the case of Charlotte, the person might feel remorse over a matter which seems to be quite trivial. Other times, as in the case of Mike, the person might seem impervious to what by any standard would be adjudged reprehensible behavior. Nevertheless, in each there was something which would not be quieted by facile reassurance on the one hand or moral insensitivity on the other. He found himself musing over Augustine's phrase, "Thou has made us for thyself, and our hearts are restless until they rest in thee."

IT IS EVIDENT that the term "conscience" has many different meanings and is used in a variety of ways. Because this is true, it is no wonder that there has often been considerable disagreement on this issue among those who study human behavior from a sociological, a psychological, or a theological perspective. One of the thorniest issues is whether conscience is simply the result of cultural conditioning, or whether there is some kind of universal moral law which transcends all cultures. There is much evidence that different cultures regard any given behavior or act in vastly different ways. Such matters as the rites of passage in the process of "coming of age," the practice of monogamy or multiple marriage, and the varying attitudes toward older people are but a few of the many that might be cited. Even more subtle are the variations within a given culture regarding what is right and what is wrong.

We saw, for example, that attendance at a motion picture on Sunday was absolutely forbidden as far as Frank was concerned. At the same time we saw that for his playmates such a behavior not only was not wrong, but was, in fact, desirable. It may be argued that Frank's idea more nearly coincides with keeping the Sabbath holy, but many would find it difficult to define holiness in such particular terms. If it is wrong to go to the motion pictures on Sunday, what about listening to the radio? By the time Frank was grown, television had become commonplace. Is it wrong to look at television on Sunday? What if the program includes the showing of a movie?

In the light of these shades of meaning and subtle variations regarding just what is right and what is wrong, it is understandable that many conclude that conscience is purely sociological in essence. There can be no doubt but that the culture in which a person is raised provides the content of the conscience, the kinds of things which are perceived to be acceptable as well as the kinds of things which are perceived to be unacceptable. But when the concept of conscience is reduced to this sort of formula only, there are other questions which are left unanswered. Why is it, for example, that from time to time there are those who stand against the patterns of culture in the name of right? Or, to put it another way, what if the conscience says that the culture is in error? Such a phe‧nomenon is by no means unusual or rare. Thus, a correct understanding of conscience requires not only a consideration of cultural forces but of individual and personal factors as well.

However it is defined, the emergence of conscience involves the whole complex matter of relationships, and the need for acceptance, which is universal. It is difficult, if not impossible, for the child to perceive his acceptance on any but a conditioned basis. "If you are good, you are loved," he reads into all of life. To be "good" inevitably comes to mean the observance of the customs, the mores, the behaviors of those upon whom his existence depends. To be sure, there are times when the relationship is in fact conditioned by behavior. Parents may themselves be so starved for love that they attempt to purchase love and obedience from their children by setting up demands which must be met. The truth is, however, that even in those instances when the love of the parents is most freely given, it is perceived by the child as conditioned.

Whenever limits are set, whenever necessities are spelled out, whenever restrictions are defined, they are seen by the child as the basis for acceptance. There was a time when this fact led to the conclusion that children should never have to encounter limits or experience the discipline of necessities. It soon became clear, however, that to leave the child without such structures was to condemn him to a world so complex that he simply was unable to cope with it, a world wherein he found himself overwhelmed by decisions he was unprepared to make, terrified by the feeling of being alone in the midst of conflicting forces, defeated by being required to run before he had had the opportunity to walk.

This fact led many to consider conscience as merely an aspect of personal development, a necessary dimension for protecting the child from dangers when the parents could not be near and an important means of transmitting the positive value judgments of the past. But when the concept of conscience is seen only in these terms, it is reduced to a kind of transitory device, useful for awhile, but to be dropped when no longer needed. In that sense conscience is in and of itself inconsistent with maturity, since, by definition, when a person becomes mature he has no further need for the assistance of this supporting device.

But, again, such a conclusion raises persistent questions which cannot be overlooked. Why is it, for example, that those who seem to be most settled in their own integrity continue to sense an inner awareness of right and wrong, together with a keen conviction of personal responsibility? Long after it becomes clear that the love of the parents is relatively unconditional, that personal behavior is most often not the criterion of acceptance, that the bonds of relationship are far too strong to be torn by negative feelings or untoward acts, there remains the sure certainty that what is done makes a difference, and that there is no avoiding the fundamental fact of moral law.

The need to recognize the genuine significance of cultural conditioning and personal development, and at the same time to avoid the pitfall of seeing nothing more than these factors, has led to a search for terms which will describe the immature conscience as well as the mature conscience. It is likely that such a search will prove futile in the end. Inevitably it tends to give the impression that these two are separate and discrete, that for awhile the person has an immature conscience and then, hopefully, a mature one. In actual life, no such fine line of demarcation can be drawn. Nevertheless, the notion behind such a search has much validity, for it calls constant attention to the fact that no simple conception of conscience will do.

WHEN WE LOOK CLOSELY at Frank's conversation with Charlie regarding the Willis contract we can see something of the struggle through which he is passing. It is a struggle which involves the tension between certain basic principles on the one hand and the pressure of circumstances on the other. He has to admit that his principles are not sufficiently strong to interfere with his behavior. Yet he has no peace within. He is haunted by a sense of guilt, and he hopes against hope that Mary will not ask him what has happened.

Even more disturbing is the similarity between what is happening to Frank now and what happened when he was a lad. It becomes increasingly clear that the same patterns of behavior have persisted throughout the years. When the time for decision comes, he is unable to resolve the conflict. He feels pushed by the necessity to do what is expected of him, and can honestly think of no convincing argument with which to answer Charlie. In effect, he can't say "no" either to his conscience or to Charlie and the office. More than once he has resolved to "set things straight once and for all," but he isn't even sure what "straight" means. "What we did *was* legal, wasn't it? Besides, in a competitive market doesn't someone always have to lose?"

On a different level, Charlotte struggles with the same tension. She sees no way to resolve her feelings about her date kissing her good night at the door. "How could I have done it?" The frightening thing, as she reflected on it, was that only part of her was against it. And now it is done, and will always be done. She could remember the lines from the *Rubáiyát*:

> The Moving Finger writes; and having writ,
> Moves on: nor all your Piety nor Wit
> Shall lure it back to cancel half a Line,
> Nor all your Tears wash out a Word of it.[1]

How could I have done it?

Strangely enough, Mike's problem is basically no different. Flagrant in his disregard for every known standard of his community, he found himself unmoved by what he would have called a lot of foolishness and old-woman talk. Yet, when at last he comes to Dr. Watson, it is evident that deep within there is a yearning and an agony that had never shown on the surface.

Frank and Charlotte and Mike, whose definitions of right and wrong would be poles apart, are nonetheless caught on the same pointed hook of guilt. It is inevitable that each seeks for some tangible act or deed to account for the inner pain. Frank sees in his business the objective cause for his distress. Charlotte is convinced that it was the kiss that proved her undoing. Mike finds no reason within the long list of ethical derelictions, and in the end, it is possible that his appraisal is the most hopeful since he sees the root of his disturbance within himself rather than in some external circumstance. In essence he is saying, "It's not what I've done, it's who I am that's out of fix." There can, of course, be no facile separation between the person and his behavior. And yet, at a deeper level, the distinction is basic.

The Apostle Paul struggled with this strange contradiction within himself, and within all men. In Romans 7 he wrote:

> I do not understand my own actions. For I do not do what I want, but I do the very thing I hate. Now if I do what I do not want, I agree that the law is good. So then it is no longer I that do it, but sin which dwells within me. For I know that nothing good dwells within me, that is, in my flesh. I can will what is right, but I cannot do it. For I do not do the good I want, but the evil I do not want is what I do.

It is a dreadful feeling. "Wretched man that I am!" wrote Paul, "Who will deliver me from this body of death?" Frank knows what he meant. So do Charlotte and Mike. But they may have more difficulty discovering that change in behavior will not be sufficient. Indeed, in certain instances the behavior may not be wrong at all, although in others it may be. Behavior changes as the person changes. The law is not abolished, but fulfilled. Paul put it, "The law of the Spirit of life in Christ Jesus has set me free from the law of sin and death."

FROM STILL ANOTHER point of view it is not easy to see that conscience is a part of every man, and that the restlessness of which Augustine spoke can never be resolved until "we rest in Thee." Frank can see no signs of conscience in Charlie; indeed, he finds himself half envious that things seem to make so little difference to Charlie. In the same way, Dr. Watson had once been quite resentful of those whose lives seemed to flaunt the moral law at every turn. It had irritated him to think that there was no retribution, that they were not troubled, that they could "get away with murder." He could still remember the day he first read Psalm 73 seriously.

> For I was envious of the arrogant, when I saw the prosperity of the wicked.
> For they have no pangs; their bodies are sound and sleek.
> They are not in trouble as other men are; they are not stricken like other men.
> Therefore pride is their necklace; violence covers them as a garment.
> Their eyes swell out with fatness, their hearts overflow with follies.

> They scoff and speak with malice; loftily they threaten oppression.
> They set their mouths against the heavens, and their tongue struts through the earth.
> Therefore the people turn and praise them; and find no fault in them.
> And they say, "How can God know? Is there knowledge in the Most High?"
> Behold, these are the wicked; always at ease, they increase in riches.

Yes, he had thought, that's true. It *was* irritating. He could understand the feeling of the psalmist as he read on:

> All in vain have I kept my heart clean and washed my hands in innocence.
> For all the day long I have been striken, and chastened every morning.

How long had it been before he understood the deeper meaning of conscience, the realization that beneath the external behavior there is inner turmoil? He hadn't seen it at first. Only later did he know that it was true, know that a man like Mike Jackson can try to flee from reality in many ways, but always has within himself a driving restlessness which would not die however often he found a transitory solace in alcohol or sensuality, feverish activity or lethargy. "Our hearts are restless."

It was then that he discovered the meaning of the psalmist when he wrote:

> But when I thought how to understand this, it seemed to me a wearisome task,
> Until I went into the sanctuary of God; then I perceived their end.
> Truly thou dost set them in slippery places; thou dost make them fall to ruin.
> How they are destroyed in a moment, swept away utterly by terrors!

It was true. He could see now that his perspective had been distorted. When he could look beneath the obvious, when he could see what was within, he knew. He knew. Mike and Charlie and those people whose names were in the papers, it was true for each of them as for all men. No one goes happily to hell.

MATURITY does not set aside the conscience; on the contrary, the sensitivity to right and wrong seems to become more acute. As the content of the conscience, so much conditioned by cultural mores, gradually emerges from legalistic bondage, rules and regulations are fulfilled in love for one's neighbor. Just now, Frank does not see this; neither does Charlotte, for that matter. Mike doesn't either, although he may stand closer to its possibility than the other two. He may never see it, nor may they. But for all three, it *is* possible.

3
Anxiety

How do you figure a guy like that! Gad, what a crepe hanger! He needs a crying towel nine feet long! Charlie muttered to himself as he walked down the hall. He never quite knew what to say to Frank, and wished he would quit always bringing up questions about the contracts. He liked Frank well enough, but it made him uncomfortable to be around him at such times as this. Trouble with Frank is he just won't let anything get settled. Like I told him, I got over that a long time ago. You just gotta make up your mind that business is business. I wish he'd quit bugging me. He knows as well as I do that these reports have to be in the post office by five o'clock. How do you like that guy! Good grief!

He could still make it if nobody stopped him. These are the sorriest elevator operators in town. They always expect you to put something in the box at Christmastime, but I'll be hanged if I can see how they have the gall to take it. He frowned as the door slid back revealing a jam of faces all looking vacantly forward into nothing.

"Step to the back of the car, please. Can you push back a little?"

He got in hoping they'd go express to the ground floor. No room in here for anybody else. Pass 'em on by. Won't hurt 'em to wait. Can't you see I'm in a hurry?

You'd think these fellows at the parking lot would be on the ball. Hot-rodders, that's what they are. Only thing they really like is to go tearing around in somebody else's car. Well, I'd sure better not ever find a dent in one of my fenders. Come on, come on, hurry it up, I haven't got all day!

He slid the package under the grill just as the clock was striking five. "Be sure that gets on the evening plane for Cleveland."

Cleveland, there is a town for you! Without thinking he

touched his inside coat pocket to be sure he had his ticket. He usually picked them up at the airport, but this time he was going to be pushed and didn't want to take any chances. They really know how to entertain you, no doubt about that. Wish I could catch the plane out tonight instead of having to wait until tomorrow afternoon.

He glanced at his watch as he got back into his car. Seven after five. No need to go home now. Plenty of time to stop by Julio's for a couple of quick ones. What about that crumby auditor trying to give him a hard time over the bill from Julio's? This was necessary for business, wasn't it? Keeping him on the road and happy was just about the most important thing the Company could do. Who else could come up with one ten-strike right after another? They knew it, too. Let 'em sweat it out as much as they wanted to. "Bourbon on the rocks and put it on the tab." The old swindle sheet has a few creases left in it.

WHO IS CHARLIE? It would be difficult to get any consensus. To the attendant at the parking lot he is a grouch; to the elevator operator he is a guy looking out for number one; to the Company he is a top flight salesman; to Julio he is an easy mark; to his secretary he is a man in a hurry who wants what he wants when he wants it, and had better get it, too; to the gang in the office he is always good for a story but you would hate to have him around all the time; to his competitors he is ruthless, the kind of fellow that lets you know you better not drop your guard. Who is Charlie? If you asked Frank, he could tell you if he didn't have to think about it. But when he stopped to think about it, he wasn't so sure. And if you asked Charlie, he'd look at you like—Well, what kind of a question is that supposed to be? You some kind of a nut or something? After awhile you come to know that Charlie has to keep running. Tomorrow in Cleveland, the day after in Chicago, back in the office by Tuesday, where are the files on that Hairston contract, and see if you can get Tom Gafney on the phone in St. Louis.

It would never occur to Frank to think of a person like Charlie as having a conscience. The restlessness he could see, but conscience—well, hardly. And if you'd asked him about anxiety, he'd probably say that Charlie is anxious to do unto others as they'd like to do unto him, and do it first.

LIKE CONSCIENCE, the term anxiety and its corresponding adjective, anxious, have many meanings. Moreover, the uneasiness which we saw to be part and parcel of conscience cannot be understood fully without an awareness of the meaning of anxiety.

We often use the term in the same sense that Frank implied when he observed that Charlie was anxious to get the best of other people. We might say "I'm anxious for you to come," or "we are anxious to see the new play." In addition, there are times when we use anxious to mean apprehensive. "You were gone so long, I was beginning to get anxious about you." Or perhaps, "I had some anxious moments until I got the word that everything was all right."

When we speak of anxiety in human behavior, however, much more is implied. Anxiety is the feeling of foreboding or dread. It may involve a tightening of the stomach or breaking out in a cold sweat. It is distinguished from fear in that fear has an object, some identifiable cause, a tangible reason. Anxiety, on the other hand, has no such objective basis, although when we're anxious we search desperately for something to account for the distress. Anxiety is a choking feeling that brings panic and, at the same time, paralysis. It is the experience of threat to one's whole being; it is the awareness of impending doom; it is the sense of meaninglessness; it is the terrible realization of finitude.

Anxiety, like conscience, can be understood only in terms of personal development and significant relationships. It can never be ignored, although all men strive with all their might to avoid it. In one sense, it is possible to write the story of every person's life in terms of the devices he employs to deal with anxiety.

Even at this more fundamental level there is still a variety of meaning attached to the term "anxiety." For the clinician, anxiety is a violent and destructive pathological condition that tends to reduce a person to abject despair. For the psychologist, anxiety is an "alarm bell" that calls attention to something so desperately wrong that it must be dealt with at all costs and as soon as possible. For the philosopher, anxiety is the possibility of freedom, the inner urge that will not allow the person to settle for less than complete fulfillment. For the theologian, anxiety is the fear of the Lord which is the beginning of wisdom.

WE HAVE SEEN that Frank was the first child. It is not easy to be a first child. It takes awhile to understand just what is expected by the bigger people who are already here. They do not always do the kind of things you like, and at times you wonder whether they love you or not. After awhile it becomes easier to know what they want, and it turns out to be better if you do it that way. You pick up your clothes, just like they say, and brush your teeth, and say your prayers, "If I should die before I awake." It would be nicer if that wasn't in there, but they taught it to you that way, so it is better to go on and say it. You hope you won't die before you wake. But it is nice to be a good boy and be told so, and anyhow, they probably never will know that you don't like the part about dying. Certainly you'll never tell them. It's not so hard to be a first child after all. You mind your Mama and do everything just right, and she will love you and do nice things for you. "God bless Mama and Papa and help Frank to be a good boy."

It was a kind of paradise, really. After awhile you don't think of those times when you wondered whether to be a good boy or not. It is far, far better to be a good boy. Only thing strange is that they do not always do the kind of things you like, even when you are a good boy. Hard to figure that out. Sometimes they are cross and other times they leave you with people who aren't Mama or Papa at all. Do you suppose they know you don't always feel like being a good boy? Do they know you don't like the part in the prayer about dying? Hard to see how they could because you never once said it. But they do know a lot of things you didn't think they knew. Would they quit loving you if they knew? Suppose they already have. It was a terrible thing to think. Only one thing to do. Be a much better boy than before. Then they'll love you for sure.

WE HAVE SEEN THAT ANXIETY is a feeling of threat to one's whole being, the sense of impending annihilation of the self. Furthermore, we have seen that anxiety is universal. It is the feeling that comes in the realization of being something but not everything, in the tension between being creative but not the creator. It takes the form of a feeling of rejection, of separation, of aloneness. Many have thought of anxiety as associated with birth, as the child is separated from its mother and must cope with a world too terrifying to be endured. The very root meaning of the term suggests the kind of choking suffocation occasioned by passage through a narrow, constricting channel. It is the dreadful sense of being finite, the awareness of personal destruction.

One of the ways we attempt to cope with such a dreadful feeling is to deny its existence by assuring our acceptance through behavior designed to please. Since it is evident that one's very security is dependent upon his relationship with others, it is concluded that this relationship must be maintained at all costs and without a flaw or the suggestion of a breach. The result of this conclusion is a constant and at times feverish rejection of the self in favor of conforming to the perceived expectations of those whose acceptance is judged to be essential, expectations which may be real or imagined. When the times of separation come, the anxiety becomes a goad which drives the person to a redoubling of the efforts which have proved successful in the past to allay the sense of rejection. For Frank, the answer was exceedingly clear: Be a good boy, and your parents will respond with love and approval. Keep the rules and receive the reward. Do right and live.

The terrible fact, of course, is that this kind of response to anxiety, though positive in its intention, carries within it the seeds of its own defeat. In the attempt to establish a more secure and permanent relationship with those whose acceptance he must have, the child comes more and more to realize the terrible gap between the way they perceive him and the way he perceives himself. He is haunted by the feeling that if they really knew who he was they would not love him anymore. Thus the breach grows wider even as he redoubles his efforts to assure the continuation of love. He is uneasy over the slightest indication of displeasure and must constantly be reassured that all is well.

LOOKING BACK, Frank was never able to determine just when the terrible realization began to dawn on him that all was not well. He certainly tried to be as good as he possibly could, and yet things were different anyhow. Mama seemed to be tired more often and she didn't pick him up like she always had. She seemed to lie down more now, and his grandmother, who was staying with them for awhile, told him to go outside and play quietly so that Mother could get some rest.

Sometime much earlier he'd learned that somebody else was coming to live with them. No one seemed quite clear about who it was, but it was to be either a baby sister or a baby brother. He could remember Mama saying that it was wonderful and that they were all so glad. She had also said that he would love the new baby and it would be nice to have someone to play with. Actually, he wasn't sure. Not sure at all. Although they never said it in so many words, it seemed likely that they were going to love the new baby so much they wouldn't have time to love him. It was upsetting just to think such a thing, and on two occasions he'd not been able to eat his supper. Once they had been very cross with him when he'd spilled his milk on the new tablecloth. He'd cried that night when he went to bed. "God bless Mama and Papa and help Frank to be a good boy." That's it. Help Frank to be a good boy. And God bless the new baby, I guess.

After awhile, when he thought of the new baby at all he was able to say how glad he was that it was coming. When Grandmother came he was the one who got to tell her the news.

"We're going to have a new baby come to live at our house, Grans. And we're going to be extra careful with her since she will be little and can't do anything right and needs somebody to help her. We'll have to be extra careful not to let her fall down the cellar steps and break her neck or get her head mashed in the screen door."

"I should say so," Grans had answered. "Those would be terrible things to have happen to her."

"Sure would," he'd agreed. "She'd die if those things happened, and we don't want her to die 'cause we all love her."

"Come in here, come in here, Grans!" he called out from the room that had been furnished for a nursery. "Come here! Come here!"

"All right, Frank, I'll be there in just a minute. Mother and I are talking right now."

"Come now! Come now!"

"Frank, for goodness sakes don't be such a pest. Grans just got here. Give her time to sit down and catch her breath. She'll be there in just a minute. You go on and play for a little while."

"But I want to show her the thing we're going to wash the baby in." He came to the door of the bedroom. Mother was sitting on the bed and Grandmother was hanging some things in the closet.

"You'll just have to see it, Grans. It sits up on legs and has a place for soap. And we have a little thing to see if the water is too hot or too cold or just right. We don't want to put the baby in boiling water. That would hurt her. Can you come now? Huh?"

Sometimes it's hard to be a first child. Just as everything is all settled and everybody loves you something happens. It takes a little while to realize that the new baby is coming no matter what you can do. But they will love you if you are a good boy. Before long all the things you say about the new baby come out just like *they* say them. This way they'll never know how you really feel. After awhile, you don't even know it yourself. Of course we love the new baby. It would be awful if she should break her neck on the cellar stairs or be scalded in the boiling water. I think.

The night that William was born Mama didn't even sleep in our house. Not that she'd picked him up for days. Several times he'd crawled up on her lap and she'd rocked him, but it wasn't like it used to be. She didn't seem to fit as well as before, and in a little while Grans would say, "Come on, Frank. Let's go set the table while Mama rests a bit." He didn't want to set the table, but you couldn't say so. Grans had rocked him several times, but she didn't rock like Mama.

"God bless Mama and Papa and Grans and the new baby and help Frank to be a good boy." After Grans had turned out the light he cried a little and she came back.

"I want to sleep in Mama's bed," he sobbed. Grans had let him.

WILLIAM was a second child. Funny thing, he turned out not to be a girl at all. "Won't it be nice," Mama had said, "having a boy to play with Frank. They'll grow up to be real close to each other. I'm glad he was a boy. We'll have a girl next time."

It is not easy to be a second child. It takes awhile to understand just what big people expect of you. Before long you discover that all of the big people are not the same size. Not only that, but they don't do the same kinds of things—to you or for you. It's pretty easy to see what Mama does. She washes you and feeds you and rocks you and puts you down. Papa does some of those things, too, but he isn't here as much. It's hardest to tell what Frank does. He brings things to Mama and sometimes he pinches and he makes noise. Mostly he pinches and makes noise when Mama isn't there. Mama doesn't like for people to pinch and make noise. She always comes running whenever anybody pinches or makes noise. That's a good thing to know when you need her.

Frank is a good boy. Everybody says so. Good boys hand people towels when they ask for them and hold the bottle while it is cooling just a little. It is not easy to be as good a boy as Frank. He can reach the towels better, and when you try to hold the bottle it drops. "Oh, William! Now look what you've done!" But she came when she heard the crash. That's a good thing to know when you need her.

People tell Frank that he is a good boy. Good boys are nice to their little brothers and let them ride in their wagon. It seems so easy to be a good boy when Frank does it. Apparently he has worked at it longer, can do it better. It is not easy to be a good boy when you try it yourself. It would be nice to be a good boy, but usually when they talk about a good boy they mean Frank.

"For goodness sakes, William, try to be more careful with the nice picture book. Why, that's one Frank had when he was your age and he didn't tear it a single bit. Hold it with both hands and don't try to carry it by a page 'cause it will tear out. There, that's better." He had wondered where Mama was and called out to her once. She said, "I'm busy right now, William. I'll be there in a minute." She came in a hurry when Frank yelled at him about the book. That's a good thing to know when you want her.

"William, I'm just going to have to punish you. You know better than to drive nails in the back porch door. I've told you again and again that nails are for the wood Papa gave you. We just can't have you destroying property. I don't know why you keep on doing things like this when you know good and well that you ought not to." He was a good pounder. She came when she heard him pounding. She hadn't said much to him all morning, but she was here, now. Only thing, it'd be nice if she didn't switch him when she came. Even that is better than her not coming, though.

ONE OF THE WAYS we attempt to cope with the dreadful feeling of anxiety is to deny its existence by compelling the attention of those whose relationship is essential for our very existence. Whatever the cost, it is absolutely imperative to know that they are for you. For William, as for Frank, the choice of means was quite wide. He would just as soon have been a good boy; indeed, he could pray "God bless Mama and Papa and Frank and help William to be a good boy." The terrible fact, however, was that he found himself in competition with an expert. Try as he might, he could never seem to do things quite as well as Frank.

Frank, of course, saw to that. It is not easy to be a first child. One's own position is precarious enough at best. It is comforting to know that they love you when you are a good boy and that usually you know what it means to be a good boy and know that you can do it. What is terrifying is to realize that William may be a good boy, too. Indeed, it is quite likely that he is a good boy since they say they love him, and why else would they? Well, he can't be as good a boy as I am. He cries more and dropped the bottle. I didn't drop the bottle. It's not always easy to understand why they seem to put up with William. It may be that they don't see that he is not half as good a boy as I am. But if I keep trying and trying they will know. I never did tear a book or drive nails in the back porch. But William did.

After awhile it becomes clear that the things you can do better than Frank is drop bottles and tear books and drive nails in the back porch. You don't necessarily want to do those things, although some of them are sort of fun, but Mama comes then when she didn't come the other times. What you really want is for her to come. It'd be nice if she would come and tell you that you are a good boy, but it is better that she come and fuss at you than not come at all.

The terrible fact, of course, is that this kind of response to anxiety, positive in intention as was the other, also carries within it the seeds of its own defeat. Indeed, the impending destruction is much more apparent in the case of William than it is for Frank. Clearly, when the summons is met by a coming which takes the overt form of rejection there can be no possible solution. What is not always quite so clear is the genuinely positive intent of the negative behavior, the yearning for a relationship which seems ever more remote, the longing for an acceptance that always appears just beyond reach. Even more difficult to see is the inner feeling that if they really knew who he was they would love him.

It is here that the contrast between Frank and William is complete. The terror in Frank's heart is that if they knew him they would not love him; William yearns for them to know him, but he is afraid to run the risk since they might not come at all. For both there is the feeling that attention has to be earned by whatever device proves most productive. And for both there is the aching sense of not really being loved. As a consequence the anxiety is in fact not allayed. On the contrary the very behaviors designed to settle it turn out in the end to magnify its pain. The paradox is that, to a certain degree, the devices are effective. So it turns out that their very success is the cause of failure.

WE HAVE ALREADY NOTED that the child always perceives his acceptance as relatively conditioned. On too many occasions this may in fact be true. Unfortunately there are parents who are unable to love their children, although in most instances they pretend to do so for their own sake. They may be too indulgent under the pretext of allowing freedom; they may be too rigid under the pretext of maintaining discipline; most often they are unable to sustain any consistent relationship at all. But the fact of the matter is that however constant the love, however consistent the relationship, the child inevitably perceives it otherwise by reason of the anxiety that is inherent in the human situation. And the usual pattern is that the older child will seek to gain acceptance by conforming while the second child will become a rebel.

Of course, it may be the reverse. If, for example, the first child rebels, then it is likely that the second child will tend to conform. And the pattern repeats itself in the third child and the fourth and the fifth. If the third child feels himself closer to the second, he will rebel to make common cause against the older. If he feels threatened by the nearer sibling, he will conform and become like the first child. The variations are endless, but the basic thrust of conformity or rebellion remains the same throughout. In each instance the child seeks to deal with anxiety by attempting to escape from the fact that he is something but not everything. Frank seizes upon the device of attempting to be everything by denying his individual integrity; William's gambit is to assert his individuality at the expense of his relatedness. Although their behavior is logically opposite, it is actually identical. However different the form, the underlying purpose is the same. And for them, as for all men, the only possible outcome is defeat.

"You'd think the father would have stopped him. Surely he knew that he would come to grief. He really didn't have enough experience or judgment to be turned loose with all that money."

"Yes, that's true. But the fact is that's the way God deals with us. When I really think about it, it scares me a little."

"It has always seemed strange to me that he would have wanted to leave. You'd think he'd have everything he needed right there. That's the part of the story that has always puzzled me."

"I can see you never did have an older brother! Believe me, that's reason enough to get away right there!"

Miss Morrison looked over her glasses at Harold. "Sounds to me like you're speaking from experience."

"You bet I am. We get along fine now, but there was a time when I would have gone in a minute if I'd had anywhere to go."

"It's not hard for you to understand his going, then?"

"I should say not. What always surprised me was that he stayed around at all after he got his share of the inheritance. I think I would have left that night."

For awhile there was silence. You never knew what would come out of this class, but you could be sure that everybody would say just exactly what he thought. When they'd started they called themselves "The Young Adults." Everybody said that the name, at least, wouldn't last long—time would take care of that. They'd asked Miss Morrison to be their teacher. She wasn't exactly a

"Young Adult," but that didn't mean she was not young in heart. For nearly four months they'd been studying the Gospel of Luke, and today they were on the fifteenth chapter.

"I don't think that's what Jesus had in mind at all when he told the story. The prodigal just left, that's all."

"Well, could be. Yet the more I read it, the more it seems to me that this story is really the way things are, in life I mean."

"You heard Dr. Watson say just last Sunday that you can't make the parables 'walk on all fours,' and that it is wrong to try to read meaning into them that Jesus never intended at all."

"Well, I can see that, all right. But, like I say, being a younger son myself I think I know how he felt."

"If you ask me, both of you are off base. The elder brother is the point of this story. If you'll look at the first two verses of the chapter, you'll see that Jesus was telling the story to the Pharisees and scribes who were upset over his receiving tax collectors and sinners."

"But that doesn't mean that the younger brother isn't real, too. He couldn't believe that the father would ever be able to love him after all he'd done."

"And yet when he came to himself, he didn't try to go back to his erstwhile friends, or the citizen who had hired him, or even to the elder brother. It was the father he turned to."

"I'll tell you this, he sure knew what he was doing, not trying out the elder brother. That guy wouldn't give him the time of day!"

"Well, can you blame him? To tell you the truth, I've always sort of thought the elder brother had a point. He'd been working the place all those years. I think he had a right to be sore."

Miss Morrison listened. It always interested her that folks tended to identify with one brother or the other. "What do you think was Jesus' point in telling the story?"

"To show that God forgives. We're all kinda Prodigal Sons, I guess." That was Harold. He knew what the far country looked like. It was good to be back, but you don't forget.

"I think he wanted the Pharisees and scribes to realize that God can and does forgive."

"I wonder if they ever got the point. You know, one way you

look at it, they were as far away from the Father as the prodigal. Yet he wanted them, too."

"As I was reading this last night, it occurred to me that what happened to the elder brother is actually just like what happened to the prodigal when you look at what the father did. He came out to meet the prodigal and he came out to meet the elder brother, too."

"Gee, I never had thought of it that way. Now that you call attention to it, I can see it, though. I wonder if he ever came in."

"You know, I guess it never occurred to me that it might be easier for the younger brother to come back into the father's house than it was for the elder brother."

Miss Morrison nodded, "It turned out that the tax collectors and harlots went into the Kingdom before the Pharisees."

"Does that mean it's better to be a sinner?"

"Maybe so." Harold, again. "I've found something I might never have known about."

Miss Morrison peered over her glasses again. "Does this mean you all don't feel that the elder brother was a sinner?"

"No, of course not. But you know what we mean. Out carousing around and all that."

"Yes, I know." Miss Morrison thought of the Elder Brothers she'd known through the years and the misery of discovering that love cannot be bought by acceptable behavior. Then she thought of the Prodigals she'd known and the agony of separation. Some of them didn't come back, either. "Yes, I know." And then, almost to herself, "It's hard to live by grace."

MOST OF WHAT we have seen about anxiety thus far has seemed generally negative. The truth of the matter is that anxiety is always experienced as destructive. Only in retrospect can it be seen as "the possibility of freedom." Charlie would never think of it that way. Indeed, he would never think of it at all if there were any way to avoid it. One of the reasons Charlie drove so hard was to escape the possibility of thinking. He was like a man on a bicycle who could stay up as long as he was moving, but knew he would fall over if he ever stopped. He couldn't let himself ease up even for a minute. "All this hoopla about conscience is nonsense. That's why a guy like Frank bugs you so. What has it ever gotten him? Wife, two kids, mortgaged to his ears. You gotta live it up, look out for old Charlie. You can bet your bottom dollar nobody else will."

It was inevitable that Frank could never see the real Charlie. "Never a care in the world," was the way he put it. And then, "doesn't it bother you at all, even a little?" To tell the truth, it irritated him that Charlie could get by with murder. Actually, at this point there was no way for him to know how it was with Charlie on the nights when sleep would not come, or to feel the rising panic Charlie felt when he couldn't stop by Julio's or somewhere for "a couple of quick ones." How could he ever suspect the knotting in the stomach when the auditor asked questions about expense account items, or the near panic over the prospect of a session with an agent from the Treasury Department to check his income tax? He couldn't know for two reasons. Primarily, he was so tied up in his own thinking just now that he wasn't able to hear what other people were really saying. In addition, Charlie was quite adept at concealing his feelings since he couldn't cope with them, himself.

It's a long way to the far country and, fortunately, the road is not easy and gets harder every step. Ironically, it seems hard to turn around, although actually it isn't. It is sad to contemplate that the road may lead to a pig pen before Charlie comes to himself. It is tragic to realize that even then he might not.

"ANXIETY is the possibility of freedom." Frank would never have thought of it that way. It had been a long time since he and William were boys. You learned a lot you didn't want to know as the years went by. He still remembered when William had left home. He always knew he'd come to no good end. Now, no one knew where he was. Well, one thing was certain. *He'd* never do a fool thing like that. Right was right and wrong was wrong. You might not always be able to tell the difference in some things, but basically you knew. It certainly wasn't right to run away, be irresponsible, waste everything, your money and your life. Whatever happened to him would serve him right. William irritated him, too. He was another one who got by with murder, but it finally caught up with him, I guess. I don't know for sure, but I reckon it did. It was even more irritating to recognize that things hadn't turned out too hot for *him*. Goodness knows he'd done his best. After all, that Willis contract *was* legal and the office expected him to pull his load. And what had it gotten him? He was mortgaged up to his ears. Well, the thing to do was just keep plugging. If you worked hard enough and did what was right things were bound to pay off in the end. It would be nice not to be so strapped financially. If they had a bigger house they could have a real party one night and invite a lot of the old friends they hadn't seen in quite awhile. But they couldn't afford it, not to really do it right, anyhow.

"ANXIETY is the possibility of freedom." Miss Morrison knew that, although she would never have used that phrase. She had never thought much about anxiety one way or the other but she knew what it meant. When she thought of it at all, she probably would think of Paul's word to the Philippians, "Have no anxiety about anything, but in everything by prayer and supplication with thanksgiving let your requests be made known to God. And the peace of God, which passes all understanding, will keep your hearts and your minds in Christ Jesus." There had been a time when this had seemed to say to her that maybe one day she wouldn't have any more anxiety. She could still remember how discouraged she had become when the troubles just kept on coming. Somewhere along the way she'd gotten the idea that it was shameful to have troubles, and if you had any you'd better not let anybody know it. She smiled at herself as she remembered. She would never forget the time she had suddenly realized that even as Paul wrote those words he had more troubles than most people know in a lifetime. "In everything." That was the clue. She wondered why she had never seen this before, really seen it. It seemed so clear now, but it wasn't then. You didn't have to hide, to try to be something you weren't, to conform or rebel in trying to gain acceptance. When you can bring everything out in the open, then you really do find the peace of God which passes all understanding. She knew what that meant, all right. You never would have figured it out beforehand; but it was something you could see in retrospect.

"ANXIETY is the possibility of freedom." Seen in this light it is the painful reminder that something is amiss, that things can't stay as they are. It is the insistent goad that presses on toward maturity, that will not let us go. But Frank doesn't know that; neither does Charlie, nor William. For the time being, anxiety to them is only the dreadful specter which terrifies with forebodings of impending doom.

4
Hostility

> By the waters of Babylon,
> > there we sat down and wept,
> > when we remembered Zion.
> On the willows there
> > we hung up our lyres.
> For there our captors
> > required of us songs,
> And our tormentors, mirth, saying,
> > "Sing us one of the songs of Zion!"

"Grace! Whatcha doing, Honey? Oh, Gra - a - ce!"

"What is it, George?" He could just barely hear her.

"Where are you, Grace?"

"I'm down here in the basement trying to match up these socks."

"Well, can you come up here when you get through? I need you to help me with something."

"All right, but it'll be a little while. Are you in a hurry?"

"Well, sort of, but you go ahead with what you're doing and come when you can."

George picked up the Bible and began reading again.

> How shall we sing the LORD's song
> > in a foreign land?
> If I forget you, O Jerusalem,
> > let my right hand wither!
> Let my tongue cleave to the roof of my mouth,
> > if I do not remember you,
> If I do not set Jerusalem above my highest joy!

> Remember, O LORD, against the Edomites
>   the day of Jerusalem,
> How they said, "Rase it, rase it!
>   Down to its foundations!"
> O daughter of Babylon, you devastator!
>   Happy shall he be who requites you
>   with what you have done to us!
> Happy shall he be who takes your little ones
>   and dashes them against the rock!

"Whew!" He shuddered as he put it down. "I'd sure hate to meet him when he had a sword in his hand instead of a harp."

"Sorry I took so long." Grace settled into the rocker with the darning basket in her lap. "The way these kids go through socks is something fierce. What was it you wanted?"

"To tell you the truth, I'm not real sure. That is, I'm not sure just how to go about it. Boy, that preacher really does give you some sticklers."

"Now George, you know better than that. What is it?"

"Well, it's my turn to lead the Bible study at the men's breakfast in the morning, and I'm bogged down in Psalm 137. We've been on the Exile, and the Preacher thought it would be a good thing to study tomorrow. Whew! Have you ever read it?"

"Yes, I've read it. I couldn't really say I know enough about it to be of much help, though."

"I'll take a chance on it. Guess what I really need is someone to talk it over with to see if my ideas make any sense."

Grace snipped off the thread and picked up another sock. They'd sure come a long way. Who'd ever have thought that George would be worrying about a Psalm, let alone be willing to lead a Bible study? "Isn't that the one where the captives are by the river weeping for Jerusalem?"

"Yeah. That's not the part I'm puzzled about, though. It's this fellow who is so bitter about it all."

"Doesn't he have a right to be bitter?"

"Well, I guess so. While I was waiting for you, I got to thinking about those refugees I saw in Korea. But this man was supposed to be religious. I just don't see how he could really want to take little children by the heels and crack their heads open upon a rock! What had the kids ever done to him? Why should he take it out on them?"

"I see what you mean. But I guess when you are blind with rage you don't have much time to be very logical about things. You just strike out at anybody or anything."

"Well, yeah. That's true enough, all right. I sure saw plenty of it in the army. It's just sort of unexpected to find something like that in the Bible. It's a long way from 'Love your enemies'!"

"No doubt about that. But you make it sound as if the people in the Bible were not real people like the ones you saw while you were in the army."

"Yeah. I guess I always thought they were sort of special, saints or something, you know."

"Well, some of them were, or came to be—that is if you define 'saint' as the New Testament does. But that doesn't mean they weren't real people just like we are. They knew what it was to be hostile and bitter and resentful."

"This one sure did. Do you think that real people can love their enemies?"

"There you go, again. They *were* real people."

"OK, but do you think they ever really loved their enemies?"

THE TERM TEMPER, like conscience and anxiety, is used in many ways. We may speak of a person's disposition or frame of mind by saying, "he has an even temper" or "he has a fiery temper." Sometimes we use temper without a qualifying adjective to mean rage or anger as when we say, "he's in a real fit of temper" or "he really showed his temper." On other occasions we use temper in a positive sense to mean calmness of mind or composure and we say, "he lost his temper" or "he kept his temper." In one way or another these all refer to the experiencing of resentment or anger or hostility or indignation or irritation and the way the person deals with these circumstances and feelings.

However defined, it is certain that temper may become quite terrifying at times. This was what George sensed as he read the ancient Psalm. There is an awesome aspect to the kind of violence which erupts in the bitterness of resentment and lashes out with blind fury and destructive rage. Part of the terror comes from an awareness of the consequences which this unleashed hostility wreaks on those who fall beneath its lash. Part of the terror comes from an understanding of the anguish and the agony of the person caught in such an outburst. But part of the terror also comes from the realization that these same kinds of forces are within oneself.

IT IS NOT EASY to deal with one's own hostility. Frank knew that. From the time he was a little boy he had been told to watch his temper. Ordinarily he was quite successful in doing so. Good boys didn't lose their temper and fly off the handle over everything that came along.

"I don't want to have to punish you, Frank, but I simply won't have you talking to your mother that way."

Whenever she referred to herself as "your mother," he knew she was displeased. He felt the old fear clutch at his heart. What if she didn't love him anymore?

"I'm sorry. I didn't mean to." He sobbed as he said it.

"I'm sure you didn't. I can't imagine what in the world possessed you to say such a thing. I know it won't happen again." Even now he shuddered to remember what it was he'd said. She had called him to come in and take his bath, but he hadn't wanted to leave right then. He and Jim were making mud pies in the sand pile, and he wasn't near through.

"Fra-a-nk!" she'd called. "I mean it, Frank. Come right now, I don't have time to wait around all afternoon."

He'd meant to mind, but maybe he could finish this one pie. He hadn't heard her come out the back door, and it startled him when she had grabbed his arm and lifted him up. "Frank, when are you going to learn to mind!"

He was still holding the tin spoon in his right hand. "I'll chop you up with this spoon."

Had he really said it? Had he actually said those words? Years later they used to laugh about it. "Can you imagine Frank ever saying a thing like that?" He could join in the laughter, although not quite as heartily as they did. It was one of the family jokes you'd just as soon they'd all forget.

What he did not forget was that it was never to happen again. That much was quite clear. Usually, it didn't. He'd worked real hard at it. When William came he was able to make himself believe that he didn't want his neck broken, or to have him scalded in boiling water. But it was frightening that sometimes he had a hard time not pinching William. Twice Mama had caught him doing it. "I was just loving him, Mama."

"Well, you'll have to be more careful with William. He's just a little baby, and it hurts him for you to be rough with him. Now, give him a few gentle pats. That's right. I know you love him and don't want to hurt him."

There were times when William had irritated him dreadfully. He seemed to get away with anything. When he tore up his books, Mama and Papa had gotten him some more. Sure, they had switched him, but it didn't seem to make any difference. Frank remembered the day Papa came in with the news that William was gone. "Good riddance," was the first thought that'd popped through his mind. "I hope he doesn't come back." Almost at once he was filled with remorse. "That's a dreadful thing to think about your own brother. What if he's in trouble, what if he's hurt? I didn't really mean that. I hope they find him."

ONE OF THE WAYS we try to deal with the negative aspect of temper is to deny its reality. There is a kind of success which accompanies this procedure. When the hostile feelings are not expressed there is no danger of having to deal with the possible negative response that might be provoked. But the success is illusory and, in the end, the result is not success at all but failure. During the early years of Frank's life he had little opportunity to deal openly with his own hostile feelings. Not only did he perceive that his overall acceptance was conditioned by acceptable behavior, but in the case of hostility, there were direct prohibitions which effectively prevented any constructive measures being taken. By the time he was grown, Frank had suppressed his anger so long that he was unable to cope with it when it did emerge.

He could not understand why he had lost his temper with Bill over the broken glass on the coffee table, or why he was so fractious with Mary these days. It terrified him to sense the bitter resentments that welled up within him, resentments against Charlie and William and no telling who else. It wasn't right. He knew it wasn't right to feel that way. He remembered how he had felt when William left, and how terrible it was to feel that way. When their first child was born Mary had wanted to name him Frank, Jr., but he'd insisted that they name him for William. Maybe that would make things up just a little, maybe the folks would feel better about that.

Deep within he was deathly afraid of his temper. That's why it was still hard to laugh when the family told the story of the spoon. Maybe he hadn't meant it, like they said, but who could really be sure? And as for William, who could forget that first of all Elder Brothers who rose up against his Younger Brother while they were in the field and killed him. "Where is . . . your brother? . . . what have you done?" O God! Help Frank to be a good boy!

IT IS NOT EASY to deal with one's own hostility. William knew that. They'd always said he had a violent temper. Why couldn't he be a good boy like Frank? Frank doesn't throw things and break windows, and have temper tantrums and scream. "Honestly, I just don't know what in the world is going to become of him. We've tried everything we can think of, and nothing seems to faze him in the slightest. For goodness sakes, William, get out of here with that drum!"

He wished they weren't always mad at him. Well, he guessed they weren't always mad at him, but it sure seemed like it. They were always yelling at him. How'd you like it if every time you turned around, there was old Frank? Brush your teeth like Frank does, pick up your clothes like Frank does, say your prayers like Frank does.

"William, did you hit Frank with that stick? Answer me, William! Did you hit him?"

"Yeah, I hit him. But he was . . ."

"It doesn't make any difference what he was doing, you know better than to hit people with a stick! If I've told you once, I've told you a thousand times that we just won't have that!"

"But he was . . ."

"William, you heard me. Now you just march yourself right upstairs this minute."

"I'll hit him again and hit you, too!"

"That you won't, young man! You just wait until your father gets home. He'll give you the switching of your life!"

"I don't care, I don't care. I hate Frank and you and everybody!"

"You don't do anything of the kind! Get on upstairs now, and don't let me hear a sound out of you until supper!"

His eyes stung with tears as he slammed the door behind him. Wish I had a big stick; I'd show 'em! He kicked the chair, knocking it over against the wall. Ouch! He gasped with pain as he held his foot. Old fool chair!

He didn't really know how it had started. That was the strange thing, he could never remember how things started. He didn't just set out to hit Frank with a stick. They were going to play cowboy, and he didn't want to be the rustler. Frank always made him be the rustler. It was OK to be the rustler sometimes, but not every time. The rustler always got caught and had to be put in jail in the tool shed. Sometimes when the other boys were there they'd put him in jail, and wouldn't let him out. One time they went off and forgot him, and he'd called and called, but they didn't come. That was the time he'd knocked a plank off the wall of the tool shed with Papa's pick. Papa was real mad about that and he'd gotten a switching. They didn't switch old Frank. He'd said he wasn't the sheriff and didn't even know I was in there, and besides, he was sorry. Frank was always sorry, but I got the switching. Like now, only he didn't even say he was sorry this time. Wish I'd hit him harder! Doesn't do any good to try, you always get switched anyhow.

William flung himself across the bed and closed his eyes tight. One thing he was sure of, he wasn't going to cry. He wouldn't give them that kind of satisfaction. I know what I'll do. I'll run away. Maybe that'll show 'em! I bet they'd be sorry, then. Maybe I'd die or something and then they'd be sad. "Poor William," they'd say. I'll go tonight, maybe.

He toyed with the idea awhile. It wasn't the first time he'd thought of it, and he guessed he knew he really wouldn't go. Mainly because he didn't know where he could go. They probably wouldn't even miss me. I'll just stay around here and show them a thing or two. Wait'll I get that old Frank off to himself. One of these days I'm going to be big enough to whip him. I think he's sort of scared of me right now.

He opened his eyes and looked up at the ceiling. It was beginning to get dark, and Papa would be home in just a little while. Gee, whiz! It'd be sort of nice if Papa didn't always have to ask, "What's William done now?" Honestly, he didn't mean to hit Frank. But he shouldn't always make you be the rustler. You just get so mad you don't know what you're doing.

"Well, William, what's the matter this time?" Papa always said that. He wished he could think of an answer. He closed his eyes and acted like he hadn't heard.

ANOTHER OF THE WAYS we try to deal with the negative aspect of temper is to give vent to it. There is a kind of success which accompanies this procedure. Expressing anger releases pent up emotion and eases tension; the storm blows fiercely for awhile, and then tends to subside. But the success is illusory, and in the end, the result is not success at all but failure. During the early years of William's life he had little opportunity to deal effectively with his own negative feelings. He came to perceive that his only means of gaining the attention of the family was to rebel, to go contrary to their expressed wishes or requests. The fact that he felt rejection in their very coming only increased his sense of frustration. He found himself lashing out at Frank or his parents.

Paradoxically, he, too, was deathly afraid of his temper. There had been a time when he seemed to have some control over it, but that was past. Now, more and more he found himself caught up in fits of rage he was powerless to stop. He really hadn't wanted to hit Frank with the stick and yet he'd done it anyhow. When his father asked him what was the matter, he honestly didn't know. He didn't even want to think about it. He didn't want to think about what he might do. He was torn up by deep resentment and loneliness, by a desire for revenge and a longing for some kind of reconciliation. It was in his freshman year that he finally reached the breaking point. It always seemed that if only they had known who he was, they would have loved him. But as he saw it, they never tried. "Always making over old Frank. I'll show 'em this time, good and proper." He was only nineteen when he left.

"How'd it go George?" Grace put down the afternoon paper as he walked up on the porch.

"Whatcha mean?"

"The Bible study, silly. What do you think I mean? You were so nervous when you left here this morning, you hadn't even tied your shoes. I kept wondering if you'd find your way to the church."

"Oh, that! Well, now, I'll just tell you. You're looking at what may well be the finest Bible teacher in the whole church!"

"Be serious, George! What happened?"

"Who's not serious? That preacher better start looking to his laurels."

"George Nelson, what on earth am I going to do with you?"

He leaned down and kissed her on the cheek, then settled himself in the rocking chair and propped his feet up on the fern box.

"You might try giving me some supper. And look, both shoes tied!"

They both laughed at the same time.

"I can see right now you're not going to be fit to live with. But I can tell you this, not one bite of supper do you get until I've heard the whole story."

"Well, if you put it that way, OK. But you're bribing me, I guess you know that." He sat and rocked for a little while. "You know, just like the Preacher said, it really went well—in spite of me, I guess. You won't believe this, but I'm really looking forward to my time coming up again. Honey, it was great, just great! Oh, I was scared to death at first, afraid they might not say anything and there I'd be. Maybe we just had a good subject, I don't know. Anyhow, I had a hard time getting them to stop when quarter to eight came. Some of them were still there talking when I had to leave."

"Did you all get everything settled about that poor old Israelite?"

"I'm not sure everybody did. What we talked about the most was whether or not you should ever get angry."

"Good gracious, George. It never occurred to me we had a choice. I don't know anyone who doesn't get mad once in awhile."

"Me either. What they were saying, though, at least some of them, was that anger is a sign of immaturity; and after you grow up, you don't get angry anymore, or at least not as much."

"Well, they may just have something there. You sure ought to be able to control your temper better as you grow up."

"Whoa, now! Wait a minute! You just shifted gears. That's really the point that stood out after we'd been going at it for awhile. It took Doc Harris to put his finger on that one. He said there's a real difference between being angry and losing your temper."

"Yeah, when you say it that way, I can see what you mean. I guess it sort of depends on how you look at it. How'd you all size up that old Israelite on the basis of this distinction?"

"Everybody pretty much agreed that he was angry and lost his temper, too. Thing was, though, a lot of them said they thought he had a right to."

"Right to what, get angry or lose his temper?"

"Actually they were saying both. Their point was that sometimes things were so fouled up that it would be wrong not to lose your temper. Old man Simpson brought up Jesus' cleansing the Temple and asked me if I didn't think he'd lost his temper. Tell you the truth, I didn't know what to say. I really don't believe that Jesus ever lost his temper, but how are you going to prove it? A lot of the fellows said they were sure he hadn't. I don't think we ever answered old man Simpson, though. He didn't say much after that, but he and the preacher were really going at it after we broke up."

"It's time to put the rolls in the oven and finish supper. Don't forget a word, now. I want to hear it all when I can pay attention."

George kept rocking as Grace went into the house. He could piece together a lot of the discussion, what this one said and that one. There sure were a lot of different ideas about the same passage of Scripture. Hard to believe that they could be so far apart on what they thought it meant. The fascinating thing was that, as they talked about it, they began to see things they hadn't seen before.

He reached in his pocket for a scrap of paper and looked at the notation he'd written.

"Grace, where's the Bible? I want to look up Ephesians 4:26–27."

DR. HARRIS hung up the receiver. How long do you suppose we're going to have to wait before they do something about that slum section over beyond West Fourth? You'd think after all these years you'd be used to seeing people suffer, but I guess you never are, really. I don't want to get used to it, he thought. Why did they wait so long to call you? He knew the answer to that, and wished he didn't. She couldn't be a day over sixteen and had no business being a mother. The baby would live despite its malnutrition. At first he couldn't believe it was nearly nine months old. There'd be a foster home, and anything would be an improvement.

On the whole, the welfare agencies did a good job with what they had, but somehow the problem always seemed to outdistance them. Too often just patching up when the whole thing needed overhauling from top to bottom. He thought about how she'd cried when they told her she couldn't keep the baby. She ought to have been able to see that. She was just a child herself, no husband, no steady job, no nothing. It was the right thing to do, no question about it. He wished he could erase from his mind the picture of her face, thin, drawn, tears streaming down her cheeks.

How could he be so sure that things would have been different for her if there had been no slum? They always asked him that. It was something you couldn't really prove. He'd heard all the arguments over and over again. "People make slums, and if you take them out of there and give them a nice place to live, they'll just make another slum out of it." "Don't you know that girls from the right side of the tracks also have illegitimate babies?" And so it went. The wretched fact was that it was true. He banged his fist on the table. Plague take it, that's not the answer! That's begging the confounded question! These people need help, and it's up to us to help them. Suppose some of them do go wrong, we still have no right to let babies be born and grow up in that kind of filth!

He reached for the phone and began to twist the dial. After

the third digit, he stopped and slowly put the receiver back on the hook. His hand was shaking as he took off his glasses and looked out over the city. You could see Chestnut Hill on a clear day. He heard the big clock striking. One. Two. Three. Four. Five. Guess I'd better keep on to ten, he thought. Hold up just a bit until you can see things a little straighter. "There's a real difference between being angry and losing your temper." Did I say that just this morning? Guess I'd better pay a little more attention to myself.

THERE IS NO QUESTION but that anger presents one of the most difficult and vexing problems of life. How is anger to be understood, and in what sense is it valid to make a distinction between anger and resentment or anger and hostility or anger and indignation? We have seen the various ways the term temper can be used, and as we have looked at Frank and William, at Grace and George, at Dr. Harris, certain of these meanings have stood out quite clearly. But the problem still remains.

It is comparatively easy to see some of the negative ways of dealing with anger. To repress all hostile and negative feelings, as Frank attempted to do, is not to get rid of them. Rather, they seem to become more virile than before. Gradually they take on various disguises until the person is scarcely able to recognize them. Often there is only a feeling of weariness or fatigue together with periods of depression. As time passed, Frank gained no real understanding of his outbursts of temper, and the only thing he knew was to resolve to do better.

On the other hand, an unrestrained expression of hostility, as was true for William, leads to feelings of guilt and fear together with a sense of loneliness. There may be a kind of panic as the realization of helplessness to control the hostility becomes ever more clear. It is possible to recognize something of the extent to which both William and Frank were reacting to their perception of their parents. But we cannot simply conclude that everything would have been different if their parents had been different.

DR. HARRIS knew the difference between anger and losing one's temper, at least at the theoretical level. In actual life, however, he found that the distinction was difficult to maintain. He hoped the day would never come when he would be insensitive to the suffering of men and women, and he was indignant when he thought of the inhumanities existing within his own city, not to mention around the world. Impulsively he had picked up the phone. But whom did you call? The Mayor? The City Planning Commission? The Municipal Judge? Your Councilman? Your Minister? And what did you say when they answered? It is a treacherous thing to act in the heat of wrath. He saw that.

It is just at this point that the subtle distinction between anger and losing one's temper stands out most sharply. Even as he put down the phone he could feel the tug toward withdrawal. Who was he, after all, to think that he could straighten out the social conditions of his own city? Goodness knows, they'd been there a long time. Weren't the poor always with us? Besides, it's not easy to say who's right and who's wrong. And what right do you have to go tampering with other people's lives? He looked at his watch. If I'm going to get by the hospital before dinner, I'd better get started. Tomorrow I'll get to work on that Fourth Street thing. He closed the door and tried the knob to make sure the night latch was on. Would tomorrow ever come?

THERE IS A KIND OF INDIGNATION which is born in the realistic recognition of man's inhumanity to man, himself and his fellows. It is heard in the word of the ancient Hebrew prophets who cried out against injustice and wrong.

> Hear the word of the LORD, O people of Israel;
> for the LORD has a controversy with the inhabitants of
> the land.

And the reason for the controversy?

> There is no faithfulness or kindness,
> and no knowledge of God in the land;
> there is swearing, lying, killing, stealing, and
> committing adultery;
> they break all bounds and murder follows murder.

Reason enough. The cataloging of evil that was true in the time of Hosea, true in the time of Christ, true today. But this is not the true reason for the controversy.

> Therefore the land mourns,
>   and all who dwell in it languish,
> and also the beasts of the field,
>   and the birds of the air;
>   and even the fish of the sea are taken away.

The controversy comes because the people die as a consequence of their sin. It is here that anger is seen as the manifestation of love, for when the one you love is in danger, there can be no peace until the danger passes.

> Woe to you, scribes and Pharisees, hypocrites! because you shut the kingdom of heaven against men; for you neither enter yourselves, nor allow those who would enter to go in. Woe to you, scribes and Pharisees, hypocrites! for you traverse sea and land to make a single proselyte, and when he becomes a proselyte, you make him twice as much a child of hell as yourselves.

There is another anger which is born in the agony of personal hurt and the feeling of rejection. It has no purity of motive nor intention of redemption. Rather it is infused with a desire for vengeance and a longing for hurt. It may have valid ground in injustice so that, in all honesty, the person can lift his face toward heaven and cry out, "I am wronged!" It may find its roots in a twisted perception of circumstance and bespeak the dark night of the soul and the terror of impending doom. Whatever the source, it is common to all men and from it spring the bitterness and resentment which darken understanding and nourish hate. It is a fearful feeling, it is a consuming fire. Frank knew this; so did William.

"DID YOU EVER FIND THE BIBLE?" The supper dishes were washed and the two younger children were in bed. Grace picked up the darning basket and sat down in the rocker.

"Yeah. It was right where I left it when I dashed out of here in such a hurry this morning. Those verses in Ephesians are really something. Wish I had known about them last night. Listen, 'Be angry but do not sin; do not let the sun go down on your anger, and give no opportunity to the devil.' How about that?"

"Well, I think it's pretty hard to do."

"Me too. But the thing I'm talking about is that being angry is not a sin. I mean, I always thought it was wrong to be angry. That's what those fellows were saying in the discussion this morning, but it isn't true. Wonder how we got that idea?"

"I'm sure I don't know. What'd that say about the sun going down?"

" 'Do not let the sun go down on your anger.' I like the way Phillips translates it, 'Never go to bed angry—don't give the devil that sort of foothold.'[1] What that says to me is that there's something you can do about it when you get hot under the collar. Remind me of that next time I start chewing out the kids!"

"And get chewed out myself? I should live so long!"

They laughed again.

"Listen to this: 'If you are angry, be sure that it is not out of wounded pride or bad temper.' "

"Phillips again?"

He nodded. "Yes. I wish I could say *I* was always sure."

They sat in silence for awhile. He knew she meant it. Yet it still puzzled him that a person like Grace could feel that way. He wished he could control his temper half as well as she did! But he didn't say that. He was afraid it might sound like he was fishing for compliments—or that he had thought she was. Funny how some things you feel the most you somehow can't always come right out and say. He thought back through the day. He saw some things a lot clearer than he had before. Sometimes you ought to be angry, sometimes you had no valid reason to be, but were anyhow. He wondered whether he would be able to tell whether his anger was the right kind or not. Trouble with me is that so often when I get mad I'm just plain mad. Even so, it isn't like it used to be. He could thank Grace for that. She really took that "sun going down" business seriously.

"Grace."

She looked up.

"Listen to this. Just four verses later Paul is saying you shouldn't have any anger at all. 'Let all bitterness and wrath and anger and clamor and slander be put away from you, with all malice.' What do you suppose he means by that?"

Before she could answer the phone rang. She was gone quite awhile and when she came back he could tell something was troubling her.

"What is it, Hon?"

"I'm not real sure. That was Mary Mason on the phone, and something's wrong. I don't know what it is. More the kind of thing you can sort of sense. I feel bad about it already. She was over here the other day and I could tell she was upset. I thought at the time there ought to be something I could do, but you know how it is. I got busy with the kids and somehow just didn't get over. She wants me to have lunch with her tomorrow. Keep your fingers crossed."

5
Decision

"The thing to do is just remember the ways people have helped you when you were in trouble, and that'll give you the clue as to how you can be of help." Grace could almost hear Miss Morrison saying that now. Goodness knows she'd thought of it many times since then. She put her coffee cup down and looked at the dishes still on the breakfast table. I've got to get up from here and get those dishes washed and put away or they'll never get done. She knew she was dawdling and that she had so much to do there wasn't any more time to be lost. Yet here she was. Just one last swallow, she thought, as she reached for the cup again. Now I really do have to get started.

Washing the dishes was no trouble. As a matter of fact, there was something sort of satisfying about it. You started off with things all in a mess, and in a little while they were straight again. It'd be nice if people could be straightened out that easily. She smiled to herself ruefully. Nobody knows better than I that it just doesn't work that way.

"Now, Honey, don't worry about a thing. I know you'll do just fine. You can tell me all about it at supper." George kissed her and dashed out the back door. In a few minutes she heard the car turn into the street. He really means it, she thought. I wish I could be that certain.

Frankly, she *was* worried about Mary. She should have gone over there several days ago when she first sensed that something was wrong. She bit her lip as she remembered how Mary had looked going back down the walk. She'd brought back the hairdryer she'd borrowed when hers was on the blink. They'd chatted for a minute while she got a pie ready for the oven. Mary'd said she was in a hurry, and when you're busy you just don't think about saying the right thing, whatever the right thing is. She'd said, "Let's get together before too long," and Mary'd said, "Yes, let's." She'd dried her hands on her apron as she walked to the door. For a minute it'd seemed that Mary was almost on the point of saying something as she went out. But she hadn't. You could almost feel the weight which seemed to press down upon her shoulders as she walked away.

It wasn't that she hadn't thought about going in the days that followed. But what do you say when you go? "See here, now, you've got a problem, and I've come to solve it!" Well, of course you'd never say it just like that, but how do you keep it from sounding like that? And what right do you have to go barging into somebody else's life? How would you like it if people came barging into yours? No, that's not the way to put it. How many times did I wish there was somebody to come? But not just anybody. Yes, that's it, not just anybody. And how do you know when you are *the* somebody? Well, I don't have to worry about that, I don't think. She wouldn't have called me to go to lunch if she hadn't wanted me. What I've got to decide now is what to say when I get there. "The thing to do is just to remember the ways people have helped you . . ."

IT IS PRECISELY the ability to make decisions that leads to the agonies of anxiety as well as to the pain of conscience. This does not mean, of course, that all decisions are anxiety producing or that the consequence of all decisions is discomfort. Nevertheless, the fact of decision does involve the awareness of responsibility and the consciousness of consequence.

Many decisions which at one time required considerable deliberation tend to decline in significance until they are no longer a part of conscious process unless some extraordinary event or circumstance introduces a new dimension into the situation. Thus, the simple act of tying shoelaces was once an intricate procedure requiring multiple decisions regarding which string to pull and which way to form a loop. After awhile no conscious effort is needed, unless the string knots or a cut on a finger requires the unaccustomed use of another. It is in this sense that habit removes the necessity for deliberation, both positively by freeing the person from myriads of relatively inconsequential decisions and negatively by obscuring personal involvement in behavior, whether constructive or destructive. Under these conditions only the disruption of the ordinary chain of events calls attention to the fact that responsibility and consequences are still present.

Other decisions which cannot be classed as habitual nonetheless involve a minimum of anxiety or sense of personal responsibility. The selection of a necktie or the purchase of an umbrella, for example, may certainly be the occasion for deliberation, but does not ordinarily involve the kind of choice which might evoke panic or lead to elation.

Just here, however, the implications of decision become more subtle and complex. If, for example, the necktie is perceived as likely to provoke adverse comment or if the price of the umbrella is out of reason, then the sense of personal involvement is more acute, in terms of both responsibility and consequence. So it is that a decision to attend the neighborhood motion picture theater might be a matter of little or no importance unless it has to be made in the presence of a prohibition, as was true for Frank. In such an event, the pressure of personal responsibility as well as the fear of consequence increases manyfold. Thus, it becomes clear that the particular content or focus of decision must always include not only that which is chosen but also that which is rejected.

Finally, there are decisions for which the awareness of personal responsibility and consciousness of consequences is acute. It is in this sense that the term "decision" is ordinarily understood, implying a deliberation, a weighing of alternatives, a consideration of implications, and the selection of a particular course of action which is final and categorical.

This does not mean, of course, that such a decision is not subject to review. It does mean that the review itself represents a new decision which, however related to its antecedents, is nonetheless subject to the same kind of process as the earlier decision which is to be reviewed. It is just because the categorical and irreversible dimension is often obscured in habitual behavior and seemingly inconsequential choice that the meaning of decision on such occasions is more likely to be distorted than when it is perceived as a discrete and uncomplicated choice. Nevertheless, whether seen as critical or irrelevant, it is evident that no decision is or can be made in radical freedom. Indeed, it is the realization of the complex roots and prior determinants in every decision, however habitual or novel, that has led to the serious question of whether freedom actually exists in any real sense.

All of these levels of decision have been apparent at every point in the lives of the people with whom we have been concerned in these pages. It has been increasingly clear that what they do at any given time is shaped by what has already been done in the past. So it is that to talk about decision in any meaningful or realistic fashion is to be aware of the fact that the very act of deciding is itself the product or consequence of other decisions, which are themselves rooted in other decisions, and on and on.

OF COURSE GRACE would never put it that way. Nevertheless she was well aware of the intricate and complex forces both within and without which affected everything she did. Now that Mary had called, there was no question in her mind but that she would go. But she knew she might have chosen not to go. She could have put forth some excuse, probably a genuine cause, and declined. She hadn't gone several days ago. Of course Mary hadn't really asked her then, but she had sensed something. You couldn't really say she had deliberately decided not to go, it was just that she never did. She wondered how much not to decide was in itself a decision. Good gracious, you can't just keep going round and round in circles like that. Grace Nelson, if you think all you have to do is stand here in front of this sink and stew around like this, you've got another think coming. It was ten minutes after twelve when she heard the horn.

"Be right there," she called through the front door. "Bobby, you and Jeff finish your lunch now and Georgeanna will give you a surprise for dessert. I'll be home by the time you get up from your nap." She picked up her purse off the hall table and took a quick glance at herself in the oval mirror. Dear God, help me say the right words.

"Hi, Mary. Hope I didn't keep you waiting too long. Jeff wanted one more hug before he'd let me leave."

IT IS THE SENSE of personal respon-
sibility and the awareness of consequence which make decisions
painful. These, in turn, depend to a large extent on the way a
person perceives himself in relation to others. Frank had thought
about this a great deal of late. It surely isn't easy to know just what
is right and just what is wrong. The point is that you have to make
a decision anyhow; you just can't wait any longer.

They'd asked him to be chairman of the program committee
in the civic club. How could you tell them you didn't think you
could do it? Guys like Craig Wheelis and Vince McLean just don't
take "no" for an answer.

"You're the man, Frank! No doubt about it. There isn't anybody in the club who can handle this job like you can."

He'd met them for lunch several days ago. He knew when
Craig called that he had something up his sleeve. They were friends,
to be sure, but he couldn't remember their ever having lunch together, except, of course, at the club each Tuesday when they
might happen to sit at the same table.

"Sure, I'd like that. Tomorrow at twelve-thirty will be fine.
Yeah, all right. I'll meet you in the lobby. Yeah, me too. See you
then." As he hung up the phone he was conscious of the old familiar
feeling in the pit of his stomach. Strange how a feeling could be
good and bad at the same time. He was pleased that Craig had
called him and invited him to lunch. But somehow it took the edge
off when you knew he didn't call just because he wanted to be with
you. Craig was the kind of fellow you wished would call when he
didn't have some reason. The rest of the feeling was pretty bad.
What if you couldn't do what he wanted, that is, in case he did want
something? You wouldn't like to say no to a fellow like Craig. If
you did, chances are he would never call you for lunch again. He
found himself wishing he didn't have to go. Just let well enough
alone. Maybe something'd come up and he'd have to call that he
couldn't make it. But that would be even worse. Maybe Craig didn't
want anything, after all. People did call people to go to lunch just
because they liked to eat lunch with them.

"That's right," Vince knocked out his pipe against the palm

of his hand. "It's no reflection against the men on the present committee, but you know as well as we do that the quality of programs has not been up to snuff recently. All of us believe that with your contacts and know-how we can reverse the trend. The District Governor was down here working us over for our poor attendance record, and goodness knows he was right. A few really first-rate programs will start 'em back, though, and that's where you fit in."

"Well, honestly, I don't know what to say. Something like that'd require an awful lot of time, and I'm not sure I could take it on right now. We're real pressed at the office."

"Yeah, I know that. It's a big thing to ask you to do. But you know what they always say, 'if you want something done right, give it to a busy man.' "

"And don't forget you'll not be working by yourself. We can line up a good committee, but we need you to sparkplug the thing. A lot of men are more than willing to work with you, but we thought you'd like to pick your own team. The field's wide open."

"Well, I don't know. You fellows sort of caught me off guard."

"We certainly didn't expect an answer today. Take your time thinking about it. And as far as your business is concerned, something like this can really prove to be invaluable. You'll have an opportunity to be thrown with a lot of contacts that may turn out to be customers. Naturally, that's not why you'd take it, but it's the kind of fringe benefit you don't want to overlook."

"Yeah, you're right about that. I guess it's just the regularity of it that gets me, having to come up with a program each week."

"Well, it's not really as bad as it sounds. A lot of the programs are already set to a large extent—the District Governor's visit, the Ministerial Association at Christmas, the kids from the Boys' Home at Thanksgiving, things like that."

"I'll still have to think about it."

"Naturally," Craig motioned for the check. "I've got a man waiting for me at two and I know you are both in a hurry.

"I'll call you in a few days, Frank, and I don't have to tell you that I sure hope your answer is yes."

Frank looked at the note on his desk. "Craig Wheelis called at 11:15. Wants you to call him at his office sometime after two o'clock today."

FOR FRANK the necessity to make such a decision was fraught with dreadful anxiety. The momentary gladness at having Craig call him for lunch was long since gone. Now there remained only the awful realization that whichever way he decided, he was lost. When he was honest with himself he knew that the decision was already made, somehow. There was no way he could say no to a person like Craig Wheelis. Just like he couldn't say no that afternoon he'd gone to the movies, or when they'd had him work up the contract figures. He knew that they needn't have sent Vince McLean along. Craig alone would have been enough. Of course, with Vince there, the die was cast.

Actually, saying yes to Craig would be easy enough. Craig would thank him and tell him how pleased he was. Then he would reassure him that he knew they were in for a better day as far as the programs were concerned and that he would call Vince McLean and give him the good news. Yes, that part would be quite simple, and he knew from experience that he would even feel good for a little while after that.

It was not the phone call, though, that knotted his stomach. How in the world would he ever be able to live up to their expectations of him? You couldn't just create good programs out of thin air. Not only that, there were several members of the club who would complain no matter who was there. If you had an out of town speaker, "Why in the world did you have to go all over creation and spend a lot of money to bring somebody like that in here?" If you had a local speaker, "Isn't there any way we can get out of the rut of hearing these same guys over and over again?" If you had a politician, "You are taking unfair advantage since the other side doesn't have an opportunity to state its case." If you didn't have a politician, "You aren't really interested in the vital issues that affect the life of every man in this club, and we have a right to be informed."

He wondered what Craig would say about him to the next fellow he approached to be chairman of the program committee. "You know, I wouldn't want you to repeat this, but that Frank Mason isn't all he's cracked up to be. We really thought he was going to be a ball of fire this past year, but, well, you know yourself how it's been!" Maybe it'd just be better all the way around to tell Craig no right now. That's what he'd do. He *was* busy, no doubt about that. And if Craig didn't understand that, he'd just have to lump it.

But what if he *could* come up with some really topflight programs? Craig and all of them would like that. "Boy, that Frank Mason really pumped some life into things this year. I believe he's the kind of fellow we ought to be thinking about for president one of these years." It had a nice ring to it. Besides, wasn't Mary always telling him that he sold himself too short? And anyhow, he'd have a lot of time to work up the programs.

Just for a split second, as the buzz of the receiver told him that Craig's phone was ringing, the pain jabbed into his stomach.

"Craig? Frank. Listen, if you guys really think I can do this, I'm willing to give it a try. Yeah. Yeah. Well, I doubt that, but . . . Yeah. OK. I'll see you Tuesday at the meeting."

For WILLIAM, it had always been just the other way. You did what you wanted to do, and whose business was it, anyhow!

"But gosh, Will, you go out of your way to get into trouble."

"Trouble? Who's in trouble? Nothing wrong with me a couple of beers wouldn't cure."

They'd been sitting in the fraternity house after supper. He'd tossed his cigarette toward the fireplace and it landed just on the edge of the hearth.

"Pledge! Pick up that cigarette! What do you think ash trays are for? Maybe it'll help you to remember if you empty 'em all right now, wipe 'em out real good, and put 'em back in their places! Move!"

"Aw, simmer down. You want to make a federal case over one cigarette butt?"

"Shut up, Freshman! You heard me! Five licks for sitting there arguing with an upperclassman, and five more for every word you say until you get 'em all emptied. Now move!"

"OK. OK. Keep your nightie on, I'm moving!"

"That's ten!"

"If it'll help you any, make it fifteen. I don't like to hurry."

He gritted his teeth at each stroke of the paddle. Thirteen. Fourteen. Fifteen.

"Thank you, SIR!" He turned and shook hands, then walked back to his chair.

"I just don't get it, Will. You seem to like rubbing people the wrong way."

"Nah, that's not it at all. Thing is, you got to watch out all the time or somebody'll run over you for sure. A guy like that, for instance, gets the big britches just because he's an upperclassman. Begins to think he owns the world and can order you around. Well, he doesn't think that quite as much now. Let him swing his paddle while he can. Before long I'll be standing on the same rung he is, and then we'll see."

"But a guy like that could keep you out of the Chapter. Don't you ever worry about what people think?"

"Worry about what they think? Why should I worry about what they think? What they think is their business and what I think is mine. Let 'em think what they want and drop dead for all I care." He tossed his cigarette toward the fireplace and it landed between the andirons.

"Bull's-eye!" He got up and walked toward the door. "I'll see you guys in the funny paper. Be on the front page so I'll know you."

"Yeah, see you, Will."

They sat in silence for a few minutes after the door closed.

"How about a guy like that? I really don't think he gives a flip about anything."

"I tell you one thing. I hope he never needs anybody."

Linden Street was dark as William walked toward the dormitory. He guessed he really ought to go in and study for the Bible quiz old Professor Tiree was going to give them tomorrow. Boy, that Bible course was sure a laugh. He was only in there because they made all Freshmen take it. Some of those guys didn't know the Ten Commandments from third base. He remembered the night they'd been assigned to memorize them. Couple of the fellows had come in and said they couldn't find them, and what chapter had old Tiree said they were in?

"Exodus 20, old fool!"

"Well, 'old fool' yourself! They're not in Exodus 20 in my Bible. Just look and see for yourself!"

"For crying out loud, you don't think they are going to be numbered one—two—three, just like that, do you? Here, hand me your Bible and I'll mark 'em off for you. Didn't you guys ever go to Sunday school?"

"Well, just listen to who's preaching. Old Reverend Mason, himself. Let's get out of here before he takes up a collection!"

"If I was going to take up a collection, I sure wouldn't pick you peasants!"

He pretended to throw his English book at them and they slammed the door in hasty retreat. They hadn't come back much after that. Might be sort of fun to study with them tonight, he thought. Ah, forget it. They're such a dumb bunch of jokers they'd probably only mess me up.

He turned on the light in his room and picked his way over to the table. Got to straighten this place up one of these days. As usual his roommate was out. Boy, when that guy falls, he sure is a ton of bricks. She is a good looker, though. I can see why. Might as well look over these notes, although there probably isn't any need. We had this stuff when I was in the Junior Department. But there are certain things old Tiree likes to ask and I'd just as well have them down pat. "Crisis and Choice of the Children of Israel." He really goes for those alliterations. Bet he wishes they had been the Children of Chaldea or something like that. I'd better memorize the exact chapters and verses. Exodus 32:26: "Who is on the LORD's side? Come to me." Actually, he never had seen why Moses put up with all that sorry bunch. They didn't do anything but complain. Boy, he'd like to have been there and told 'em off. He'd have straightened 'em out quick or known the reason why. Deuteronomy 30:19: "I call heaven and earth to witness against you this day, that I have set before you life and death, blessing and curse; therefore choose life, that you and your descendants may live." He could almost hear old Tiree boom out on that one. Joshua 24:15: "Choose this day whom you will serve . . . as for me and my house, we will serve the LORD." 1 Kings 18:21: "How long will you go limping with two different opinions? If the LORD is God, follow him; but if Baal, then follow him."

He looked up from his notebook and wrinkled his brow. Let me see, now: Exodus 32:26. Three, two, two, six. OK. I got that.

Deuteronomy 30:19. Three, oh, one, nine. Three, oh, one, nine. That's a little harder. Joshua 24:15. A quarter after twenty-four. Yeah, man! 1 Kings 18:21. In eighteen hundred and twenty-one Elijah whipped the son of a gun. That'll do. Well, I'll snow him on the old "Crisis and Choice" question.

Odd thing that old Tiree should have picked those four as the ones to illustrate crisis and choice. Goodness knows there were plenty of others. What about the time at Kadesh when they were afraid to go into the Land of Promise? What about the times they went running off after Baal or who knows what? He'd brought this up one day when old Tiree asked if there were any questions. Must have riled him. Anyhow, he'd glared at him like he'd committed the unpardonable sin. "Mr. Mason, it is true that Israel often turned its back on Yahweh. But in these crucial instances they stepped forward and decided in positive and unequivocal terms to commit their ways unto him." He'd paused and glared around the room. "And I might add that it would be well if more of you here would make the same decision."

William had started to say that a precious lot of good it'd done them to come out so flat-footed for God when it didn't last long enough to mean anything. Sort of like the old man Gramps used to tell about who was the town reprobate but who would always come down and join the church every August when they had the protracted meeting in the big tent by the Court House. He never did get a chance to bring it up, though. Before he could get his mouth open old Tiree had launched into a kind of sermon on the general theme of commitment. No need to argue with him. If he didn't see it now, after teaching Freshman Bible all these years, there was just no hope for him.

All this stuff about decision was just a lot of bunk. Like those New Year's resolutions he used to make. Why, he'd even believed that things might be different. He'd even prayed about it. Really prayed, not just his Now-I-Lay-Me's. "God, help William to be a good boy. Can you, God? Can you, please? Keep me from hitting Frank and let Mama and Papa love me. If you'll just do it I won't talk in church or write in the hymnbooks or make airplanes out of the Sunday school papers, ever. I want to do what's right. For Jesus' sake. Amen."

He'd gotten up the next morning and it was a New Year. And then old Frank had started riding *his* bicycle he'd gotten for Christmas and wouldn't let him have it and when he'd asked him please he'd just kept on going, and so he'd pushed him over and he'd skinned his elbow and Papa came running out and said William you might have hurt Frank real bad and just for that you can't ride the bicycle for a whole week. He could still remember stumbling into the house and running up to his room. All right, who needs 'em? What good does it do to try to be nice to old Frank or Mama or Papa or anybody! They didn't know it, but he'd cried that day.

He guessed that was when he knew things were not going to be any different. He guessed he'd made a decision that day, but it sure wasn't what old Tiree had in mind. From now on I'm going to look after William, and anybody that doesn't like it can lump it. You get along better that way. He remembered something he'd read somewhere, "Blessed is he that expecteth nothing for verily he shall not be disappointed." That's going to be me right down to the wire.

Well, that was one decision he'd kept. Who needed 'em? Like that joker who'd hit him with the paddle tonight, or those two guys sitting there so bug-eyed scared somebody might come along and decide to hit them, or those dumb jerks who didn't even know the Ten Commandments. Let 'em all drop dead!

He glanced at his watch. Only five minutes to ten. It'd be sort of nice if his roomie didn't go out every night. Well, what of it? Hadn't he decided he could go it alone? Just for a split second, as the tower clock struck ten, he felt the pain jab into his stomach. Had it really been a decision? Was there anything else left? He slammed his book down. What a crazy thought! Of course this was what he wanted. Sink no roots and gather no moss. He flipped off the light as he went out the door. Guess I'll go down to the Old Bucket. There's usually a bunch hanging around there.

MARY tugged on the corner of her crumpled handkerchief.

"It's just that I . . . well I don't know what to do, and I guess I felt like maybe you could help me."

"I'll sure do my best, you know that. What's troubling you, Mary?"

The waitress took their sherbet dishes and filled their coffee cups again.

"Is it all right if we sit here for a little while?"

"Of course. I'll just take these things out of your way and you can stay as long as you want. Call me if you need anything."

All during lunch they had chatted mostly about the children. Grace sensed that Mary wanted to wait until they would not be interrupted before she told her what was on her mind. Strange how you can play a kind of never-never and both know that you were doing it and both know that it had to be done. To a casual observer they wouldn't appear to have a care in the world. She's ready now, Grace thought. The thing to do is just to remember . . . Dear God, help me remember.

"That's just it, I honestly don't know how to put it into words. From almost any standpoint I ought to be supremely happy. Frank is a good husband, he's got a good job, we have a nice home and two wonderful children. What else could you want?"

Grace nodded. She knew how hard it was to say that your life was falling apart. Her heart ached as she saw Mary's chin tremble. More than anything in the world she wanted to reassure her, tell her that things would work out all right, to keep her chin up. And then she thought of all the well-meaning friends who'd tried to reassure her during those dark days and how it'd only made the burden heavier since it'd meant she had to carry it alone. Thank you, dear God, for helping me to remember.

"I guess what you really want is to enjoy these things and see Frank and the children happy."

"Oh, yes, I do! I do! And somehow everything's gone wrong." She was fighting to keep back the tears. All at once she buried her face in her hands. She scarcely made a sound, but her shoulders shook with sobs. After awhile she lifted her face and dabbed at her eyes with her handkerchief.

"You'll have to forgive me. I promised myself I wouldn't cry."

"Sometimes crying is something you can't help. Besides, a good cry often sort of washes things clean."

"I cry so much these days, and there's no sense to it. It really doesn't change anything or help anything, and I feel so foolish."

Grace bit her lip. How quickly the easy reassurance came out even when she knew it didn't help. "I understand. And particularly when you try so hard not to."

"Yes. You've no idea how hard it was for me to call you. Oh, please don't misunderstand me. It wasn't that I didn't want to see you. It was just that I was embarrassed to burden you with my troubles. I almost said something about it when I was at your house the other day, but I just couldn't. I could hardly bring myself to pick up the phone."

Grace recalled how many times she'd thought about calling Mary, and had not. It had been hard for both of them. Strange how we can be so close and yet so far. What were we afraid of? I guess I was afraid of not being able to help and didn't want to run the risk of being inadequate. So I stayed away while she sank deeper and deeper in her misery. And I guess Mary was afraid that I wouldn't understand, and didn't want to run the risk of getting her troubles out in the open only to find that she was really alone with them.

"I'm so glad you called. Just sorry that it was so hard."

"I feel better already, just having somebody to talk to. Frank and I can't talk anymore. I think that's what scares me the most. We used to talk the way you and George do. But not any more. I guess it seems strange to you that we could get so far apart. I mean, you all are so close and everything."

"I can understand. You're right, it's wonderful now. But it wasn't always that way. I can remember a time when I wondered if we would ever be able to talk to each other again."

Mary looked at her with incredulity. "Grace, you're kidding. Not you and George."

"I know it sounds strange, and sometimes I find it hard to believe myself. It's like another world, or maybe you could say it's like a nightmare that was real, but you've waked up now. But we didn't come here to talk about that. I brought it up just so you'd know that I do understand what you're saying. I always feel that since it happened to us, it can happen to anybody."

" I wish I could be sure of that."

"And yet you can't. You can't be sure of anything right now."

"That's right. I've gotten my hopes up so many times. I'm

always saying maybe when this happens things will be different, or maybe after that's over then things will change. But they never do."

"Until after awhile you're ready to give up."

"Yes, that's true. But Grace, I don't want to give up. I can't give up. There just must be a way. But I've looked and looked, and it doesn't seem to come, or I can't find it."

The words tumbled out one after another. She realized she wasn't getting everything straight but somehow she just couldn't stop, and besides, nothing was really straight anyhow. And what could you put your finger on as the trouble when it seemed that everything had gone wrong, all their hopes and dreams, all their wonderful castles? Grace let her talk. The only time she spoke was to be sure that she understood what Mary was trying to say and to let Mary know that she understood.

". . . and so I guess that's really why I'm just not willing to sit by and let things completely fall apart. And I don't think Frank wants that, either, although it's pretty hard to tell what Frank wants these days. Anyhow, it gave me the courage to call you last night, I guess. That and the fact that I just kept hoping you'd understand."

"I believe that's one thing you can be absolutely sure of. Well, that is, as sure as you can be of anything these days."

Mary smiled. "Thanks, Grace. You're right. I'm not sure of much of anything these days. I'm surer right now of some things than I was before we got here today, though. You're one of them."

Grace sat in silence. Anything she thought of to say seemed rather lame. What she really wanted to say was thank *you,* Mary. She was just afraid it wouldn't come out right, and she didn't want to sound like a mutual admiration society.

"There's something else, too, Grace. I guess this may sound strange to you, but I'm surer of God than I was."

"I think I know what you mean, but it is hard to say."

"Yes, because I'm not even sure I know what I mean myself. It's not that I ever lost faith in him. At least I don't think I did. I didn't want to, that's certain. But I prayed so hard last night that you and I . . . that you . . . well, I guess what I'm trying to say is that you . . . you're . . . well, an answer to prayer."

"That's just about the nicest thing anybody ever said to me, Mary."

Mary reached for her purse. "We've been here much longer than I intended and I'd like to stay the rest of the afternoon, but you've got to get home to your children and I've got to take Bill to the dentist at four."

"It's been so good to be with you. Can we get together again soon?"

"For my part, you can count on it. I've needed this for so long. I might even be civil to Frank for a change."

DECISION is an intricate and complex matter with roots in the past which determine the possibilities available to the person at any given time. Each decision, however large or small, opens a door to areas of choice not heretofore attainable; but each decision also closes myriads of doors that can never be opened again. Thus, each time of decision or crisis, as the old Chinese proverb puts it, is made up of both opportunity and danger.

The Bible everywhere assumes the reality of choice, the importance of decision. The simple yet profound words of Jesus, "Follow me," take for granted that the hearer can in fact choose to do so and, having so chosen, act upon the decision. At the same time, the Bible everywhere recognizes the bondage which makes choice an illusion. The moving, yet profound, words of Jesus from the cross, "Father, forgive them; for they know not what they do," bespeak an awareness of the lack of genuine choice on the part of some, at least, who did him to death.

Between the freedom and the bondage, between the desire and the reality, between the dream and the fulfillment there is opportunity and danger, responsibility and consequence. It is clear that certain choices tend to limit freedom so that genuine decision is possible less and less. In a sense, Frank recognized this. So fearful was he that he might make the wrong choice, so anxious lest his choice be the occasion for rejection, that he found himself paralyzed when confronted with alternatives. He felt caught yet driven, and when the time for decision actually came, he realized it had already been made.

In the same way, although with widely varying manifestations, William knew the same bondage. So disillusioning had choice become, so futile was deliberation, that in time he concluded that all decision was meaningless. In this way he sought to avoid facing alternatives by denying their presence, and when the time for decision came he, too, realized that it had already been made.

By way of contrast, there are certain choices which tend to increase freedom. Mary was discovering that. Within the midst of her confusion and dismay she found it possible to call Grace. Like all choice, it was an act with antecedents and was made in the context of the narrowly constricted world in which she felt herself a prisoner. It is evident that the possibility of choice came as a consequence of factors introduced into Mary's perspective—factors which had not been present before, at least not in just the same fashion. It is also evident that having made the choice, the realization of greater freedom was not in and of itself automatic. Not every choice made by Frank had been negative. The same was true for William. Indeed, his cynical caricature of the Hebrew nation bespoke the more basic truth that decision, however positive, may nonetheless conclude in defeat.

Here, then, are two fundamental aspects of choice: namely, the introduction of some factor which makes positive choice possible, and the negative consequences which may follow positive choice. Because these aspects are so crucial in the process of maturity, we turn in the following chapter to a more extensive consideration of them as we look at the nature of freedom and bondage.

The law of the Spirit of life in
Christ Jesus has set me free
ROMANS 8:2

6
Freedom

"You aren't listening to me."

"Yes I am, George. Sort of."

"Grace Nelson, you haven't heard a word I've said all evening, and you know it."

"Yes I have. You were just saying that you were going fishing on Saturday and had a new lure."

"Well, that's close. It's a week from Saturday and I haven't got a new lure, Harold has. I can tell when you're a million miles away. You're worried about Mary Mason."

"Oh, George, I am. She's having such a hard time. I just wanted to cry this afternoon."

"I can imagine. But you didn't, and that's good."

"I wonder. Anyhow, you're right, I didn't. Not until I got home, that is. George, how well do you know Frank?"

"Not very well at all, I guess. I see him at church every time we go, and I know he's got a right responsible job at Martin's. He's the sort of fellow I never really feel I'm talking to. Hard to put your finger on it, it's something you feel more than know. You probably know him as well or better than I do."

"I don't think I know him at all. Of course, you never can tell. All I've heard is Mary's side of it, and goodness knows no one has to tell me that a wife can get things pretty garbled."

He smiled at her. "Particularly when all you've got to go on is pretty garbled itself."

"No, I mean it, George. She's hurt and mad and scared all at the same time, and you just can't see things straight when you're like that."

"Like that fellow in the Psalm."

"Yeah. But that doesn't mean you are either right or wrong, just that you don't have any other glasses to look through."

"I'll bet she saw things a little clearer after being with you today."

"I hope she did, but I'm not sure. Anyhow, we're going to get together again."

"Like I said this morning, you can do it. There's no doubt in my mind about that."

"George Nelson, you're impossible! You know as well as I do that you can't ever be sure how things will turn out with people."

"Gee, Honey, this thing really *is* hurting you."

She nodded as she bit her lip. "I guess I'm just about 'Exhibit A' for not seeing things very straight. I know you didn't mean it like that. I just wish it really was possible to be that sure."

LIKE SO MANY OF THE OTHER TERMS we have considered, freedom has many shades of meaning. Sometimes we speak of freedom *from* certain things, such as fear, oppression, want, and the like. In these instances we are thinking of the circumstances and situations which inhibit or restrict the exercise of choice in such a way that a person is not able to pursue a course of action as he would wish. On other occasions we use the term freedom with the preposition "of," and speak of freedom of religion or freedom of assembly or press or speech or what not. In these instances we are concerned with particular areas and activities which seem desirable and which may be denied or curtailed in certain instances. The use of the term freedom with the infinitive form of the verb carries with it this same notion of that which is to be done, such as freedom to work or freedom to marry or freedom to vote. In both of these senses the freedom, or lack of it, is generally considered to be a function of forces outside the person. Thus there may be prohibitions or restrictions imposed in the curtailment of freedom, or, on the other hand, there may be rights and privileges granted in the assurance of freedom.

There is, of course, a subtle tendency to think of freedom in some sort of an absolute sense, although it is clear that such is never the case. Beside the manifest fact that certain choices are mutually exclusive there is the corresponding and, at times, seeming paradoxical fact that certain curtailments of freedom result in the enhancement of freedom. Thus the prohibitory imposition of traffic regulations makes possible the use of an automobile on city streets and open highways. So it is that freedom is always relative, or, to put it another way, freedom without restraint destroys itself.

Quite apart from these notions of freedom which in some way or other depend on forces outside the person, there is the much more subtle and by far the more significant matter of freedom within the person. Since it is this inner freedom or lack of it which relates primarily and directly to the matter of maturity, it is here that our attention is focused in this chapter. The paradoxical relationship between these two aspects of freedom is seen in the fact that a person may be externally free but internally bound or, on the contrary, externally in bondage but internally free.

GRACE NELSON knew that. She wasn't really sure that Mary Mason would be able to "see things straight." She knew the kinds of bondage which distort and twist your perception of things and persons until it becomes difficult to know just what is true and what isn't. She would never forget the afternoon that Miss Morrison had come to see her when she was hurt and embarrassed and lonely.

"Can I come by this afternoon, Grace? I've made a new kind of blueberry roll, and I'd like for you all to try it out and tell me how it is. When you don't have anyone to cook for but yourself you don't always know what's good and what isn't."

Grace had glanced at her reflection in the mirror above the telephone table. You can't let Miss Morrison see you looking like this. She bit her lip as she searched for words to make some kind of plausible excuse.

"Well, uh, you're mighty nice to think about us, but . . ."

"Now Grace, I just won't take no for an answer. I'll only have a minute, so if you're busy don't think you've got to stop what you're doing and entertain me. Please say I can come."

What do you say to people like Miss Morrison? She hung up the phone and started making what repairs she could. When you've cried a lot there isn't much you can do, even if powder does help some. But that really isn't the most important thing. What do you say to Miss Morrison after she gets here? Everything's fine? Thank you for the blueberry roll? Come to see us again sometime? Look pleasant and laugh as you say you shouldn't have brought so much, we all need to watch our weight? What do you say to Miss Morrison? You have no right to come into my life like this? You know you just trumped up an excuse about the blueberry roll, you don't really care whether we eat it or not? Why don't you tend to your own business and let us alone? What concern is it of yours what happens to us? What do you say when she comes? Thank God you're here? I've wanted to call you many times but just couldn't? No one comes any more and I'm about to lose my mind I'm so lonely and frightened?

"Hello, Miss Morrison. Won't you come in?"

She took the berry roll neatly wrapped in foil.

"Oh, you shouldn't have brought so much. We'll gain five pounds eating all this. Do sit down while I put it in the refrigerator."

"I've really only got a minute. But I will sit down and catch my breath before I brave the traffic again."

"Can I fix you a cup of tea? The water is already hot."

"Grace, I shouldn't, but I just can't turn it down. Yes, I'd love a cup of tea."

Miss Morrison listened to the tinkle of cups on saucers and the whistle of the kettle. O God, help me find the right words. What do you say to Grace when she comes back with the tray? That looks lovely? You have such pretty china? My grandmother always said there was nothing a cup of tea wouldn't help? What do you say to Grace? Let's not beat around the bush—you're in trouble and everybody knows it and the sooner we get started doing something about it the better? Most of us don't see how you can stand to stay with George and wouldn't blame you if you took the children and left? It's up to you to show some initiative and spunk of your own—you can't just keep on like this the rest of your life? What do you say when she comes? Dear child, I'm not sure I ought to be here, but I couldn't live with myself any longer unless I came? I've prayed for you so often these past few months and want you to know that if there's any way I can be of help, I do want to do it? All of us in the church miss you and hope you'll soon be back?

"Just one lump, please, and no lemon or cream." She held the cup and saucer in her left hand while she slowly stirred until the sugar had dissolved, then sipped a bit. "Ah, that's just right."

She sipped again, and put the cup on the coffee table. She could hear the clock tick.

"Grace, I wanted to come by not just to bring the berry roll, but to tell you that I've missed you at church."

"I appreciate that. We're going to start coming again real soon."

"I hope so. Grace, you'll probably think I'm just a meddlesome old lady who should be worrying about her own troubles. Goodness knows I have plenty. But if I can be of help, I want to. And I believe you know me well enough to tell me if I've spoken out of turn about something that's none of my business."

"Why, of course not, Miss Morrison. You know I'm always glad to see you anytime. It just hasn't been convenient for us to make it recently, but we'll be back before long."

"It'll surely be nice to have you. And now I've just got to be running. Thank you for the tea. It saved my life."

"You're more than welcome. And thank you for the berry roll. Do come again, won't you?"

Grace watched her as she got into her car. Oh, Miss Morrison, come back! Come back now! Please come back right now! The car turned the corner and she was out of sight. Grace closed the door and began to gather up the cups and spoons. Suddenly she sank into the big chair and cried as if her heart would break.

After awhile there were no more tears. She picked up the tray and went into the kitchen. Why didn't you tell her? She was right here, and wanted to help. But what could Miss Morrison do? What can anybody do? George could do something if he just would. And that's what irritates me; he just won't try. Seems to me he could see what's happening to us. All he needs to do is make up his mind and then stick to it.

Could I have ever believed it was that simple? That people could just make up their minds? That there was no real bondage? I suppose I never did really believe it. Actually, it was a part of my not being able to see things straight, just as I couldn't see, or wouldn't let myself see, that Miss Morrison could help if I'd just open the door. Grace had thought about that afternoon many times. Even now it seemed like a miracle had happened. She'd not quite been able to understand just then that things were already different. Miss Morrison had come and she'd held her aloof, and then she'd gone. But she was never quite the same again.

It was two days later that she'd picked up the phone and slowly dialed the number. "Miss Morrison? This is Grace Nelson. Miss Morrison, can I see you? I need help."

THERE IS A FUNDAMENTAL SENSE in which freedom is always a gift. To say this is not to be unmindful of the fact that men have fought for freedom, have given their lives in the struggle to throw off the yoke of oppression and the bondage of slavery. But those who have done so are already free in the internal or personal sense of the word, and are striving to make real in an external or circumstantial sense that which has come to be so dear within. It is for this reason that tyranny can never prevail in the fight with freedom. However many the seeming victories won by oppression, however heavy the crushing burdens imposed by tyranny, the power of freedom once it has been experienced is irresistible. And, by the same token, however free may seem the actions and decisions of those who are internally bound, as long as the inner freedom is lost, the external freedom is mockery.

MISS MORRISON knew this. She had not always known it. As she drove away that afternoon she had ample time to wrestle again with the difficulty of freedom. How hard it is to give a person freedom. Even as she said it, she found herself wondering if that was just the right way to put it. Isn't it presumptuous to think that freedom is something you have and can give? Probably so, she thought. And yet even if that's not the best way to say it, there's something true about it, nonetheless. She could remember asking herself, how do you give a person freedom? Even as she'd raised the question, she knew it wasn't by letting them alone. There was no freedom in that. No, something more overt, more tangible, more personal was needed. And yet it certainly was not by compelling them, either. Where did you find the middle ground?

She still could feel the thrill that had come to her as one evening she had been reading in the third chapter of Revelation. "Behold, I stand at the door and knock; if anyone hears my voice and opens the door, I will come in to him and eat with him, and he with me." How many times do you suppose I'd read that verse before? But this time it was different. Maybe this time I was different. She couldn't help but smile at herself as she recalled how eagerly she'd seized upon it. That's it! That's it! I know that's it! "Behold I stand at the door and knock; if anyone hears and opens, I will come in." Why, that's the whole story of the Incarnation. He comes and knocks and we hear and open the door and let him in. It was later that she'd realized there was much more to it than the simple one-to-one solution she had first imagined. Nevertheless, she was sure that within the figure of Christ at the door there was the basic clue to the question of how freedom is given.

It was nearly dark when at last she turned into her driveway. How easy it is to be genuinely convinced that when you've offered to help, you must be just as willing to have the person refuse, and still be ready to go again and again without at any time demanding that they accept your definition of what help is or when it is to come or by whom. How hard it is to leave when, in fact, the person does not open the door. She was always plagued by many unanswerable questions. Did you really say the right words? If you'd said it another way would she have been able to let you into her life? Can you be sure that she heard your voice? Maybe she would have opened the door if you had knocked harder or spoken more clearly. She turned on the light in the kitchen and began to put the groceries away. As the years had passed she'd felt that she could understand just a little better how Jesus must have felt when he'd said to the disciples, "Will you also go away?" or the sadness in his heart as he watched the rich young ruler turn back. After awhile she wasn't sure just when she began to understand that she'd not seen the rest of it, at least not at first. But she knew in the end that what really helped was to know that he understood how she felt. Like right now, about Grace. Dear Lord, give me patience. Help me to see where I could have spoken more clearly, but help me also to see that Grace must be free to open the door or to keep it closed so that I will not in any sense violate her freedom or treat her as less than a person.

Two days later she answered the phone.

"Why I'd love to see you. I'm free right now, if you can come. Then I'll be looking for you."

Slowly she hung up the receiver. Thank you, dear Lord; she's opening the door.

IT IS EASY to say in retrospect that freedom is a gift. It is not always so easy to perceive it as a gift at the time, at least not in the ordinary meaning of the term "gift" as something that is desirable and pleasant to receive. On the contrary, the very possibility of freedom may be dreadful, as we have seen. The paradox is that the very chains which hold a person in bondage come to be perceived as indispensable so that freedom must be avoided at all costs. To be more precise, it is not the freedom which is terrifying; rather it is the unknown world of personal choice and meaningful responsibility which makes the deadly escape from freedom so tempting.

GEORGE knew that. He would never forget that awful feeling he'd had the time he'd really blacked out. There is a kind of fear that chokes you and you want to scream and no sound comes and you look around and realize you don't know where you are. How did I get here? How long have I been here? The questions jab their way into your brain as you fight to keep them out, keep them out, keep them out; for there are no answers and when the answers come they will be worse than the questions. Seven forty-five. Is it still running? Yes. Is it morning or night? Oh God! I don't know! Where am I? Where have I been? What have I done?

How can you tell in retrospect where it all began? Is there a way to trace a beginning to this thing which happened in childhood or that thing which was done in adolescence? He'd wondered about it many times. It would have been somewhat of a comfort to know that there was a cause, some reason, a particular twist of fate or circumstance, anything that would help to explain and maybe point the way out. Not that he lacked excuses. He'd always found plenty of those. But the answer was not there.

He couldn't even remember when he'd had his first drink. He was sure it was while he was still in high school, but the actual situation was beyond recall. As a matter of fact, it was in college that he'd begun to drink with more regularity. As he thought back on it, the drinking he'd done in high school seemed pretty inconsequential by comparison. And yet even then there were probably clues if only he'd been able to see them. But you didn't think about such things in high school. Not if you were sort of uncertain about yourself to begin with. It'd be real bad if the gang thought you were chicken. You'd show them that you were just as grown-up as anybody. No real way for them to know that you were pretty scared.

It was harder in college. You weren't even worried much about what the folks would say since they were back home and you were on your own. Nearly everybody got drunk every once in awhile, and mostly they thought it was a big joke when they talked about it afterwards. He'd laughed as hard as anybody when the stories made the rounds. After awhile it got to be a little more difficult to laugh so easily. He had realized even then that he was drinking too much. But he always told himself that as soon as he got out of college and settled down things would be different.

And, things had been different for awhile. He and Grace were married two weeks after graduation and moved into their own apartment. She'd never wanted him to drink, and for nearly a year he'd kept a fairly tight rein on himself. Not that he'd been a tee-totaler but, as he often said, there's a difference between a few bottles of beer or a couple of highballs and really getting drunk. Then the Korean war broke out and somehow all the resolutions seemed to lose their meaning. When he got home he promised Grace he'd do better. He went nearly a year that time. It was May when their first child was born, and he'd gotten drunk that night. Of course Grace didn't know, she was in the hospital, and besides it wasn't every day that your first son was born, and couldn't you celebrate something like that? It was a kind of hollow excuse but you had to say something. The worst part was that nobody had really asked, but that didn't keep you from having to give a reason. There was no way to admit that you wanted the reason for yourself and so wished there could have been one that made some kind of sense.

After that things sort of ran together. The time comes when

there are no more resolutions to be made, no more promises to be given, no more pardons to be asked. The dreadful thing is that the occasions which call for pardon, for resolution, for promise still come, and come again. How could they know the terrible hurt that burns like a fire deep within when they asked him why he didn't do something about it? Sometimes they begged or pleaded.

"George, for my sake, don't take another one."

"Can't you get off my back? I know what I'm doing, and if there's anything I can't stand it's a nagging woman."

"I don't mean to nag, George. It's just that I hate to see you hurt yourself this way."

"Who's hurting themselves? Can't you shut your mouth for fifteen minutes? When I need you to tell me what to do, I'll let you know!"

Usually he stormed out of the house and slammed the door behind him. If he could just get away, if he could just run, if he could just hide. By the time he got back home Grace would be asleep. How could you tell her that you couldn't stop, that something just came over you, that you'd tried, really tried? How could you tell her? You couldn't even tell yourself.

Sometimes they criticized and blamed. That was the way some of the fellows in the office did.

"I'm going to help you out this time, but I want you to be absolutely clear that this is positively all."

"Okay. I understand. It won't happen again."

"That's exactly what you said last time and the time before that."

"I know, I know. But I've learned my lesson now, and things are going to be different."

"Look George, you're old enough to run your own life; but you're making a mess of it. What you've got to do is just make up your mind that you won't take the first drink."

"Yeah, sure. That's right."

"Won't you go to a meeting of Alcoholics Anonymous? I know a couple of fellows they did wonders for. What about it?"

"Look, I don't need anything like that. I already told you things were going to be different, didn't I?"

He'd gotten off pretty light at that. Who's this guy think he is, giving out with all the advice? I'd like to tell the big jerk just what's what. Hope the old man's in a good mood. Well, here goes.

"George, I've called you in because I think the time has come for us to have a frank understanding."

"Yes, sir."

"I don't know any other way to say this than just to come right out with the bald facts. I don't believe I've ever been as disappointed with anyone as I have been with you. When I took you into the business, I had real high hopes for you. Right now I've put up with more from you than I ever thought I would from anyone. I've done it because of Grace and the two boys. You ought to be horsewhipped for what you're doing to them. Haven't you got any pride in your family? Haven't you got any sense of responsibility?"

"Yes, sir."

"Well, you certainly don't show it. Now George, I've been thinking a lot about this. Actually, I may be partly to blame by being too lenient. I just hated to see Grace having to suffer for your stupidity. But whether or not I have been too easy on you, the time for kid gloves has passed. Either you straighten up and fly right beginning right now, or you're out for good. Is that clear?"

"Yes, sir."

"All right. Now get back to your work and really mean business this time."

He closed the door as gently as he could and slumped into the chair at his desk. What does that old windbag know about what you are supposed to do and what you aren't? And what business is it of his what Grace does? Besides, she is getting along all right. I make a good living. How can they expect you to work when they are always yakking at you? His hand trembled as he picked up the pen from its holder. Steady, now. The figures ran together on the page. He clutched the arm of the chair and for a terrible moment he wondered if he was going to scream. Slowly he got to his feet and started toward the stock room. Not too fast now; no one will notice. It seemed an eternity before his hand felt the bottle hidden behind the cartons of envelopes. His throat burned as he gulped once, then twice. Ah-h-h. Now maybe I can get back to work.

Sometimes they neither begged nor scolded. They just walked away and didn't come back. Well, who needs them? All they do is criticize, anyhow. Better that they keep out of my hair. How do they know what it's like to sit at your desk and not be able to hold a pen? When did they ever have to go home and know there was no way you could face your wife and children? How many times had they dreaded to look into a mirror because of what they would see? "Exert your will power!" "Just make up your mind and stick to it!" "Won't you please try for my sake?" "When are you going to get wise to yourself?" O God, what do you do when you know all the questions and know all the answers and still are helpless to do what you know?

He looked around the strange room in terror. He had to have a drink before he could do anything else. He swallowed hard to keep the rising panic from rolling over him. The bottle on the dresser was empty. He'd known it would be even before he found it. How did I get here? Where have I been? What have I done? The questions came over and over. He had to have a drink.

Someone was at the door.

"George! Are you in there?"

He wanted to answer, but couldn't.

"George! Can you let me in?"

He tried to say that the door wasn't locked, but he didn't know whether it was or not. Instead he lay on the bed in terror. Who was it? What did he want? Go away and leave me alone! I don't know who you are.

"George!"

He heard the knob turn in the door and closed his eyes. Someone was standing by the bed.

"George, I'm Harold Clark. You don't know me, and I don't know you very well. I'm a member of AA and I'd like to help you if you'll let me."

WE HAVE SEEN that freedom is always relative and that the very exercise of freedom may result in the loss of freedom. Gradually the possibilities of choice diminish until life is prescribed by patterns of behavior which are best described as compulsive. It is as though the person is so shackled in the bondage of his own narrowing channels of response that he finds himself unable to break out into a different manner of life. Caught in the vicious spiral of predictable behavior he often longs for release but cannot attain it. Thus there is a literal helplessness which nonetheless is accompanied by a sense of responsibility and an agony of guilt in the awareness that freedom is lost through the exercise of personal choice. It is the paradoxical tension between the realization of failure and the acknowledgment of helplessness which may lead to deeper bondage, but which may also make possible the renewal of freedom.

It is in this sense that freedom is essentially a gift. It is that which is offered, that which brings a different and radically new alternative, that which creates again the reality of choice. It is not a choice in the order of behavior already established; it is not a piece-meal patching of this or that activity within the general framework of habitual response. Rather, it is the perception of a genuine reversal in which the lines are not clearly drawn and in which there is seen no security or guarantee of success. It is a gift which may be rejected. But it is a gift which, in the very act of giving, creates the capacity for choice and waits for the choice to be made.

HAROLD knew this. He had not known it in just that way, at least not at first, but looking back he could see it in a way not possible at the time.

"It does seem strange to me that Jesus would have asked the man, 'Do you want to be healed?' You'd think he'd known that already."

"Maybe so. But the story says he'd been there thirty-eight years."

"That's just the point. He certainly must have wanted to be healed, or he wouldn't have come down to the pool so long."

Harold listened to the discussion. He often wondered whether Miss Morrison could read their thoughts.

"Were you about to say something, Harold?"

"Yes. It seems to me that Jesus had to ask this question. If this man had been there for thirty-eight years, he really might not want to get well."

"That's the craziest thing I ever heard of, Harold. Why wouldn't he want to get well?"

He hesitated for a minute. Lou always made him feel rather uncomfortable and it was hard to get his train of thought together. He started to tell Miss Morrison that she'd gotten him into this, and it was up to her to get him out. He wasn't sure he could make it clear since it wasn't too clear to him, either.

"Well, from one point of view, it would be wonderful to be well. But there's more to it than that. If he was well, he'd have to do a lot of things he'd never had to do before. For one thing, could he make a living?"

"But that's nothing compared to being sick all the time."

"Maybe so. It surely seems that way to us. But maybe it didn't to him."

"Oh, Harold, you're always trying to read something into things. Jesus just asked him, that was all."

"You might be right, but even so, I think the point is that he *did* ask him. He didn't just heal him. The man had to say whether this was what he wanted or not."

"Do you think there was any real likelihood that he would have said no?"

"Yes, I believe there was."

Miss Morrison listened. She wasn't surprised that Harold saw that the question of healing was an open one. They had been discussing the eighteenth chapter of Luke and why Jesus had asked the blind man, "What do you want me to do for you?" She had suggested that while they were on the subject, they might also like to look at John 5.

"What do you think, Miss Morrison?"

"It's hard to be sure since, as far as I know, the question is never answered in the negative. Yet at the same time, I think Harold is right that the person had to make the choice. And it does say that in Nazareth Jesus could do only a few mighty works because of their unbelief."

"But that means they didn't believe that he was the Son of God, doesn't it?"

"Yes, but it isn't that simple. The kind of faith they needed was more like trust that would let them turn loose of the things they were doing."

"I still think Harold wants to make things too complicated."

"Maybe so. But I can't seem to say it any other way."

"Lou, are you saying that life is not complicated or that Harold is making it sound more complicated than it is?"

"Well, certainly not the first. I know there is more to it than meets the eye. I just wish we could get a few things a little more simplified. It upsets me to look for meaning in everything we talk about. Harold makes it sound like there isn't any such thing as a simple question."

"And after awhile you get tired of 'straining at gnats.'"

"I sure do. But I'll keep on coming. Sometimes Harold does say something good, as much as I hate to admit it."

They all laughed. It seemed so strange to Harold that Lou couldn't see it, or wouldn't. The chains might be ever so heavy, might be cutting into your flesh, but you come to depend on them and aren't sure you'd know what to do without them. For him the chains had been alcohol. He hadn't needed anyone to tell him everything was going to rack and ruin. But that was something else again from being able to face life without alcohol. Do you want to get well? You don't know. You want to get rid of the misery, the loneliness, the guilt, the fear. But that's different from asking whether you want to get well.

Miss Morrison glanced at her watch. Time had run out again. The children would be out of their classes, clamoring at the door. After all the times they'd met together, she still found something new each session, still came to the close with a kind of regret. It was not surprising that Harold could understand the meaning of choosing freedom. The intriguing point was that right now he couldn't see that Lou was not able to look at the deeper factors in personal behavior. Harold could see it in an alcoholic. It was harder for him to see it in a person like Lou. She bowed her head as the class closed with prayer. It was as she was driving home after the morning worship service that she thought of her own hesitation to let them go at the end of the hour.

WHEN WE WERE DISCUSSING the meaning of conscience, we noted the way in which Paul wrestled with the bondage which comes as a result of sin. "Wretched man that I am!" he wrote, "Who will deliver me from this body of death?" There is in this agonizing cry the recognition of helplessness, the sense of being trapped, the consciousness that there is no freedom at all. Moreover, there is the dreadful realization that in some fundamental degree the bondage has come through one's own choice, a choice made in the presence of forces which were not fully understood and over which there was not complete control. Nevertheless, it is clear that the choice was made, that there is a deep responsibility, that there is personal guilt in the wretchedness of the bonds. The paradox is that once the freedom is lost, it cannot be regained. It is here that the helplessness is seen in all its aspects. The freedom can be received, but in order for this to happen, it must be given to the person. So it is that Paul recognizes that "the law of the Spirit of life in Christ Jesus has set me free from the law of sin and death." It is in the context of freedom that he is able to describe the experience of bondage. The realization of Romans 8 makes possible the confession of Romans 7.

There is another aspect of the possibility of freedom which can never be overlooked. When freedom is offered, it carries with it the freedom to be refused. Whereas at the depths of bondage the person has no possibility of choice at all, he now has the choice between leaving the bondage or remaining caught in the web which holds him fast. Thus, the ultimate paradox emerges, that the freedom which comes in the offer of freedom may be used to reject freedom.

This basic fact stands out most clearly in the Incarnation. At every point the possibility of freedom, of deliverance, of new life is offered. There is the moment of encounter, the crucial weighing of the alternative, the decision. Some, like the rich young ruler, turned away and followed after him no more. Some, like Paul, responded in faith and discovered that in fact "the law of the Spirit of life in Christ Jesus has set me free from the law of sin and death."

In this statement by Paul is seen the genuine meaning of freedom. It is in no sense unrestrained or irresponsible. There is still a "law." The difference is in the nature of the law rather than in the absence of the law. There is a bondage in the new freedom just as there was bondage in the old. Paul saw himself as the "slave" of

Christ. It is in this sense that the critical factor of choice is seen, the choice that is made possible by the coming over of the possibility of freedom. The choice to reject freedom does in fact lead to death, but the death seems to be postponed, and for the moment there is a kind of security in the structures of the bondage. The choice to accept freedom does in fact lead to life, but the life seems to be shrouded in mystery, and for the moment there is the feeling that what will come is not life but death. For this reason Paul's metaphor of death of the "old man" is not simply a figure of speech; just so, the "rebirth" of the new man carries with it the meaning of newness of life.

As we look at Grace and George we can see something of the struggle that comes in the midst of human suffering. Their situation is not basically different from that of William, who finds himself driven by hurt and fear to destroy the things he wanted most. It is not different from that of Frank, who knew that, whichever way he decided in the choice put by Craig and Vince, he was already lost. But for Grace and George there has come the possibility of freedom. It is in the coming that we begin to understand the crucial significance of faith. Can the new life in fact be real? Can the securities of the old life be dropped? The answer is found in the emergence of faith.

Even so, to say that what happens is an act of faith is itself subject to many interpretations, for the word faith has many meanings. Thus it is to an investigation of the meaning of faith that we turn in the next chapter.

This is the victory . . . even our faith
1 JOHN 5:4 K.J.V.

7
Faith

IT WAS AFTER TWO O'CLOCK when Dr. Watson got back to the church. He was never sure just what was accomplished in making a speech to a civic luncheon club. Not that he didn't enjoy going. Indeed, it was always most pleasant to see men with whom he had little other contact. And they seemed to enjoy it, too. Many had said that his talk on faith had meant a great deal to them. Most of them probably meant it. But there is a difference in a person's enjoying a talk and having it make any real difference in his life. Maybe it wasn't his responsibility to "make any real difference" in a person's life, at least not at a civic club luncheon. But if not, then what was his purpose in going? He always came back to this question and always had trouble settling on the right answer. He knew all the words about sowing the seeds which would possibly bear fruit in days to come, and felt there was truth in such a notion. The thing that bothered him was that this kind of passive dealing with something as crucial and as vital as faith just seemed out of balance.

"Now faith is the assurance of things hoped for, the conviction of things not seen." He smiled as he thought of how often he said "substance" instead of "assurance," and "evidence" for "conviction." When you'd learned something a long time ago and had said it enough, it just tended to come out that way, no matter how deliberately you made an effort to say it in other words. Quite a few of the men had said they knew it the other way and wished it hadn't been changed in the new revision. He could understand what they meant since he often felt the same way himself. At the same time it troubled him to realize that he could become so accustomed to the well-known words and phrases that the meaning was no longer clear or even essential. You could just say the words without thinking, and they sounded right, and that was that.

It'd be interesting to know what the various members of the

club thought he'd said about faith. What would be even more interesting would be to know if what he'd said had actually made any difference in their lives. There, he'd come back to that question again. But it was important. And anyhow, how did he know for sure that it hadn't made a difference? Maybe what you need is a little faith, Preacher. He pondered the admonition and sighed. All right, I agree. How do I get it?

There was a stack of mail on his desk neatly arranged with the letters on top, followed by circulars and magazines. You sure do get a lot of trash these days. He looked up as his secretary stood at the door.

"Miss Morrison is on the phone and wants to talk to you. She called a little while ago, and I told her I thought you'd be back shortly after two."

He picked up the phone and sat down.

"Miss Morrison? Howard Watson . . . Yes, I do."

He reached for a pencil and wrote on the pad as he listened.

"Yes . . . Yes . . . Yes, I'm sure of that . . . I see . . . I'm going to the hospital in about half an hour, but I could drive by your house while I'm out that way . . . All right. I'll see you about four-thirty then."

He nodded as he held the receiver to his ear. "All right. Thank you for calling. Good-bye."

What do you really mean when you talk about faith? He thought back over the address he'd made at the civic club. He'd tried to point out the difference between faith as assent and faith that implies trust or confidence. Maybe he was splitting hairs. How could you have faith unless there was some evidence to go on? That was certainly the way he thought about his own faith. All around were the evidences of God's goodness. But of course there were evidences of other things, too. What did it mean to believe "in the face of conflicting evidence"? That one wasn't so easy. You did believe, but you couldn't be absolutely sure. Maybe what you believed was that there was a possibility. Like now. He hardly knew the Nelsons. They'd been cordial enough when he'd gone to call, but they'd always kept him at a distance. How good it was to have somebody like Miss Morrison. She could reach people who wouldn't let him get anywhere close. And when she called him she always made it sound like he could do anything. She knew better than that, but it was nice to have somebody like Miss Morrison who had confidence in you.

Whenever anyone spoke of people being saints, he always thought of Miss Morrison. No doubt in his mind that she could qualify, although, of course, one didn't qualify to be a saint in the strictest sense of the word. One thing was sure, Miss Morrison had faith. In that sense she was truly a saint. Was he a saint? He did have faith, but there were times when it was difficult to see the ultimate meaning in things that happened. He found himself remembering the words of the man whose son the disciples could not heal. "Lord, I believe; help thou mine unbelief." Those were the old words. But they were the words that had had meaning long ago, and still did.

"Do come in, Dr. Watson."

Miss Morrison's house always fascinated him. It had been built before the turn of the century and she'd grown up in it. Her mother had been an invalid, and after her father's death she had been the sole means of support. Everyone had thought she would sell the house and move into a smaller place, but she never had. Now that her mother had died, she lived alone. The living room furnishings were just as they had always been through the years; a horsehair sofa, a marble top table which held a lamp with a green colored glass shade that had beaded fringe all around the edge. Two heavy carved oak chairs stood at either end of a massive library table. A rocker with needlepoint upholstery and two ladder-back chairs completed the circle. He was sure that this was what a parlor looked like. There was a dignity which had a timeless quality. In one way it tended to intimidate him. In another way it reminded him of those qualities of life which endure. He often thought that it was just the kind of place you could expect to find Miss Morrison, and he was glad she had never sold the home.

"It's good to see you, Miss Morrison. I hope I'm not too late. It's hard to judge how much time the hospital calls will take."

Miss Morrison motioned him toward the sofa as she sat in the rocker. He could feel its unyielding firmness.

"No, I knew you'd be here when you could. As I said on the phone, I need your help with the Nelsons. Grace was here this

morning and is just about at her wit's end. She hasn't seen George
for three days and she's having a real hard time with her own feelings. One minute she's so filled with resentment over everything
he's done that she doesn't care what happens to him. The next
minute she is overwhelmed with worry and ashamed that she resents
him so much. It really is a most dreadful situation, and I don't
know whether there's any solution or not."

"It's not like you to see anything as hopeless. I guess this one
is really bad . . . enough to make you wonder."

"It surely is. To tell you the truth, Dr. Watson, I'm always
pretty helpless when it comes to alcoholics. I just can't make any
sense out of what they do. I wish I could look at it like you do. You
seem to have so much patience and understanding. Honestly, it's
hard for me to hold my temper when I think of what George is
doing to that child."

"Just like to turn him over your knee and paddle him."

"I'm not at all sure I'd stop with paddling. A good horse-
whipping is more like what I had in mind!"

"You'd want him to have a much more severe punishment
than a mere paddling, then."

"Yes. After all he's done, he should be made to suffer some,
too."

"Is this to say that you don't see him as suffering now?"

"Well, not as much as he deserves."

"So he needs to be hurt much more."

"No, I really don't mean that. It just shows that I'm a vindic-
tive old woman. That's why I wanted to see you. I don't think I can
help Grace, and I know I can't help George."

She sat staring at the floor. Dr. Watson had an almost uncon-
trollable urge to say something like there, there, of course you can
do it, or if anybody can do it, you can. He wondered why he'd
pushed her to see that George was suffering, why he'd chastised her
for being so irritated over what was happening to Grace. Then he
realized that he didn't want Miss Morrison to have any weaknesses.
It was disturbing to see that she couldn't understand the kind of
agony George was going through. Even as he thought about it, he
knew that what he perceived in her was also true for himself. He
had wanted to scold her for being who she was, just as she wanted

to scold George for being who he was. "Lord, I believe; help thou mine unbelief."

"I'll help if I can, you know that. Where would be a good place to start?"

"I guess the only place to start is with Grace since she's at least come. I asked her to call you and I believe she will. And I told her that I was going to try to see you and tell you the whole story as I saw it."

"If she doesn't call by tomorrow, I'll go by to see her."

"I think she'll call. At first she wasn't sure she could talk to you. She thought you'd never be able to understand how she felt. She's so ashamed and embarrassed that it's hard for her to hold up her head. I told her that you could understand, and she could trust you. When she left here she intended to get in touch with you either today or tomorrow."

He wanted to say that he wasn't as understanding as she thought. He couldn't even understand her. He couldn't even understand himself. He knew it wouldn't be right to make her bear these burdens, though. Of course Miss Morrison needs a pastor. I know that, or at least in a way I know it. It's just that she's so good, I tend to forget. "What about George?"

"I thought we might ask Harold Clark to look for him. While Grace was here I called his office and they told me he was out of town for the day. She's supposed to call him tonight. Harold will know what to do."

That's right, he thought. Harold will know what to do. He'll know where to look, too. He's been in all the places himself. "That makes sense. I've got to run now, but I'll keep in touch with you. Let me know if anything develops. Let's pray together before I go."

She bowed her head.

"Dear Lord, we thank thee for the assurance that thou art working out thy purpose in all things. Just now we ask thy particular blessing on Grace and George and their two boys. Be with Miss Morrison and be with me as we seek to find ways to help them. Forgive us as thou dost forgive them and all thy children through Jesus Christ, in whose name we pray. Amen."

"Thank you for coming. I feel better about things already. It's wonderful to have somebody you can turn to when you don't see the way clearly. And thank you for Grace and George until they can say it themselves."

THUS FAR in our discussion it has been possible to identify certain aspects of human behavior which are inherent in the process of moving toward maturity. In each instance we have noted the struggle which marks the path of life, and have seen how varied and intricate are the deviations as each person strives to grow up in the presence of forces which inhibit or block his progress. It is not difficult to see the emerging understanding of right and wrong as a mark of maturity; in like manner we tend to think of a person as mature when he develops the ability to deal with such factors as anxiety and hostility. When we come to a consideration of faith, however, a curious paradox becomes apparent. For although it is proper to speak of a mature faith, it is also certain that, in some situations, it is considered desirable to have a childlike faith. From this point of view, it would seem that something is lost in the process of growing up, something that can be regained only when the person becomes like a little child.

MISS MORRISON had pondered this strange fact a great deal in the past few days. Even as she had prayed for patience in allowing Grace to set her own pace, she had been conscious of how difficult it is to believe that God is working out his purpose in the lives of his people. At the same time, she was sure that her faith could be no naïve notion that all would be well. She had lived too long, seen too much tragedy and heartache to believe that. Whatever else the years had taught her, she was convinced that it was not the mark of genuine faith to go blithely on one's way in the belief that no matter what you did, things would turn out all right in the end. But wasn't that the way a child would look at things? She never was real sure, now that she was old. Had she ever looked at things that way? Probably.

She remembered the games of make-believe. She'd never had a sister or brother, so she'd had to invent them. But after awhile you knew that there was no gold at the end of the rainbow, that there was no fairy godmother who would come and turn you into a beautiful princess, that there wouldn't be any real brother or sister, that mother would never be well, that you would have to stay here and take care of her. It wasn't so much that the faith you had as a child was shattered, although at times there were some crushing blows. It just gradually eroded and crumbled. You weren't even sure just when it had gone, but you knew it was. Was that the kind of thing they meant when they spoke of childlike faith? She was sure it wasn't. Perhaps a better term would be childish. But if that were so, then what did it mean to talk about childlike faith? And was having childlike faith something you could just do at will? She couldn't believe that it was.

She remembered what Grace had said when she came that morning. "How can you have faith when you've tried and tried and nothing seems to work?"

"I don't know an easy answer to that, Grace. I wish I did. I guess for you faith is just a word that doesn't have much meaning anymore."

"I don't know; I just don't know. I'm not really sure of anything right now. The other day somebody said that the only way George will ever be any different is for me to believe in him, to have faith in him. And I want to, Miss Morrison, honest I do. But it just won't come. He's disappointed me so many times. He's lied and stolen and . . . Well, I just can't depend on him any longer."

She honestly did wish she knew the answer. She could understand how Grace could at last come to the place where she found it impossible to believe in George any more. Somewhere along the way there had to be some evidence, some ground for confidence, some basis on which to stand. And if there was nothing? How could faith be "the evidence of things not seen?" There had to be something tangible. Didn't there?

GRACE started nervously as the doorbell rang. She'd never gotten used to being alone. The big clock in the hall chimed the quarter hour. Eleven-fifteen. I'm sure that's Harold Clark. Nobody else would be coming here at this time of night.

"It's Harold, Grace. Can I come in?"

"Please do. Can I take your hat?"

"No, I'll only stay a minute. But I did want to find out a little about George before I started out looking for him. From what you said on the phone, I don't think we'll have any trouble finding him. I just sort of wanted to know what I would find when I got to him."

Grace sat in the rocker. How can you tell him what George is like? Do you say that he is a grand guy who was a hero in Korea but who somehow just never grew up? Do you say that he is irresponsible and thoughtless, and can stay gone as far as you are concerned? Would you say that he is worried and frightened, and be gentle with him when you find him? "Chances are he'll be down in one of those cheap rooming houses beyond Eighth Street. He hasn't been home for three days, so I guess he won't look like much. Do you want me to go with you?"

"No, I believe it would be better if I went by myself this time."

"It's awfully late. Are you going to look tonight?"

"For awhile. A couple of the other fellows will be helping me. If we don't find him in an hour or two, I'll get some sleep and check with them first thing in the morning. A trip like the one I've been on today takes most of the starch out of me."

"I want to thank you, but somehow I can't find the right words. I can't really understand why you'd do this. You don't know George. You don't owe him anything. He's not really your responsibility."

Harold looked down at the floor. He still found it rather hard to find words, himself. You couldn't say, "Aw, Grace, it is nothing really." But how did you tell your deepest feelings? "Grace, there was a time when a man I didn't know very well came and stood by me when my life had tumbled in and I had no place to turn. He didn't ask me to do anything, he didn't chew me out for being where I was, he just said he wanted to help me. I couldn't believe it. It didn't make any sense. Maybe it doesn't make any sense, now. But whenever I have a chance to go out like tonight it's one way I have of saying thank you to that man. And I'll never get tired of going. At least right now I don't think I ever will."

Grace nodded as though she understood. She knew she didn't, really. This just wasn't the way things were. But when you were desperate, you didn't have much right to question the motives of somebody who did seem willing to help.

"You'll call me when you know something?"

"You bet I will."

She watched him as he went down the walk to his car. Was it only two days ago that she'd stood here as Miss Morrison had driven off? It seemed much longer. That was a different world. She turned off the porch light, and started upstairs. Nothing had changed, not really. And yet it was different. It's different because there's someone with me. I'm not alone anymore. I've been alone so long, so long. Dear God, thank you for Miss Morrison, and thank you for Harold Clark. I don't deserve either one of them, and yet they're here. They're here. It was twelve o'clock when she turned off the bed light. She felt that she would sleep tonight for the first time in a long while.

WE SAID EARLIER THAT FREEDOM is always a gift, always that which comes over to the person, that which makes the possibility of choice a reality. It is clear that the person might choose to reject freedom, might decide to remain in bondage, might fear the consequences of liberty. At an even deeper level, it is certain that faith is also a gift. It is that sense of trust which wells up within the person in response to someone whose attitude and behavior provide the foundation upon which to stand with increasing confidence. It does not come at once. Its struggle is with fear—fear of painful circumstances, fear of unknown situations, fear of conflicting feelings within the self. Faith cannot come until the fear begins to diminish. Thus it is always born in the presence of fear, in the trembling of the soul, in the dreadful sense of destruction. Thus it is always born in response to love, for only love can conquer fear, and only perfect love can cast it out altogether. Thus faith always struggles with fear, always feels the tug of doubt, always knows the sting of temptation. "Lord, I believe; help thou mine unbelief."

HAROLD thought of what he'd said to Grace. It was true, he was sure of that. And yet was that really all? Not quite. Why had he felt the need to tell her that he didn't think he'd ever get tired of going? Even as he'd said it, he knew it didn't sound just right. He was tired right now. Going to look for a fellow who'd been drunk for three days wasn't any picnic. Harold Clark, you know you're going because this is the only way you can live. It's either you doing the looking or it's you who has to be looked for, and you want to keep it headed in this direction. Why didn't I tell Grace that? Well, she probably wouldn't have understood. But she probably didn't understand what I said, anyhow. Quarter to two. Better go home and sleep awhile or you won't be any help to George when you do find him. He'll make it until morning, and that's when he'll need you. Probably out cold right now.

He would never forget, that much was sure. There had been many times when it had been hard to keep his thinking straight. But the struggle of those first days had burned into his memory. He'd never have made it without Jim. He could understand how Grace might wonder why he was going. How many times he'd wondered that about Jim. Well, he knew now—or thought he did. At least he knew part of it. Jim had come. He certainly had no reason to come as far as I was concerned. But for that matter no one could have had a reason. And yet he had come. And that had been the difference between death and life. You don't say it that way. It would sound so melodramatic. But it is true. Because of him, I am alive.

He turned into his driveway and drove into the garage. For just a few minutes he sat in the dark. Heavenly Father, I thank you that I didn't take a drink today. Forgive me for not coming clean with Grace Nelson. Help me to find George, and when I find him help me to do the right thing. In Jesus' name. Amen.

DR. WATSON picked up the Testament from his bedside table. For as long as he could remember he'd read it each night before he went to sleep. He turned to the second chapter of Ephesians. "And you he made alive, when you were dead through the trespasses and sins in which you once walked, following the course of this world, following the prince of the power of the air, the spirit that is now at work in the sons of disobedience."

Paul certainly had a graphic way of putting things. Sometimes he wasn't sure that the words were meant to be taken literally. They hadn't really been dead, at least not as you usually thought of someone being dead. But the meaning was literal, of that he was convinced. For they were dead as far as living was concerned. "But God, who is rich in mercy, out of the great love with which he loved us, even when we were dead through our trespasses, made us alive together with Christ (by grace you have been saved) . . ."

It was easy to talk about the love of God. He realized that many times he used the phrase without actually feeling its real depth and meaning. He wondered whether Paul ever felt that way. When he wrote "Out of the great love with which he loved us," you knew he was trying to get beyond the ordinary meaning of the words. "For by grace you have been saved through faith; and this is not your own doing, it is the gift of God . . ." That part he understood. Love that offers the gift of faith. Only God can love like that. But because he does, it is possible for us to love, too. And faith does come when we really love.

He thought again about the talk he'd made at the civic club. There was a difference between "a faith" and "faith." He remembered reading somewhere that everyone has a faith, but not everyone has faith. It had a kind of catchy ring to it and when he'd quoted it today he'd made his point. Like most catchy sayings, however, this one tended to obscure nearly as much as it enlightened. What did it mean to say that a person had faith? Not that you "believed" the light would go on when you flipped the switch. Not that you "believed" the sun would rise tomorrow. Not that you "believed" the plane would arrive safely at its destination or that the bank would keep careful records in the handling of money. In a sense, of course, such things were matters of faith, but that wasn't what you meant when you said that a person had faith.

What did it mean? Not that a person went blindly ahead regardless of the evidence. Not that you refused to exercise reason or judgment. Not even that you were determined to act as if something were so. These things, too, could be said of faith, but would still miss the basic meaning. In all likelihood most of the men at the civic club "believed" that what he had said was so, but had it made any difference in their lives? There is that nagging question again. But isn't that just the crux of the matter? That faith does make a difference? That the person is changed? That he's able to move in a new direction, and will, however hesitantly? For then faith is understood as trust.

Sometimes it seemed so clear, and at other times it seemed to elude him. He wondered whether his ability to see it clearly or not could have something to do with his own faith. "Lord, I believe; help thou mine unbelief." He was tired now, and it was harder to keep his thoughts in clear focus. Faith is a gift. It is God's gift in Christ. But they did not all believe. There is freedom not to believe. He knew how hard it was to believe. To trust—really trust, to know that all things are working together for good, to be sure that nothing can separate us from the love of God which is in Christ Jesus our Lord. He put the Testament on the table and switched off the light.

IN TIME THE TERM FAITH comes to be used with the definite article, and we speak of *the faith*. In this sense we refer to the whole scope of belief which has come as the heritage of the church. This is the "faith of our fathers living still"; it is the affirmation of that which they came to know to be real, that by which they lived, that by which they died. It is an expression of strength, of reassurance, of hope. As it is spoken, it bridges the gap between one generation and another, it provides the evidence of that which is not yet seen, the assurance of that which is still only in the realm of hope. But *the faith* and faith are never the same. *The faith* may call out that faith may respond; and in time, faith is expressed as *the faith*. But *the faith* is always corporate, faith always personal. That which is most surely believed by the church must become that which is, in fact, believed by the individual. This personal faith never happens apart from *the faith,* but until it happens there is no salvation. So it is that Paul writes in Romans 10, "For man believes with his heart and so is justified, and he confesses with his lips and so is saved."

It is in this sense that *the faith* can be certain and settled as representing the belief of the church, but at the same time it is tentative and formative as representing the emergence of faith within the person. Rooted in the heritage of *the faith* of the church, that which is becoming *the faith* of the person represents the tension between historic belief and personal response. This is not simply to say that each generation must make the faith of the fathers its own; beyond that, the faith of the individual grows and changes as it finds a confidence in experience.

The early beginnings of faith often bear little resemblance to *the faith*. There is an inner longing which responds to the gracious act of love in hesitant trust. Something of the self can be given, but only very little. The commitment is only tentative. The fear is still there, and the risk still seems enormous. The emergence of faith is often painfully slow and its course uneven.

It may have been more than two years before the disciples were able to answer the question, "Who do you say that I am?" with a word that was truly *the faith*. It is certain that the faith they declared in the words of Simon Peter did not represent a mature and settled faith of their own. Many times on the road to Calvary their hearts were to fail within them, and on the night in which he was betrayed they all were to forsake him and flee. So it is that faith struggles with doubt and fear and disappointment and failure; so it is that faith is battered by circumstance and undermined by events which seem to belie its very foundation. How could Christ be crucified? O God, why?

It is an old question. Job knew its sting and Jeremiah its agony. John the Baptist cried from the darkness of his prison, "Are you he who is to come, or shall we look for another?" Jesus' reply points to the evidences of grace, the tangible demonstration of the love of God. "Go and tell John what you have seen and heard: the blind receive their sight, the lame walk, lepers are cleansed, and the deaf hear, the dead are raised up, the poor have good news preached to them." Here is the substance from which faith can spring, here are the deeds of loving-kindness in which can be found the basis for belief. But there is more. For though these things were to happen all around so that every eye could see them, they were not bound to happen always to everyone. John found no release from prison. Thus Jesus concluded, "Blessed is he who takes no offense at me."

It is in this sense that we can see how faith is born in response to the tangible evidences of love, but always in the presence of conflicting evidence which renders proof impossible. So it is that while faith is nurtured by a thousand blessings it also must withstand a thousand scourgings. It can never be forced, but it may be awakened. And once it is born, it is the power to move mountains; it is the victory that overcomes all obstacles; it is the conviction that will never die.

GEORGE heard a chair scrape across the floor and knew that someone was sitting beside the bed. He tried to open his eyes, but he was paralyzed with fear.

"Believe me, I know how you feel, George. You don't know who I am and you didn't ask me to come here and you don't know what I'm liable to do to you and you wish you could die but you're afraid to."

He could feel his heart pounding in his chest. That's true, but what you don't know is that I've got to have a drink. Can't you understand that? If you're so smart and know how people feel, you'll know that I've got to have a drink. He couldn't tell whether he'd said the words or thought them. He clinched his teeth and closed his eyes tighter.

"You're dying for a drink right now, and I'm not against your having one. I'm just against the agony that will have to be gone through again if you take a drink. You're already this far along, and I just hate to see you get set back."

George tried to wet his lips with his tongue.

"Gimme a drink. I gotta have a drink." His voice sounded far away. What did this guy know about suffering? He was suffering now, right now. To hell with tomorrow. If he didn't get a drink he wouldn't make it until tomorrow anyhow.

"Not right now George. Like I said, if you get pressed to it, I'll see that you get a drink, but not right now. I think I can help you to make it without one if you're able to try.

What does this guy think he's doing here, anyhow? What business is it of his what I do?

"One more thing, George. Like I said, I think I can help you if you want me to try. But if you don't, then that's your business. I'll pick up my hat and get out of here, and that's all there'll be to it."

Who is this guy? He opened his eyes but it was hard to focus. How can I tell him that I want him to get the hell out of here and want him to stay and help me? Maybe if he'll stay he'll get me a drink. "Don't go. I want you to stay. Help me get my shoes on."

"All right, George. You don't have to take anything I say that you don't want to. But if you come with me, we're going to do it my way. Right now that means we'll go home so you can get a shower and a shave and some clean clothes. Then we'll go by the clinic so you can get checked out by a doctor. Chances are you could use some vitamins after this whing-ding. Then, when you are a little more squared away, you can decide whether you want to keep on with me. The door's always open. You can run out or run me out any time you want to."

George could hear the words, but he couldn't follow their meaning. Something about getting cleaned up and running out the door. Wonder what he's doing here. He looked at Harold again. His eyes could focus a little better now. He really was sort of glad he was here. Something about the way he was talking made him feel better. He didn't know what he was saying, but his voice sounded good.

Looking back he never was able to piece out just what had happened. He could remember getting dressed, and stumbling down the stairs with Harold holding his arm. There were times when he thought he would explode. His hands were shaking, and his knees felt like rubber. When they got to the street, he knew he was going to be sick. Even then, Harold didn't seem to mind. Now they were riding along Eighth Street and the sun hurt his eyes. He put his head in his hands and wished he could die.

It was three o'clock before they left the clinic. His head was still hurting, but he was feeling much better. Harold looked at him as they drove toward home.

"It's been a rough day, George, and it's not over. Like I told you this morning, I can understand what you're going through. You don't know me or anything about me, but I had it mighty bad, too. I resented anybody messing with me just like you feel about me right now. Then the time came when I knew I couldn't make it by myself, and that was the hardest decision I ever had to face. Right now I can tell you it was the greatest day of my life, but it didn't look like it at the time. I asked the good Lord to help me stay sober that day, just twenty-four hours. I knew I couldn't make it any longer than that, but with his help I thought I might make it that long. When he taught us to pray, "Give us this day our daily bread," I know he was thinking about me. That's two years ago now, and so far I've been able to make it with his help. I don't know where I'll be tomorrow, but today I'm sober. He'll help you, too, if you want him to."

They rode along in silence. George knew that he had to say something. What is there to say? Who is this guy? He doesn't make any sense at all. What in the world does he mean with all this stuff about daily bread? Who said anything about bread?

"You don't have to decide now, George. I know you can't rush these things."

"Aw, it's not that at all. I appreciate your coming to get me, and all you did. Don't you think I'm not grateful. I'd like to talk to you about it, but I know you probably have a lot to do today. Suppose you drop me off at the house, and we'll get together later on this week and have lunch."

"OK, that sounds like a great idea. Here's my card with my number on it. I'll be looking for you to give me a call." He watched him walk up the front steps to his house. Help him, dear Lord. I've done all I can do. Now it's up to you and him.

By the time he went by the office and tended to the things that had to be done that day, it was nearly six-thirty when he finally got home. He could hear the phone ringing as he came through the back door.

"It's for you, Harold."

He picked up the receiver.

"Oh, Harold, he's drinking again. I tried to stop him, but he wouldn't listen. Where he got it I don't know."

"I'm so sorry, Grace. I'd hoped that he might be able to make it this time."

"I did, too. And he seemed so much better this afternoon when he came in. But I should have known not to get my hopes up. He hasn't changed at all, not at all. I'm ready to give up."

"I wouldn't blame you for that. You've had just about all you can take."

"I guess it wouldn't do any good for you to go looking for him, and besides I couldn't ask you to do it."

"No, it wouldn't. I'd go if I thought it would. He knows where I am and he'll have to call me. If I went after him now, he'd never be able to stop." He searched for some words to say. He knew something of what she was going through, but he guessed he'd never really understand what it was like to be the wife of an alcoholic. She had been hopeful last night, he knew that. But now all that was gone. How can you have hope when all the props are swept away? And when hope is gone, can you still believe? "Blessed is he who takes no offense at me."

"Grace, will you let me call Miss Morrison? I know you'd hesitate to worry her, but she'd want to know. Maybe you'd like for her to spend the night with you."

"No, Harold, thank you just the same. I suppose I'll make out all right. I always have."

He sank heavily into the chair. He'd never get used to the feeling of helplessness he always had at a time like this. Grace can't understand why I didn't do something. How could she? And George must be going through torture. But Grace can't see that, either. He longed for some way to help her right now. How can I tell her that there is hope? She's built up hope before, only to have it dashed to pieces. Anything I'd say now would be just words. Dear Lord, if there is any special blessing you have right now, Grace and George could use it.

8
Hope

"God grant me the serenity
to accept the things I cannot change,
courage to change the things I can,
and wisdom to know the difference."

Harold looked at the plaque on the breakfast room wall. The
words were so familiar he really didn't need to read them. How
many times had he prayed for that kind of serenity, that kind of
courage, that kind of wisdom? Sometimes he thought the hardest
part was the serenity. He'd never been one to sit by and let things
just happen. If something didn't go right, he had to get into the
thick of it and do something.

He knew it would be wrong to go looking for George again.
Some of his friends would question whether he should have gone
down to the hotel in the first place. They'd argued the point many
times. Sure, you can't decide for somebody else just like you can't
quit drinking for somebody else. Yet he was certain that for him it
was necessary to go. How else would somebody like George ever
know that you really want to help? It's sort of like "hanging out
the flag," a tangible way of saying that, when you want help, here
is where you can come.

It was so clear to him; he wondered why so many of the
others disagreed.

"The trouble with you, Harold is that you just gotta be doing
something."

"No, that's not it at all."

"As long as you run around wet-nursing these fellows, they're
not going to have any reason to do anything different. That's
what's the matter with most of them right now. Somebody's always
standing around to pull their chestnuts out of the fire. The only
way they can really start back is to hit bottom, and hit it hard."

They often sat in the clubroom arguing the point over cups of coffee. He wondered why they kept at it. Everybody knew what everybody else would say, and that when they were through, they would all be of the same opinion with which they had started. But it was good to know that you didn't have to agree with everybody to be a member. As Jim often said, who would ever expect a bunch of drunks to agree on anything?

"But what keeps bugging me is that maybe there is some way you could raise the bottom, some way you could keep him from losing everything before he starts back."

"Well, I dunno. It takes a pretty hard jolt to shake these guys out of their rut."

"But can't you remember how much you wanted to quit if you'd only seen some way out?"

"Yeah, I guess you could say that. Most of the time what I wanted was to con somebody out of a drink. But underneath, I was mighty miserable when I got sober."

"Now that's my point. You were miserable, but the only thing you knew to do was to get drunk so you wouldn't feel miserable. And although it seemed to work for a little while, it never did, really. I believe if you'd thought there were some other way to stop the misery, you'd have tried it."

"Naw, I doubt it. Everything anybody suggested was already out since it started off with no drinking."

"But that's the way AA starts off, isn't it?"

"Yeah, but by the time I got here I was so desperate I was even ready to try that. I was really on the ropes, but you know about that as well as I do."

"True. But I still say that when the fellow can believe that the misery of doing something about it is less than the misery of staying where he is, he'll change."

"That's exactly what I've been saying all evening."

"OK. We're agreed, then. I guess where we really differ is how you let him know that what looks like death is really life. Right now, for me, that means going to him at least one time and telling him that I'm ready to stand with him, that if I can make it anybody can, and that I'm willing for him to make up his own mind. After that, it's up to him."

"OK, I'll buy that—for you. For me, I'll not budge until he calls and says he's ready."

It always ended there. Who was really right? How can you really accept things you cannot change? How do you know you can't change them? Maybe there is something you can do. Maybe if I go out and find George just one more time, that would do it. How do you know until you've tried? Grace had wanted him to go. She couldn't bring herself to say so, but he knew she did. Wish she'd let me call Miss Morrison, or somebody. It is hardest to do nothing. But this was something, just the fact that he wasn't going. He so wanted Grace not to give up, not to let hope die. All at once he wondered if he was thinking more about himself than Grace. The fellows are right, I do need to be doing something. But that doesn't mean I'm not right, too, and it certainly doesn't mean that going out after George last night was wrong. No, it was right, even if he is drinking again. God grant me the serenity to accept the things I cannot change.

WHEN WE DISCUSSED FAITH we saw that it is both the mark of maturity and at the same time representative of a childlike trust unmarred by the sophistication of experience. There is a similar paradox in the idea of hope. On the one hand, hope signifies a confident expectation, a genuine trust, a settled faith that reaches out beyond the narrow channel of present circumstances toward that which is most surely to come. On the other hand, hope may simply be the expression of a vain wish, a futile longing, a pathetic yearning for that which can never be but which appears so enticing and so desirable that its possibility cannot be lightly dismissed. Hope may also be seen as the link between reality and desire, between sorrow and joy, between suffering and release. It is the promise of tomorrow which makes today endurable; it is the possibility of victory which makes the struggle worthwhile; it is the assurance of life which transcends the agony of death. Apart from faith, hope cannot exist; indeed, there is a sense in which hope is simply a synonym for faith in the future. Yet hope is not identical with faith in that it includes a yearning for that which is yet to find fruition and which may in fact undergo change in form and definition before its final consummation. Apart from hope, no life is possible. The old proverb "While there's life there's hope" might well be reversed, for there can be no life when all hope is gone.

IF GRACE NELSON had thought about this at all, she would never have been able to agree without rather drastic redefinition. As it was, she knew that life has a way of going on in all its wretchedness when hope has faded and the dark night of the soul is not pierced by even a single spark of light.

She hung up the phone and walked slowly back to the kitchen. After awhile you learn to go through the motions of doing what must be done. It was already dark and the boys had to have their supper. She could hear them playing in their room upstairs. They'd come running in as George had left.

"Isn't Daddy going to stay for supper? He said he'd help us make a birdhouse. Where did he go, huh, Mommy, huh, Mommy?"

"I don't think he'll be back for supper, Stuart. It's too dark now to build a birdhouse. You can do that later. Now you and Spencer run upstairs and play until I call you for supper."

"Can't we eat now? We're hungry now, we're hungry now!"

"Don't argue with me, Stuart. Now get on upstairs this minute and don't come back down until I call you."

"Make Spencer come, too. Spencer's not coming. I don't want to go if Spencer doesn't have to go, too."

"Stuart, you march yourself right straight up those stairs before I switch you. I've told you not to argue with me, and I mean it, young man! Spencer is coming, but that's no concern of yours. Hurry now."

"Yes'm." She could see his lip quivering as he turned to go up the steps.

"Wait a minute, Stuart." She sat on the second step, and gathered him in her arms. He buried his head on her shoulder and sobbed as she swayed back and forth in a rocking motion. "There, now, don't cry. I didn't mean to speak so harshly to you. Mommy's tired and out of patience. Supper will be ready in just a little while. Can you and Spencer build me a castle with your blocks while I get it ready?"

She forced a smile as they went up the steps. "Close your door so you won't be disturbed. I'll call you in just a little while."

It was then she'd picked up the phone to call Harold. It was the kind of thing you did hoping against hope that maybe there was something you didn't know about, something that somebody might do, something that could change the terrible fact that things would never be any better. Not now, anyway. She stared vacantly at the mirror as she listened to Harold saying he wasn't going to go this time. She wasn't even bitter. She had been, but that was past now. Seeing Stuart cry had taken the sting out of her resentment. Right now it was hard to feel anything. What is there to feel when hope is dead?

"No, Harold. You don't have to do that." What could Miss Morrison do? What could anybody do? She'd already done everything she knew how. She couldn't face Miss Morrison, anyhow. Right now she couldn't face anybody. Poor Harold. It must be hard for him. He had tried to help.

"Thank you just the same. I suppose I'll make out all right. I always have." She wished she could sound more convincing.

All at once nothing seemed to matter any more. It was as though she were living in a dream. She knew what was happening—that George was gone, that the boys were hungry, that she was talking to Harold on the telephone. But it was like watching it happen to someone else. She looked into the mirror. Everything looked real enough. She could see the newel post with the cut glass goblet, the hall chair where Stuart had thrown his jacket when he came in, the frayed place on the rug. An hour ago George had been standing right there.

"Please don't go, George. I don't know what you're looking for, but I know you'll never find it if you leave. Think of the boys. They need you here. They're getting old enough to wonder where you are all the time, and I don't know what to tell them."

"Oh, you'll think of something. I'm sure of that. Why don't you tell them their old man is a war hero and has gone out to lick the world? Yeah, tell 'em that. Tell 'em he doesn't need old Iron-pants' job, that he's a real hero who got his picture in the paper."

He swayed a little as he turned toward the door.

"George, you *are* a hero to me. You'll always be a hero to me.

I know it was hard coming back this afternoon with Harold, but don't stop now."

"Yeah, this Harold must be pretty great stuff. You tell the boys about him? He'll be around here when their old man is gone, I bet."

"George Nelson, you know that's not so. You ought to be ashamed of yourself even to think such a thing."

"Well, well, not so, huh? Just what I thought."

He stood in the doorway. She could hear the boys in the side yard.

"George, if you go this time, don't come back. I can't live like this the rest of my life. I don't want you to go, but if you do go, that's it."

He slammed the door and stalked across the porch and down the steps.

"Daddy! Are you coming right back, Daddy? Can we build the birdhouse this afternoon, Daddy? Daddy, can't you hear me?"

DR. WATSON drove slowly along Summit Avenue. It was a little out of his way, but he'd wanted a few minutes to collect his thoughts. He was troubled by the fact that Grace hadn't called. He knew that Harold had found George, and he tried to dismiss not hearing from Grace on the grounds that she had been so happy over his return that she had completely forgotten to get in touch with him.

He was nearing the top of the slope now and could see the city stretched out below with its thousands of lights. He stopped the car in the turnout and switched off the motor. He'd sat here many times, but the feeling of awe never seemed to leave him. Who could know what went on in the city? What thousands of dramas played themselves out in the streets and alleys, in the hospitals and precinct stations, in the apartments and the hotels, in the mansions and hovels? There was something wonderful about the city, and something terrifying. At times he felt overwhelmed by it and at other times he seemed to be at peace with it. He knew that to look at it from this vantage point was to blot out the faces of those whose lives and fortunes moved between laughter and tears. And yet he had to come here ever and again to see things whole and to know that there was a perspective which gave a long range view.

What would he find when he got to the Nelsons? He'd started to telephone before going by but had changed his mind. Now he wasn't sure this had been a wise decision. Ordinarily he let folks know he was coming, particularly at night. It wasn't just that the time might be inconvenient or that they might not be at home. The real reason he phoned was to give them an opportunity to pick things up. For him this meant not only straightening up the living room a bit, but also an opportunity to get their thoughts somewhat "picked up." He knew how uncomfortable it made his wife feel when someone dropped in unexpected. Not that things should always stay neat as a pin, but the children did leave things strewn around, and she hated for the place to look like a cyclone had struck it when people came to call. Some of his friends in the ministry thought it better to "catch folks where they are." He wasn't so sure. If "where they are" was wanting to appear different, it would be taking unfair advantage to call unannounced. He knew all the reasons pro and con and wondered why he hadn't called the Nelsons. *I guess this time I just don't want to take the chance that they might say don't come.*

He knew something of the frustration Miss Morrison felt about alcoholics. You could try and try and fail again and again. He often wondered just when you do give up hope. As he looked out over the city, the ancient words came back to him as they did so often when he stopped here. "O Jerusalem, Jerusalem, killing the prophets and stoning those who are sent to you! How often would I have gathered your children together as a hen gathers her brood under her wings, and you would not! Behold, your house is forsaken!" Had all hope been abandoned when Jesus said those words? Sometimes he thought so. Yet, even as he did, he remembered there were those who had followed. Would Jesus have forgiven even then? He thought of Simon Peter's question, "Lord, how often shall my brother sin against me, and I forgive him? As many as seven times?" He was sure that the answer had been as difficult for Peter as it was for him. "I do not say to you seven times, but seventy times seven." *All right, I'll try.* He switched on the key to the car and touched the starter. I do hope George was able to make it.

He had some difficulty in finding the house. They all seemed to look alike in this new subdivision, one split-level after the other. How could a person find a real identity when everything looked the same?

"Mrs. Nelson? I'm Howard Watson. This may be an awkward time, but if it's not too inconvenient, I'd like to come in."

"Oh . . . why, yes . . . do come in. George isn't here just now, but do come in."

"I could come back tomorrow, Mrs. Nelson. You're at kind of a disadvantage here, and I don't want to impose on you. My main purpose in coming by was to say that Miss Morrison told me of George's difficulty, and I wanted you both to know of my willingness to help if there is anything I can do." The words sounded hollow to him even as he said them. What do you say that will really express how you feel? She may not want any help. Then, again, she may want help but not from you. How do you offer in such a way that she does not feel coerced?

"No, please come in. I was going to call you, but so many things came up I never did get the chance."

He was sorry she felt the need to defend herself. It would be nice if you could just wipe the slate clean and get to the things that really matter. But how do you know what really matters? With somebody like Grace Nelson it isn't too hard to guess. What matters to her is that George get sober and stay sober. But it's just not that simple. You can't ignore George or his drinking, but at the same time, it is Grace who is here now. He sat down on the sofa as she sank into the rocker.

"I've left George." There was a coldness in her voice that cut like a knife.

"I see."

"He was here. Harold found him in one of those cheap hotels over beyond Eighth Street and brought him home. I told him if he went through that door I would leave him."

"You've just come to the end of your patience."

"Yes, I guess you could say it that way. I've put up with all I can stand." She rocked slowly back and forth. He began to wonder if she was really aware of his presence.

Suddenly she turned toward him and spoke in low and measured tones. "What would you do if you were in my place?"

"Mrs. Nelson, you won't think I'm being facetious when I say that, in all honesty, I haven't the faintest notion of what I'd do. I suppose I'd be sitting there wondering what was right and what was wrong."

"I don't know what's right and what's wrong anymore, and I don't know whether anybody does. But that doesn't include you. You're a preacher—I'm sure you know what's right and what's wrong. Isn't that what you came here to tell me? Because if you did, you can save your breath. I'm not the slightest bit interested in what you have to say."

"All right. It was the farthest thing from my mind to try to tell you what to do, but I guess that's pretty much all you thought you could expect from me."

"Isn't that what all you preachers do?"

"Well, I can't really speak for all preachers. Some do, I guess, and some don't. But the point is that if I had any notions along that line, I might as well forget them."

"You can as far as I am concerned."

"Then that's that. I should tell you, though, that I do it not simply because of your wishes but because I had no intentions of that sort anyhow."

"What did you come for, then, if not to tell me what I ought to do?"

"I came by to see if there was any way I could help. It just never occurred to me that telling you what to do would be of any help, even if I knew what to say, which I don't."

"What kind of help do you have?"

"That's not an easy question to answer, although it is a fair one. What I have may not look like much help, but it's all I have. I'm here to let you know that the church wants to stand with you in these rough places, and to remind you of God's grace which is sufficient."

"No miracles? No flashing lights? No legions of angels?"

"No magic, Mrs. Nelson, no simple waving of the hand. I could wish very much that there were."

She'd stopped rocking now. Her hands gripped the arms of

the chair. He could feel the tension in her voice as all of the frustration and bitterness began to pour out. "You ought to be able to do better than that. You're a minister, a man of God! Well, where is God? I've prayed to him, and what good has it done? Do you know what it's like to sit here night after night in fear and loneliness, crying until there are no more tears? Do you know what it is like to see the person you love most, slowly turning into a stranger before your very eyes? Do you know what it's like to have two sons who need a father and who don't have one? I don't think you do! Yet you knock on my door and tell me you want to help."

"Yes, that's true. I do very much want to help. But I take it that you see my coming as pretty useless and really resent my being here since I haven't had these things happen to me."

She bit her lip as tears welled up in her eyes. "I didn't mean it. I really didn't mean it. You'll have to forgive me for speaking that way."

How could he tell her that he felt no anger, that he had no ill will toward her? "I can say the words of forgiveness, Mrs. Nelson, yet no matter how sincerely I mean them, I guess you will still feel embarrassed by what you said."

She nodded, but no words came. Slowly the tears ran down her cheeks.

"The way I see it, all these feelings were tied up inside of you, and I just happened to be the first one along. You'd held them in as long as you could, and now they just had to come out."

She nodded again. The tears continued to course down her cheeks, but the fury of the storm was over. After awhile she reached for her purse and found a handkerchief. "I am sorry I said all of those things. But you're right, I guess, that they just had to come out. At least I didn't seem to be able to stop and now I do feel better, somehow."

"So that even when you wanted to quit you just couldn't somehow."

"Yes. And even though I'm ashamed of having lashed out like that, I do feel better."

"I'm glad. The thing is, then, that this isn't the way of doing that you'd choose, and in one sense you really regret it; and yet, at the same time, you're sort of glad, or maybe relieved."

"Relieved is more like it, I think. I just don't feel quite as beaten as I did before you came."

She leaned back in the rocker and closed her eyes. After awhile she opened them. "I said I'd left George, and I meant it then. But not now. He needs help, and so do I. Somehow I believe we'll get it."

"Not too sure what that help will look like, but really hopeful now that it will come."

"Yes. Yes, I am." She paused a bit and then went on. "I am, because for me I guess it already has. Now it's late and I know you have to go. Thank you for coming. I think I'm going to be all right now."

He started to rise, but realized she had something else to say.

"It's terrible how you can get swamped in your own resentments and hates. I was so mad at George this afternoon I could have killed him. Then when he came back with Harold, I began to feel that everything was going to be all right. So when he began to talk just like he used to, I guess I just lost my balance. But, you know, I don't feel that way now. I don't know what is possible now. I had hoped that somehow he'd just change overnight, that we'd be able to put all this behind us, close the door on the past. I'm not putting this very well, but it makes some sense to me."

"I'm not sure I understand all you're saying, but the thing I hear most is that your expectations of both you and George are different now, and perhaps more realistic."

"Yes, in a way I suppose that's it. But it's not real clear to me even so. I was thinking of the words from something we used to sing in the College Choir. 'Out of the depths I cried unto Thee.' Do you know it? I can't remember it, somehow."

"I don't know the song, but those words are from Psalm 130. Maybe it's the same. Let me read it, now."

> Out of the depths I cry to thee, O LORD!
>> Lord, hear my voice!
> Let thy ears be attentive
>> to the voice of my supplications!
> If thou, O LORD, shouldst mark iniquities,
>> Lord, who could stand?

> But there is forgiveness with thee,
>> that thou mayest be feared.
> I wait for the LORD, my soul waits,
>> and in his word I hope;
> my soul waits for the LORD . . .
>> more than watchmen for the morning.
>
> O Israel, hope in the LORD!
>> For with the LORD there is steadfast love,
>> and with him is plenteous redemption.
> And he will redeem Israel
>> from all his iniquities.

Grace nodded. "That's the one. That's really how it is, I think."

WE HAVE NOTED that hope implies expectation and promise of something yet to be, which is able to sustain and encourage in the presence of doubt and despair. At the same time we have also seen that hope may be vain, may be based on unrealistic desire, may be an evidence of naïve longing. In point of fact these two are inevitably intermixed. Only slowly is it possible for the substance of hope to be enlarged so that it becomes the hope which "does not disappoint us," as Paul put it in Romans 5. It is inevitable that we will set our hope on that which is unrealistic and which would be unsatisfying if it were in fact attained. Yet the struggle which marks the painful transformation of that for which we hope, is both the evidence and the means of maturity.

The paradox is that hope must die before hope can be born. The crucial moment comes with the death of that hope which had in fact proved to be the means of sustaining, at least for awhile, but at length is discovered to be unrealistic. In such a crisis moment there is the possibility of overwhelming despair which ultimately leads to death, or of the birth of that hope which reaches beyond the agonizing longing of the moment to that which is even more satisfying than could have been dreamed.

DR. WATSON drove slowly along Summit Avenue. Some of the lights of the city had gone out now. O Jerusalem, Jerusalem. It wasn't that you had no hope, but that you hoped for the wrong thing and could never really change. Yet some did. It was possible. He thought of the two who walked on the road to Emmaus after the crucifixion. All of the despair seemed to be summed up in three words, "We had hoped." It was as if they were saying, "there was a time when things seemed possible to us, when our expectations ran high, when our fulfillment appeared near . . . we had hoped . . . but that was then and this is now and there is nothing left." No way for them to know that, before the day was out, their whole lives would be changed forever.

He stopped at the last turnout before the street began the long descent. The remarkable thing was that they had already heard the words which were to be the basis for their transformed hope: "O . . . slow of heart to believe." How slowly, indeed, is genuine hope born from the death of hope that could never be. How painful and dismaying is the death of hope in the unfolding events which reveal its vanity. He thought of Grace Nelson. How many times had her hopes been shattered, how many times had she felt the wounds of despair, how many times had she turned again to hope that would never be? He knew that the events of the past two days were too recent, too close to form the basis for any confident judgment or evaluation. Nevertheless, he was sure that, for her, there had begun to emerge a different kind of hope than that which had disappointed her so often before. It was a hope which had its roots in God, not in the expectation of some magical resolution of all the problems of life, but rather in the awareness of forgiveness. "O Israel, hope in the LORD! For with the LORD there is steadfast love, and with him is plenteous redemption. And he will redeem Israel from all his iniquities."

He watched the lights of the city. Somewhere in the vast expanse of streets and buildings of light and darkness was George. Was he sitting in a bar, was he walking aimlessly through the dark alleys, was he lying unconscious in some rooming house?

"I'll be so glad to go look for George."

He'd stood in the doorway as he was leaving.

"No, Harold is right. This time he has to come back on his own. It's hard to say, but it's true. I can see that now."

He'd said good night and gotten into his car. He'd been willing to respect her wishes, but even now he wasn't sure. How could you know whether this was like the rich young ruler whom you had to let go away without being followed or like the one hundredth sheep lost out on the mountain? He knew there was a difference, a vast difference. How many times he'd longed for some measure which would clearly mark off the difference in this person or that. Right now, he was willing not to go, if that was right. Indeed, he recognized that in point of practicality he wouldn't know where to begin if he did go. Yet he never could be sure that someone like George would be able to come back. "O, Jerusalem, Jerusalem. How often would I . . . and you would not."

"IT'S HERE SOMEWHERE. I know I have it somewhere." George fumbled in his pockets. What if he'd lost it? He'd never remember his name. He had to find the card. What had he done with it? Put it in his pocket, he knew. Or thought he had. But it wasn't there. It wasn't there. He knew they were looking at him, and probably didn't believe him.

"All right, Mac. You'll do better to get on back and sleep it off a little. We'll let you call your friend in the morning."

"I want to call him now!"

"Yeah, I know. But you can't call him if you don't have his number and don't know his name. You'll feel better tomorrow. Probably even be able to remember who you want to call."

He really didn't have the strength to argue. He found himself shuffling down the hall and before he knew it the door clanged shut and the key rattled in the lock. He fell across the hard cot as the world slowly drifted away. There was a terrible roaring in his ears and the lights seemed to be going off and on, brilliant flashes and inky darkness. "Gotta call him. Gotta call him now."

Slowly he became aware of a sharp pain jabbing through his right shoulder. He winced as he tried to turn over and fell back on the cot. His head pounded as though it would split. This time he was able to sit up. He realized he had been sleeping with his arm twisted under him. The pain streaked through his neck as he tried to raise his head. It was awhile before he remembered where he was. Gradually he was able to piece together at least something of what had happened. He remembered stumbling down the street as the squad car pulled up beside him. He'd tried to turn away, but had fallen against the curb.

"You'd better get in here with us, Mac."

He'd wanted to protest, but couldn't find the words.

"Tell us where you live, Mac, and we'll take you home. You're liable to get hurt staggering around town like this."

"Got no home."

"Aw, sure you got a home, buddy. Everyone has a home. What's your address? They're probably looking for you right now."

"Got no home."

By the time they reached the precinct station he knew what he had to do. But the card—he couldn't find the card.

It was daylight, now. His shoulder didn't hurt quite so much but his head was killing him. What was that fellow's name? Look again, through all your pockets. Slowly, now. Don't panic. He pulled a crumpled piece of paper out of his coat pocket. As he held it in his hand he could feel the old fear clutch at his throat. He guessed it was really final this time, written out officially on company letterhead. "As of this date you are no longer employed . . ." When he'd opened that envelope something just seemed to snap within him. Everything had sort of been going better, then this. Grace had told him not to come back and he knew she meant it.

"You're awake now, I see."

He nodded his head and tried to answer but no words came.

"The night sergeant said you wouldn't let them take you home. Did you ever think who it was you wanted to call?"

He shook his head. The card must be here somewhere.

"You know what you want to do now? We got no charges against you, and we can't keep you here forever."

"I want to call a fellow. Got his card here somewhere. Just give me a minute to find it."

"Sure, take your time, Mac. Just call me when you're ready."

He could feel the beads of sweat standing on his forehead. When he pulled the handkerchief from his breast pocket the card fluttered to the floor. That's it. Why do you suppose I'd put it there? He picked it up and looked at it. Harold Clark. Yes, that's him. I just couldn't think of it. "Hey Sergeant! Can you let me out? I've found it! Sergeant!"

"OK, OK. Sarge says you can come up to the desk. Take it easy now."

He dialed the number. O God, let him be there. It was then that he noticed something printed on the back of the card. "God grant me the serenity to accept the things I cannot change, courage to change the things I can, and wisdom to know the difference." The phone was still ringing.

"Hello. Harold Clark? Harold, this is George Nelson, I need you real bad. Can you come?"

"GEORGE?"

"Yes, Hon."

"Are you listening this time, George?"

"You know I always listen to you."

"Yeah, I know. In one ear and out the other. Put your paper down now and be serious. I need to talk to you about Mary."

"OK. I'm all at attention."

"George, I want you to call Frank Mason and see if you can get him to go to lunch with you."

"I thought you said you wanted to talk about Mary Mason."

"Well, I do. But we ought to do something about Frank, too."

"Grace, you know I'll do this if you really insist. But honestly, Hon, I can't see myself barging into his office and saying 'See here, Frank Mason, you are now a Nelson project, and I've come to reform you'!"

"No, of course not. And when you say it that way I know my idea was foolish."

"Well, I wouldn't say foolish. I'm just not sure that's the best way for me to go about it."

"I see what you mean. I am worried about them, though. Do you think there's any hope for folks like that?"

He watched her for a minute as she rocked slowly, looking into space. "You know the answer to that as well as I do, Grace."

"Well, I don't mean that there's really no hope. What I wonder is, do they know it?"

"I'll bet Mary does tonight. And if she does, then Frank will know it, too."

"I do hope so, George. I really do."

WE HAVE SEEN THAT HOPE must die in order to be born, that the horizons of hope must always stretch beyond the boundaries of sight, that the substance of hope must forever transcend particular expectations however earnestly desired. It is in this sense that hope is always rooted in faith, and like faith is ultimately a response to one who comes to speak a word of grace, and in that word to bring again the confidence that through the darkness there yet will be a ray of light. But if its roots are in faith, then like faith, its nurture is love. For without love neither faith nor hope can endure. In the first verses of Romans 5 Paul wrote:

> Therefore, since we are justified by faith, we have peace with God through our Lord Jesus Christ. Through him we have obtained access to this grace in which we stand, and we rejoice in our hope of sharing the glory of God. More than that, we rejoice in our sufferings, knowing that suffering produces endurance, and endurance produces character, and character produces hope, and hope does not disappoint us, because God's love has been poured into our hearts through the Holy Spirit which has been given to us.

There can be no question but that faith, hope, and love endure, but there can also be no question that the greatest of these is love.

9
Love

JOHN MASON picked up the evening paper and closed the front door. "Anything interesting in the mail today, Martha?"

"Not very much. Mostly circulars and things like that. I believe there was a bill from Taylor's and a couple of magazines. It's all in there on the hall table."

"I thought we might hear from the Robinsons today. They were planning to reach Seattle on Monday, weren't they?"

"I believe that's right. You can't tell about the mail, though. We'll probably get a letter from them tomorrow. Supper will be ready in just a few minutes. Florence and I went by the hospital this afternoon to see Mrs. Thompson and we were a little late getting home. You'll have time to glance at the paper if you'd like to."

"All right. How's Mrs. Thompson getting along?"

"Oh, John, I don't know. As well as could be expected, I suppose. She's nearly eighty, and looks so frail. She seemed in good spirits, though, and is talking about going home."

He picked up the paper, and sat in the big chair with the ottoman. Kind of hard to concentrate on the news. He listened to Martha's steps in the kitchen. She'd tried to sound casual, but when you've lived with anyone that long you can read her moods. If a letter didn't come tomorrow, they'd have to wait until Monday. Maybe that was better. Everybody always said that no news was good news. He wasn't so sure. Sometimes it was harder to wait, not knowing.

Of course we don't even know for sure that William is in Seattle. It's been over two years since we've had any word at all. But after a while you just don't talk about it. It doesn't do any good when all you can do is ask yourself "why" over and over again. But you have to ask the question even when there isn't any real answer. Not that you can't always think of dozens of answers, but that doesn't mean you've found the real one. If there is a real one. You ask the question in different ways at different times.

"To be perfectly truthful, Mr. Mason, I'm not at all sure I know why he's doing it. He didn't want me to call you, but I insisted. I told you you had a right to know."

There had been a kind of insistence in the way the phone rang. Probably it was just that he'd been uneasy about William ever since Christmas. They'd had real hopes for him when he went away to school. Maybe he'll find himself, they'd said. Somehow it hadn't worked out the way they had hoped. He'd gone home with his roommate at Thanksgiving, and all during the Christmas holiday he'd seemed distant.

"I appreciate your calling, Dr. Thompson. I can catch the plane first thing in the morning if you think I should come."

"I hope you'll understand when I say that I believe it would be better if you didn't, Mr. Mason. William has decided to do a two year hitch in the Army, and since he has to work it off sooner or later, I honestly think this is the best time. Things haven't gone too well with him this fall, and it was a pretty bitter blow when he didn't make the fraternity. I don't know what was behind that, but I do know he took it pretty hard."

"I understand. Let me know if there is anything I can do. We'll arrange to have his personal things shipped home if you'll let me know how to proceed."

He could still feel the heaviness in his heart as he'd gone back into the sitting room.

"Martha, it's William. He's left school to join the Army. That was the Dean, Dr. Thompson. He thinks it's the best thing to do."

How do you keep your voice steady when your throat is choking back the tears? How do you speak the words of comfort when you ache for comfort yourself? How do you find the strength to hold her in your arms as she sobs in anguish for her child when your own agony is more than you can bear? "O, Absalom, my son, my son!"

"Isn't there anything we can do?"

"The Dean thinks we should let him go."

"But he's so young, he's not yet twenty. Oh, John, we have to do something!"

"Yes. Yes, we have to do something. And yet I guess it's not what we'd want, not what we'd choose."

"Can't we stop him? Is it right just to let him go without saying anything?"

These were some of the ways the question had to be put. Even when there would be no answer, it had to be asked. It surged up from the depths of the soul and demanded some course, some strategy, some reason. In time the form of the question would change.

"Did the Dean know why he wanted to go?"

"He wasn't sure. He did say that the fraternity had not initiated William when they took in the pledge class. Maybe that's not the whole answer. Apparently they do that sometimes, then take them in later."

"Did you have any inkling that he would do it?"

"I don't know, Martha. I knew something was wrong when he was home Christmas. But I couldn't talk to him. I don't know; it's been a long time since I've been able to talk to him. Sometimes I wonder if I ever could."

"I just hate to think of his leaving without telling us."

"Yes, I think that's the hardest part."

Gradually the question moved toward its inevitable form.

"Where did we fail, John?"

"I don't know. I've wondered many times. William was so different from Frank. I always thought I knew what to expect from Frank, but never William."

"Didn't we love him enough? I did try, I tried real hard, but I can't help wondering."

"Now, Martha, you can't blame yourself. You did what you thought was best, just like I did."

"I know; but sometimes I've wondered whether he felt we were too hard on him."

"You just can't torture yourself that way, Martha. You corrected him because you loved him. It would have been heartless to do anything else."

Even as he said it, he wished there had been some other way to tell her what was in his heart. He was conscious of defending himself as he defended her. Not that he didn't honestly believe what he had said. There could be no doubt in his mind that love did not imply a kind of sentimentality which refused to take a stand or confront another person with the negative aspects of his behavior. The theory was easy, it was putting it into practice that was hard.

THROUGHOUT OUR DISCUSSION we have spoken often of love. Indeed, it is evident that here as elsewhere myriad meanings cluster around the word. How is it possible to penetrate its depth, to understand its subtle tenderness, to comprehend its firm conviction? The task is made more difficult by the superficial usage which is part and parcel of common speech. "I'd love to go," or "I'd love to do it," are phrases heard every day. In such form we express whim and fancy, we signify attraction and personal preference, we indicate wish or desire. At an even more disturbing level the term "love" is used to characterize all manner of human relationships which exploit rather than create, which enslave rather than set free, which bring death rather than life. The possessive tyranny of a selfish parent, the facile protestation of a seductive suitor, the irresponsible declaration of an unscrupulous public servant all echo in hollow mockery the verb "to love."

Can such a word be rescued from destruction? Can some enduring definition so mark its nature and its being that forevermore men recognize its deep and awful splendor? Can the phrase "I love you" be confined to that self-giving act of prime devotion wherein the saying signifies the reaching out of heart and life, wherein the hearing opens wide the door of hope and sets the firm foundation of triumphant faith? Can the term "love" be used only to designate that relationship which is patient and kind, is not jealous or boastful, is not arrogant or rude, does not insist upon its own way, is not irritable or resentful, does not rejoice at wrong but rejoices in the right, bears all things, believes all things, hopes all things, endures all things—and never ends?

LOOKING BACK NOW, Dr. Watson couldn't be sure that there really ever had been a time when he actually thought that such a thing was possible. More likely it was the kind of vain wish you had in the eager naïveté of youth when you thought for a little while that you could set things straight once and for all, including a distortion of meaning in the use of words. He smiled as he thought of his own impetuous zeal. Only later did he realize that love actually does not insist on its own way—even in the matter of definition. Could he really have been so positive that he was able to define love once and for all? Right now, for the life of him he couldn't recall his definition, but he was sure of one thing: the meaning of love had slowly but surely become more real to him. He thought of those whose lives had withered when the tap root of love had been cut. And of those whose radiance was evidence supreme of the life-giving nature of love.

How easy it was to say! He had long since learned that the words draw meaning from and express the experience, not the other way around. When experiences differ, the same words have different meanings, no matter how much there may be external agreement in regard to definition. He sat gazing through the window of his study. The clock chimed the halfhour just as he saw his secretary turn in the driveway and park her car. He glanced at his watch through force of habit. Was it eight-thirty already? He'd stood around talking with some of the men after the breakfast. It'd been hard for George to close the discussion on time. "Will you lead us in prayer, Dr. Watson?"

The chairs scraped as they stood and bowed their heads.

"We thank thee, O God, for the occasions that bring us together in thy name. As we go from this place help us to be conscious of thy presence in everything we do, that we may show forth thy praise not only with our lips but also with our lives. Through Jesus Christ, our Lord, Amen."

He wanted to speak to George, but saw that several of the men had gathered around him so that there was no opportunity. He noticed Crandall Simpson moving toward him and knew that if they got started he would never get over to George.

"What'd you think of the discussion this morning, Howard?"

He could feel himself tightening up, and wished he wouldn't react that way. "I thought it was excellent."

"Well, I don't know. Some of these fellows have a pretty unrealistic view of life. They seem to think that everything should always be sweetness and light."

"Um-hum." He tried to concentrate on what Crandall was saying, but his mind was on George.

"I know the Bible says to love your enemies, but you can run that kind of thing into the ground. There's just entirely too much talk about love these days. Understand, I'm not against love, but to hear some of these fellows talk, you'd think this was the only thing they knew."

"Um-hum." He saw George reaching for his hat, and knew he'd be gone in just a minute.

"Now you take the discussion this morning. A lot of those fellows thought Jesus never lost his temper. It's sort of part and parcel of this whole kid-gloved approach to life. You know as well as I do that religion is more than love."

"That's true. But I guess it sort of depends on what your definition of love is." George was at the door, now. "Excuse me just a second, Crandall." He turned as he spoke. "Oh, George. Don't stop, I know you're in a hurry. Just wanted to say 'thank you.' I thought it went off well."

"Thanks, Preacher. See you later."

"Excuse me, Crandall. Now, you were saying that folks were putting too much emphasis on love?"

"Well, it seems that way to me. Maybe I'm just old fashioned, I don't know. I believe you need more than love. Kids have to be disciplined, I know that."

"But that isn't different from loving them, is it?"

"Well, like you say, I suppose it depends on what you mean by love. I better be getting down to the office."

Dr. Watson watched him as he walked away. What does he mean by love, he wondered. What do I? Suddenly his heart was heavy as he went into his study. Whatever I mean by it, I didn't show it very well just now.

As he sat down he reached for the New Testament and turned to the third chapter of 1 John. "We know that we have passed out of death into life, because we love the brethren." But what did it mean, to "love the brethren"? Sometimes it didn't seem too difficult. Sometimes the "brethren" were lovable. But even when they were not, there was a difference. He recalled the wretched times through which Grace and George had passed. They hadn't been very "lovable," yet his heart had gone out to them in their misery. But what about Crandall Simpson? Why was it that just being around him seemed to set him on edge? He read on. "He who does not love remains in death." An awesome notion. Yet he thought he understood, at least in part, what it meant. But you can't just say, "Here, now, I'm going to love!" It's not that simple.

What do you mean when you use the term "love"? It probably would not have helped if he had had a concise definition already formulated when he was talking to Crandall Simpson. He thought of what he had said. What would have helped was simply to love him. Slowly he realized that when he really tried to think of the meaning of love, what stood out was not a definition but an action, a relationship, something that happened. It is the tenderness of the mother who looks into the face of her firstborn child; it is the stirring in the heart of a man and a maid in the first sweet bloom of youth; it is the deep yearning that causes the shepherd to leave the ninety and nine and search for the sheep that is lost; it is the depth of devotion of the friend that gives his life that another may live; it is the patient understanding of the husband and wife whose lives have intertwined across the years so that they two have become one; it is the longing in the heart of a father who eagerly scans the road to the far country for the first glimpse of the son who so slowly returns; it is the figure of a man on a cross who prays "Father, forgive them, for they know not what they do."

WHEN WE SPOKE OF FREEDOM, we saw that it was a gift, that which comes over to the person and in its coming creates the possibility of freedom. At a deeper level we saw that the same thing could be said of faith, for faith, too, is a gift. In both instances it is clear that, in the deepest sense, both freedom and faith are born of love which is the greatest gift of all.

It is possible to resist love when it is given, to turn away into the wasteland of isolation. It is not possible to love until love has been received, until the experience of being loved has brought to birth the freedom and the faith in which love can be given. Yet, once this love is given and received, all else is changed and life is filled with meaning and with hope.

MARY did not really know that, at least not in just that way. But she did know that things were different, although it would have been difficult to point to any particular change. As it was, she scarcely had time to think about it.

"Did it hurt, Bill?"

"Not a bit. And I did just like he told me, and I don't have to come back for a long time."

The trip to the dentist had taken a bit longer than she had planned. Bill hadn't said anything as they waited in the office, but she could feel the tenseness in him as his turn grew nearer. She squeezed his hand.

"We're going to have something special for supper tonight, something you'll like."

"Oh, boy! What is it?"

"I can't tell. It's a surprise. But I can tell this much, you and Dad really like it."

The supper dishes were cleared away now, and Betty had long since gone to sleep. Bill kneeled by his bed and closed his eyes. She bowed her head.

"Now I lay me down to sleep . . ." It is different tonight. Thank you God. "If I should die before I wake . . ." Maybe I can talk to Frank, but what would I say? Yet, somehow . . .

". . . Daddy and Mama and Betty, and help Bill to be a good boy . . ." O, God, why does it get this way? It wasn't always this way. "Thank you that going to the dentist is over, and thank you for the chocolate pie . . ." Grace said there had been a time when she and George couldn't talk, but is that any reason that it will ever be different with Frank and me? "Amen." Why should I think it would be any different tonight? "I already said 'Amen,' Mama, and you still have your eyes closed!"

"I guess I didn't hear you say it, Bill. 'Amen.' Now, off to sleep with you. It's been a good day. Have nice dreams."

She turned out the light and walked slowly back to the living room. She could feel her hands trembling. What on earth is the matter with you, Mary? But the trembling didn't stop.

"Frank," she began.

"Uh-humm." He was buried in the evening paper.

"Frank. I love you."

"Uh, hum? What'd you say?"

"I said, 'I love you.' "

"Well, gee, thanks. What's that supposed to mean?"

"I . . . I don't guess it's supposed to mean anything, except that I do love you . . . and I don't think I've acted very much like it, lately."

"You all right, Mary? Is something wrong?"

"Oh, Frank . . . I don't know. I think so, that is, I think I'm all right. But something is wrong, too . . . and I don't know for sure what it is. But I do love you, and I want you to know it . . . and I want to act like it . . ."

He put the paper down and looked at her for a long time.

"Mary . . ." He shook his head. "Mary, you're not making any sense. If you've something to say, come on out and say it and quit talking in riddles!"

She closed her eyes, and pressed her hands tightly together. O God, I'm not doing very well. How can I say it so it'll make some sense?

"Look, Honey, I don't mean to be dense, but you sort of hit me with the water bucket, and I guess I'm kind of off balance."

"It's not your fault, Frank. I just don't know how to say what I feel. I know this isn't fair, and I wish I could do it better. I haven't been very nice for a long time, and I've been miserable, and I know I've made you miserable, too. And Bill and Betty. And I want to do better." She could feel the tears running down her cheeks. Please, God, don't let me cry. I don't want him to feel sorry for me.

"Gosh, Mary, I don't know what to say. I'm sorry I flew off the handle this morning like I did, but . . ."

"Oh, Frank, I don't want you to apologize. I don't want you to feel like you have to apologize. I want you just like you are. I want you . . ."

Slowly he walked across to the sofa and took her hand as he sat down beside her. For a moment he was quiet as he searched for words. "I guess I really am dense, Mary. I can hear the words you're saying, but . . . gosh, Honey, I . . . but I want to . . . to know what you're telling me . . . I really want to . . . Mary . . ."

"Oh, Frank . . . I do love you, Frank." She leaned against his shoulder, and he put his arms around her. He could feel her trembling as she pressed against him. He wanted to say, "And I love you, Mary," but the words wouldn't come. Instead he drew her closer and kissed her gently on her hair, and forehead, and lips.

"YOU CAN COME TO SUPPER NOW, JOHN."

He folded the paper and put it on the end table. "They're predicting that the bond issue for the new wing on the hospital will pass."

"Well, we certainly do need it. When Florence and I were over there this afternoon they were putting up an extra bed in the ward at the end of the hall."

They bowed their heads as they sat down.

"Lord, make us thankful for these and all our blessings. Pardon our sins. For Christ's sake. Amen."

"John, do you really think the Robinsons will be able to find William?"

"You never can tell."

They ate in silence for a while.

"John, I think he had to go. I didn't want to think that. I didn't want him to go. But now, I think he had to."

He nodded. She was right, he knew that. He wished it wasn't so, "O, Absalom, my son, my son. Would God I had died for thee."

"More coffee?"

"Just about half a cup. I probably shouldn't have it, but it's particularly good tonight. Can you reach the Bible?"

She handed it to him, and then poured the coffee. "Are we still reading Hosea?"

"Let's see." He turned the page. "Yes. Two more times, today and tomorrow. Today it's from the eleventh chapter."

He sipped his coffee, and then began to read.

> When Israel was a child, I loved him,
>> and out of Egypt I called my son.
> The more I called them,
>> the more they went from me;
> they kept sacrificing to the Baals,
>> and burning incense to idols.

> Yet it was I who taught Ephraim to walk,
>> I took them up in my arms;
>> but they did not know that I healed them.
> I led them with cords of compassion,
>> with the bands of love,
> and I became to them as one
>> who eases the yoke on their jaws,
>> and I bent down to them and fed them.

He paused and sipped his coffee. He knew what she was thinking. Sometimes children really don't know that you love them. Sometimes there's no way for them to realize that what you do is the very mark of love, not the absence of love. You want them to know, you wish they could understand.

> How can I give you up, O Ephraim!
>> How can I hand you over, O Israel!
> How can I make you like Admah!
>> How can I treat you like Zeboiim!
> My heart recoils within me,
>> my compassion grows warm and tender.
> I will not execute my fierce anger,
>> I will not again destroy Ephraim;
> for I am God and not man,
>> the Holy One in your midst,
>> and I will not come to destroy.

He paused, then began to read the devotional booklet.

> In this passage which is one of the most moving in all the Old Testament, the Prophet helps us see yet another aspect of the steadfast love of God. This time we see him not as a husband wronged by an unfaithful wife but as a father whose love for his son has been met by disobedience and waywardness. Nevertheless, his fierce anger is softened in warm and tender compassion. He will not destroy, for he is God and not man. This is the love we see in Jesus Christ. It is not dependent on our good

behavior. It does not wait for our faithfulness. There are no conditions which must be met before it is given. Rather, as Paul put it in Romans 5:8, 'God shows his love for us in that while we were yet sinners Christ died for us.' God loves like that!

He closed the book and started to bow his head.

"John, before you pray. . . You know, when you first began to read, I thought about William. We did love him. We taught him to walk and all those things. And still he went away, just like it said. But John, I think now that I had it wrong. We're the ones the prophet is talking about. We're the ones that God forgives. I believe I see it clearer than I ever did."

He nodded. "Yes, Martha. Yes, of course you're right. I really hadn't thought of it that way, but I know it's true."

After awhile he bowed his head. "O, God, we thank thee for thy love and thy forgiveness. Bless William tonight, wherever he is. Be with Frank and Mary and the children. For Jesus' sake. Amen."

"SAY YOU LOVE ME, BABY."

"Why sure I love you, Kid. What on earth would make you think any different?"

"Well, I just like to hear you say it, Baby. Sometimes you don't act like you love me."

"OK, I love you. There. Now, how about shutting up for a while and let me finish talking to Dave. You just sit there and look pretty, how about that."

"Now, there you go. I want you to talk to me, Baby. You don't love me."

"Listen, Kid. I told you I loved you twice already, haven't I? That ought to be enough for awhile. Just save it for later on. I'll tell you again."

It had begun to rain when the plane landed in Cleveland. Charlie hated rain. It was depressing, and, ye gods, it was hard enough to get some pleasure out of life without it raining. By the time the cab got to the hotel it had turned into a downpour. The doorman held the umbrella, but he got wet anyhow.

"Tell the valet I'll need to have this suit pressed right away."

He signed his name on the register and glared around the lobby. "Any calls for me?"

"Nothing here, Mr. Bowman. Will·you be with us more than one night?"

"Yeah, probably two at the least. But don't put it down definitely. I'll let you know in plenty of time."

Why hasn't Dave left word?·He knew I was coming on this plane. You don't suppose some of the boys from Pittsburgh have moved in on me, do you? He swore under his breath as he waited with the bellhop at the elevator door. This Cleveland trip is really getting off to a hot start. Getting so you just can't count on anything any more.

"Will there be anything else?"

"Naw, I'll call you if I need you." He shoved a dollar bill into the outstretched hand and watched the door close behind him. What a bunch of leeches. A lousy buck to bring up one lousy bag. Better have a good stiff drink. He rummaged through his things until he found the bottle. Should have gotten some ice but it's too late now. Dave will be calling any time. Or he'd better. As he reached for a glass he caught sight of himself in the mirror. What's happened to you, Charlie? What's wrong? He shrugged. Nothing that a good stiff drink won't cure. He'd said it so often he almost believed it. Why, sure he believed it. Look, Boy, you're in Cleveland. Dave'll call in a minute, and everything will be rosy. What's with the gloom? He stood at the window watching the rain pelt down on the streets. The lights of the cars glistened on the wet pavement. It was a long way down from the seventeenth floor. It'd all be over in a minute. What was it about every hotel room that was just the same? Why didn't Dave call? He jumped as the telephone shattered the silence. "Yeah?"

"Charlie, Boy! When'd you get in?"

"Just this minute walked in. What do you know?"

"I'll pick you up in twenty-five minutes. Got you a swell date, a real looker. Everything set?"

"Fit as a fiddle. Will you come up for a drink?"

"No, too much trouble to park. How about you meeting us at the side entrance, OK?"

The loneliness came back as he hung up the phone. The rain

danced in the street and the endless line of traffic crawled hesitantly through the intersection. What's happening to you, Charlie? It'll be all right just as soon as they pick you up. Wonder who he's brought this time. Wonder if she's a blond or a brunette. Does it matter? The light turned red and the line stopped.

It was nearly three hours later when they finished eating. He need not have worried about Dave or that bunch from Pittsburgh moving in. Dave was really a pushover. It was just too easy.

"Honey, why do you have to be talking business all the time?" She'd turned out to be a brunette.

"Well, you know the old saying, 'business before pleasure.' " He'd tried to make it sound witty and she'd laughed. Too loud, he thought.

"Yeah, I know, Honey, but I'm ready for the pleasure. Let's dance."

Dave had said for them to go ahead, he was tired of business, too. They got up and walked toward the tiny floor. For a fleeting minute Charlie wished he was at home and could take off his shoes.

She leaned against him as they swayed in time to the music.

"You're cute. And you do love me, don't you Baby?"

"Look, Kid. Do we have to go over all that again? What's with this 'do you love me' bit?"

"Well, nothing, Honey. Except that I wouldn't want you to think I go out with just anybody. I think it's important that people love each other, and everything. I mean. . . well, you know."

She had pulled away from him just a bit and was looking up into his face. Suddenly it struck him that she couldn't be more than twenty years old. He took her hand and walked back toward the table. "You ready to go, Dave?"

"Ready to go! Why, Charlie, what's the matter? The party's just beginning!"

"I guess I'm sort of beat tonight. You all stay here. I'll catch a cab."

"Aren't you going to take me with you, Baby?"

"No, Dave'll see that you get home."

"See there, you don't love me after all. You were just saying it. You didn't mean it. I believed you, and you didn't mean it."

"Maybe you're right, Kid. Maybe you're right."

By the time he got back to his room the rain had stopped. He looked out of the window. Most of the traffic was gone. Guess they've all gone home. Guess they had a home to go to. It's a long way down from the seventeenth floor. It'd all be over in a minute . . . What's happening to you, Charlie? Slowly he sank to the floor and leaned his head against the foot of the bed. Maybe it's true that you can't go home again. Maybe you've never been there at all. Try as he would, he couldn't erase the picture of that face. She wasn't much older than Doris. Why had she kept on telling him to say he loved her? What did love have to do with it, anyhow? If she'd kept her mouth shut she'd have been here right now. Maybe if she hadn't been a brunette. She had brown eyes, just like Doris. You've got to quit thinking like this, Charlie. Doris is at home with her mother where she belongs. But doesn't this kid have a mother? Where is her mother tonight? Maybe her old man is off on a trip somewhere and doesn't know she's out. He wouldn't let her go if he knew it, would he? Why, if she even thought about it he'd slap the tar out of her. And what about the guy who took her out? Yeah, what about him? This is crazy. Doris is home, home in bed. I'd kill anybody who tried anything fresh with her. I'd kill him! I'd kill him! I'd kill him! I'd kill him! I'd kill him! The tears rolled down his cheeks as he pounded his fist against the floor. O God, where is Doris tonight? Can she actually be nearly twenty? It was just yesterday that she was a little baby. Where have the years gone? O God! Of course I love her. Doesn't she have everything she wants? What else could I have done? He pulled himself up slowly and fell across the bed. Far below the wail of a siren told the mournful tale of tragedy. Then all was quiet.

"GEORGE."

"Hmmm."

"Are you asleep, George?"

"Hmm?"

"I said, are you asleep?"

"Um."

"I've been thinking about Frank and Mary some more."

"Um-hum."

"I think you're right about not calling him, at least not right now. He might get the idea that we are sort of ganging up on him. Forget what I said. OK?"

"Um-hum."

"Goodnight, George. Love you."

"Love you. Night."

She stared up at the darkness. Thank you, God, for this day and for everything that has happened. For the children and for George. She was conscious of his breathing, deep and regular. Help me to know what is right for me to do about Mary and Frank. Somewhere she could hear a dog barking in the night. Dear Lord, how many people are sad tonight? How many are afraid? I don't want to forget what it's like to be afraid. I don't want to feel that because things are working out so well for us, nobody else has any trouble. A car drove by. Much too fast, she thought. What strange sounds come in the night! There is a peace in the darkness, and also a terror. Help me to keep the proper perspective, dear Lord. I don't want to neglect people, but I don't want to force my way into their lives when they aren't ready. Keep us this night, and always. For Jesus' sake. Amen.

IT IS EASY to talk about love; it is not so easy to understand its gentleness and its depth. It is possible to describe the pain in love; it is not always so possible to sustain the hurt and despair which love may bring. It is certain that love may be perverted; it is just as certain that love never ends. Faith and hope do endure. But the greatest of all is love.

10
Joy

"Here Dad, catch!"

Frank whirled almost instinctively and threw up his hand to stop the ball. It dropped to the ground and rolled a few feet away.

"You caught me off guard, but I'll be ready next time. You won't get another one by me! Your time now. Catch!"

He watched as Bill brought the glove around. The ball hit solidly in the pocket.

"You're getting pretty good at that. Before long you'll be gobbling up grounders and line drives like a pro. Wait 'til I go in the house and take off my coat. We've got a few minutes before Mama calls us to supper, just time enough for a little infield practice. OK?"

"OK. But hurry." Bill watched him go up the steps and through the door. Gee, it was nice to have him come home from the office in the afternoon in time to play ball a little before supper. He didn't used to do that. Guess he was too busy or something. Maybe he really hadn't known how much fun it was to play ball. Sometimes grownups didn't seem to know much about having fun. But maybe Dad was learning. You'd think he'd have known about it years ago. Still sort of hard to believe that he really did have time to play these days.

"Hurry Dad!" He pitched the ball into the air and caught it before it hit the ground. Of course it didn't go very high, but he did catch it. Dad had taught him how to do that. Dad could throw it lots higher and it was harder to catch. But he was doing much better. Dad said so. He'd almost gotten so he didn't have to close his eyes when the ball came right at him. Sometimes it was hard, but Dad was sure he could do it.

"Here I come, ready or not!"

Dad always said that. Of course, Dad already knew he was

ready before he said it. But it was fun to have him say it. "I'm ready."

"Knock it to me on the ground." Bill ran to the corner of the yard near the rose bushes.

"OK. Better move over to the right a little. I might hit it into the rose bed."

Bill caught the first ball and threw it back.

"Nice going." Dad said it just the way the big boys at school did and it sounded great. He caught the next one and the next one and the next one.

"You can hit it even harder if you want to." He leaned over and watched the ball rolling across the grass. Just before it got to him it hit a rough place and bounced crazily to one side. He lunged for it and missed. The ball headed straight for the roses. Before he could think, he dashed after it.

"Be careful, Bill!" But the words came too late. The brittle canes snapped and the blossoms lay in the dust.

"I'm sorry, Dad. I didn't mean to do it. I didn't mean to, Dad." He tried to choke back the tears. How many times had he been told never to play in or around the roses? He stood quite still with the ball clutched in his hand.

"Are you hurt, Son?" Frank ran across the lawn. How do you hear the answer which has already come in the pleading justification? How do you heal the wound that goes deep into the heart, the wound that gives rise to fear when something goes wrong? How do you say it's all right after thousands of times of reproach and blame, of bitterness and resentment? How do you help him to know that roses are nothing compared to a child?

"I . . . I don't think so, Dad. But the roses . . ."

"Yeah, looks like they're in pretty bad shape. That ball sure did take a rough bounce. But I thought for a minute you had it."

"I almost did, Dad. I really almost did." He rubbed his sleeve across his face. He guessed maybe those really weren't tears after all. It was only then that he saw the trickle of blood down the back of his hand where the sharp thorn had dug into the flesh. "Guess I did sort of get a little scratch or something."

Frank picked up Bill's hand and looked at it. "Yeah. I don't think it's too bad, though. Try it out, and if it doesn't hurt, we'll have time for a few more grounders before Mama calls us."

"What's Mama going to say about the roses?"

"She'll probably fuss a little, but she'll get over it. Tell you what let's do. Let's pick up some of these blooms that got broken off and take her a bouquet."

"All right. Gee, Dad, you're swell."

IT IS THE PECULIAR CHARACTERISTIC of joy that it is always experienced in relation to sorrow or mourning. In a basic sense it represents an emergence from darkness into light, from the gloomy shadows of night to the brilliance of the new day. It is as though the depth of joy can never be realized apart from the depth of sorrow to which it stands in contrast. So it is that the true fullness of joy retains the consciousness of that despair which has been transformed and redeemed.

It is also the peculiar characteristic of joy that it often encompasses the bittersweet paradox that includes both laughter and tears, the strange but common experience of weeping for joy. In this seeming irrational response is seen the evidence of triumph through suffering, of victory through defeat, of life through death. From still another perspective, it is apparent that joy is the incredible consciousness of attainment, the awareness of fullfillment.

FRANK had discovered that it was not easy to piece together all the parts of what had been happening lately. He was sure that something was still happening in him, but it was the kind of thing you couldn't really see, at least not clearly, precisely because you were standing too close to it.

He could hear Mary singing a good night song to Betty.

> Lullaby and good night, with roses bedight,
> Creep into thy bed, there pillow thy head.

He found himself humming along with her. He had been reading the paper, but for the past few minutes he had become more conscious of what was happening back in the bedroom than what was written in the headlines.

If God will, thou shalt wake when the morning doth break.
If God will, thou shalt wake when the morning doth break.

The paper slipped out of his hands and dropped to his lap. It startled him out of his reverie and he picked it up again. The words of the song kept running through his mind. "If God will, thou shalt wake when the morning doth break." That sort of described how he felt. It was kind of like waking up to a new day. Maybe not just the same because he hadn't exactly been asleep. More like he had stumbled through a long night. When you wake up from a nightmare you know it was a dream, but this had really happened. "If God will, thou shalt wake when the morning doth break. If God will, thou shalt wake when the morning doth break."

As Mary closed the door to Betty's room Bill suggested they come back to the living room.

"Can we read the story in here, Dad?"

"Sure, Son." He put down the paper. "What's the story about tonight?"

"Zee . . . Ze-rub . . . Zerub . . . Gee, I can't say it. Here, you can read it if you want to. Mama says this was your book when you were a little boy."

The years fell away as he took the frayed copy of *The Story of the Bible*. Even before he opened the front cover he knew what he'd find: "THIS BOOK IS THE PROPERTY OF Frank Mason." There was a lump in his throat as he saw scrawled underneath the bookplate, "William, too."

"Where'd you find it, Mary?"

"It was in that old trunk you took to college. I was looking through it last week for my high school yearbook and came across it. We've been reading it some every night. We didn't start at the front. Bill saw a picture that caught his interest and we began there."

"Here's the place, Dad. It's about Zee . . . uh . . ."

"Zerubbabel."

"Yeah, that's the one. Do you remember him?"

"A little, I guess. When I was your age it was easier for me to say Ezra than Zerubbabel. They built the temple and the walls of the city, didn't they?"

"Yeah. Gee, I guess you know about everything, Dad."

Frank laughed. "Well, maybe one or two things got by me, but it's nice to have you think so."

"Are you going to read?"

"No, let's let Mama read. She's a better reader than I am." He listened to the words he had heard so long ago.

" '. . . When the foundation of this house was laid before their eyes, [they] wept with a loud voice; and many shouted aloud for joy.' "

"Weren't they glad to have the temple built again?"

"Why sure they were. It had been so long since the old temple was destroyed."

"Well, if they were happy, why did they cry?"

"Sometimes people cry when they are happy."

"Gee, I don't see why. Looks like they'd laugh or something."

"Well, I think they did. They were shouting for joy and crying at the same time."

"That's sort of crazy, isn't it?"

"Yeah, I guess it does sound sort of crazy. Anyhow, that's what they did. Better tell Dad good night now. It's time to be in bed. We can read some more about it tomorrow."

"Good night, Bill. How's the hand?"

"It's OK, Dad. Can we play again tomorrow?"

"Sure thing. Sleep tight." He listened as they walked down the hall. How did you explain tears of joy to a child when you didn't even understand about them yourself? It really didn't make sense. He found himself thinking of a verse worked in cross-stitch that used to hang on the wall in a brown frame at Grans' house. "Weeping may endure for a night, but joy cometh in the morning." He wondered what had happened to it when they sold the house after Gramps died. Grans had cried a lot then, but that was different from weeping for joy.

He opened the cover of the book again. "THIS BOOK IS THE PROPERTY OF Frank Mason." He could remember when he had written his name on the line so carefully. And he remembered how mad he'd gotten when William scrawled "William, too" below. It'd be nice to be able to tell him it was all right. He could feel the lump again. Mama had cried when the letter finally came from the Robinsons saying that they hadn't found William in Seattle. They did find out that he'd worked for awhile in an auto garage, but apparently had left with no forwarding address. One of the men thought he'd gone to Alaska, but wasn't sure. He leaned his head against the back of the chair and closed his eyes. Mama's tears weren't tears of joy.

By the time Mary came back he had fallen asleep. She picked up the new magazine and sat down on the sofa. Had it been only six weeks? But marking time by the calendar really didn't tell the story. Six days, six weeks, six years. It was the kind of thing you couldn't measure by time alone, or any other standard that made logical sense. Everything looked the same—same house, same dishes, same furniture. But really, everything was different, or rather, everybody was different. Looking back, she wouldn't have believed it could be possible. But it was real. It was real.

The phone rang, and she got up to answer it. When she came back, Frank was awake.

"Must have dropped off to sleep." He yawned and stretched his shoulders.

"I'll say you did. And snored so loud it's a wonder you didn't wake yourself up."

"Me snore? Why I *never* snore. Never!"

"I hear what you're saying, but I also hear you snoring." She laughed. "One of these days I'm going to start the tape recorder and then you'll see. Or perhaps I should say, You'll hear!"

"No fair. That's taking advantage of my defenselessness. Anyhow, how'll I know it's me on the recorder?"

"Give up. That was Grace on the phone. Wanted to know if we could have supper with them Saturday night. George is going to charcoal some steaks. I told her I thought we could, but would check with you when you woke up. Can you do it?"

"Sounds great to me. You and Grace have gotten to be real friends. I'll be glad to get to know her better, and George, too." He yawned again. "Must have slept a crick in my neck. What time is it?"

"Nearly ten."

"Ummm. Sorry about the roses. It was really my fault. We shouldn't have been playing on that side of the yard."

"They'll grow back. I wish you could have seen Bill when he came in with the blooms. Kind of a peace offering—I don't know, it's sort of hard to describe. I just wanted to hug him. Frank, you've made such a difference in him. He's, he's . . . I don't know how to describe it, but . . . I'm so grateful."

He sat staring at the fireplace without really seeing it. What did you say when you had the same difficulty finding the right words? You couldn't say, "Aw it's nothing, really." It *was* something—something that was making a difference in his life, something that was making a difference in Bill's life. But it made him uneasy that Mary seemed to think he should be thanked for what was happening, that somehow he should get credit for it. But how could you say this without seeming to take lightly something which is deep with meaning?

"Frank, you'd better get to bed. I know you're worn out after working all day and then playing ball with Bill when you come home. But I'm so glad you do—play ball with him, that is. It means so much to him."

"Look, Honey, this may sound crazy to you, but playing ball with Bill isn't a kind of chore. I want to. I get a bigger bang out of it than he does. He's getting pretty good, too."

She nodded. Somewhere within her she knew that it was tragic that they had to talk about it. It was the kind of thing that should be so much a part of their lives it would never be an issue. She wondered if that time would ever come, could ever come, after all that had happened to them. Yet even as she wondered, she realized that it was a miracle that they were able to talk about it at all. It was not surprising, really, that they couldn't find the words. They were like children just beginning to talk. Yet they *were* beginning. Thank you, God. We should have been along this way years ago. But I'm so glad we're this far, even if we are late. At least we're moving, and . . . help us to keep on.

Frank yawned as he got up slowly.

"You know, it's something, your finding that Bible story book. Mama used to read it to William and me every night. I hadn't thought of some of those things in years. The captivity, and their coming back. I dreamed something while I was asleep, but for the life of me I can't remember exactly what it was. Sort of started out with the rebuilding of the temple, but Bill was in it, and the rose bushes. Then, somehow, it got to be William, and I was picking a switch off the big shrub by the front walk for Mama because William had let the chickens out of the coop. We chased around to catch them, but never did find them all. While we were looking, we realized that William was gone and we couldn't find him. When the phone rang it seemed to be somebody calling about William, and that's when I woke up. Real crazy and mixed up."

"You've thought about William a lot recently, haven't you?"

"Yes, ever since the Robinsons said they'd try to look him up in Seattle. Seeing what he'd written in the Bible book sort of got me. I guess William never really did feel like he had anything of his own."

"OK KID, what'll you have?"

"Just a cup of coffee will be OK."

"Now look, Kid, you can't get along on nothing but coffee. You gotta have something that'll stick to your ribs. How about a hot roast beef sandwich with plenty of gravy? That sound good to you?"

"Just coffee's OK."

"Aw, Kid, look. So you're down on your luck. You're never gonna get anywhere sitting around starving to death. OK, so you're broke. So lemme buy you one crummy roast beef sandwich. Tell you what I'll do. I'll loan you the price of it, and you can pay me back when you get on top again. OK? OK! Two hot roast beef sandwiches and go heavy on the mashed potatoes and gravy."

He nodded. The jukebox blared through the noise of rattling dishes and the heavy sighs of trucks pulling into the crowded parking area. The girl brought the coffee and stared at him as she set it down.

"Say ain't you the fellow that came through here about four months ago?" He nodded. "I thought so. You looked familiar when I saw you come in. But I almost didn't recognize you. You've sure lost a lot of weight. Where you been?"

He shook his head. "Around."

"You shouldn't have took off like you did. Boss was as mad as hops when he went out there and found you hadn't emptied up the garbage in the dumpster. Tell you the truth, I didn't blame you for not liking it. But you ought to have told him you were leaving."

He sat looking at the coffee cup.

"Say, if you're still looking for a job, I'll be glad to put in a good word for you. Boss has cooled off by now. But you gotta promise you'll stay longer than a couple of days. We sure need somebody to push that mop around."

He shook his head.

"Thanks, Kid, but let him alone right now. He's not feeling too hot. He almost didn't come in with me. I didn't know he'd worked here. Does he owe you anything?"

"Naw. Actually he left without collecting what pay was coming to him. Guess that's one thing that kept Boss from really blowing his stack. Tell you the truth, it's a pretty smelly job. You pick him up?"

"Yeah. He was standing by the road about a hundred miles back. But keep your trap shut about it. He's not hurting anything."

"You know me, big boy. Tight-mouthed as a clam, that's me. I see Cookie shoving your sandwiches through the window so I'll run get 'em. If you change your mind about the job, Fellow, just let me know."

William stirred his coffee and looked down at the floor.

"You want to spill it, Kid? I'm no headshrinker, but sometimes it helps to get it off your chest."

He shook his head.

"Well, it's up to you. Eat your sandwich now, and we'll get rolling."

He stirred the gravy into the mashed potatoes and raised the fork to his mouth. He was hungry, no doubt about that, but somehow it was sort of hard to swallow. Maybe a drink of water would help wash it down. It was ironic that they'd stopped here. Yes, he remembered. How well he remembered! He closed his eyes as if to shut out the sights and sounds that pressed in upon him. But how do you close out the memories, the bitter dregs from the cup of yesterday?

"Ain't your sandwich good, kid?"

He nodded, and picked up his fork. This was a nice guy, a real nice guy. He didn't have to stop and he surely didn't have to stake him to a meal. He'd like to talk to him, but what was there to say?

The record on the jukebox scraped to a close, and for a moment there was a kind of quiet in the midst of the din while the mechanism produced another disc. Then the music started again, and somebody with a nasal twang began to sing, "Look down, look down that lonesome road, before you travel on . . ."[1]

He clenched his teeth. There was no turning back, now. He knew that. He'd already decided that. Painfully, he'd traced the road every step of the way, as in his imagination he traced the miles that stretched out before him. "Look up, look up, and seek your Maker, 'fore Gabriel blows his horn . . ." If it were only that easy. But it never worked out just that way. Somehow it seemed easier to run, although that wasn't easy, either. Funny how things sometimes popped into his mind. He couldn't remember when he'd learned the verses, but they'd come to him over and over again. "Whither shall I go from thy spirit? or whither shall I flee from thy presence? If I ascend up into heaven, thou art there: if I make my bed in hell, behold, thou art there. If I take wings of the morning, and dwell in the uttermost parts of the sea; Even there . . ."

"You ain't touched that beef, Kid. That's your business, but it sure will do you good. Go on and eat some of it anyhow."

He nodded, and picked up his fork again. It was good roast beef, and he knew he should eat it. He could remember wondering why anybody would ever make their bed in hell. But that was a long time ago. A long time ago. The record was on its second time through the song. "Look up, look up, and seek your Maker . . ." He knew it was the other way around. He'd run as long as he could. Now he wouldn't run anymore. "Weary toting such a load, trudging down that lonesome road . . ."

"Had enough, Kid? Finish up your coffee and we'll get rolling again."

He got up and waited at the door while the cashier rang up the money. The wind had started to blow. You could tell it would soon be winter. He could smell the garbage as they passed the kitchen door. Had it just been four months? He climbed into the cab and pulled the door shut.

"Thanks for the sandwich. It was real good. I just didn't have much of an appetite."

"Glad to do it, Kid. Hang on, now, while I get this baby back out on the road. That was something, you having worked there and that gal recognizing you. Haven't you got any folks?"

He nodded. "Yeah." He started to say, "I guess so," but changed his mind. He remembered the first time the Chaplain had asked him that. Strange how people asked you that. He'd wondered what difference it would make whatever you answered. If you said yes then what would they say? Maybe, "Why don't you get in touch with them?" What if you said no? They'd feel sorry for you, probably, but it really wouldn't change anything. He could feel the ridges in the pavement thumping against the wheels. The words of the Psalm kept running through his mind. ". . . If I take the wings of the morning, and dwell in the uttermost parts of the sea; Even there shall thy hand lead me, and thy right hand shall hold me."

"That's strange . . ."

"Huh? Did you say something, Kid?"

"Uh, no. Guess I was just thinking out loud." All at once he realized that the words said something he'd never seen before. He'd always thought it meant that, well, you tried to get away and couldn't, and that sooner or later you got caught up with and that was bad. But, actually, it said something different. ". . . shall thy hand lead me, and thy right hand shall hold me . . ." He knew he'd never thought of it like that. But maybe . . . why that's sort of like . . . He closed his eyes. All at once he felt as if he were going to cry. He clenched his teeth, and tightened his fists until his fingernails dug into the palms of his hands. Could it really be true? He shook his head in disbelief. He couldn't remember the rest of the Psalm. Something about darkness and light. He said the words over again. ". . . Even there shall thy hand lead me, and thy right hand shall hold me . . ." Even in hell . . . It had been hell . . . Oh, there had been times that weren't as bad as others, but when you looked back, it all sort of ran together. Besides, it hurt to think about it and it made him sick. "Search me, O God . . ." That was it—that was how the Psalm went. "Search me, O God, and know my heart: try me, and know my thoughts: And see if there be any wicked way in me, and lead me in the way everlasting."

That was the hardest part. How could he say, "*any* wicked way?" Was there any way that wasn't? ". . . Even there shall thy hand lead me . . ." The words kept coming back. ". . . lead me in the way everlasting." Could he find it now? Could this be it? How did you know? And yet, there was no turning back. No matter what he would find, he had to keep going. "Search me, O God, and know my heart . . ." Guess there isn't any way to hide, no matter what. But I don't want to hide any more . . . I . . . I want to go home . . . The pavement thumped against the tires and he leaned his head against the back of the seat and closed his eyes.

"Hey, Kid." It was grey dawn when he opened his eyes. "This is it, Kid. I'll have to let you off before we get clear into town. I'm going to leave the highway at this corner, anyway, and you'll have a better chance to catch a ride at this junction than you would farther on. Good luck."

"Thanks. Thanks more than I can tell you. I hope I can do something for you, someday. I don't know when it'll be, but I'd like to . . ."

"Forget it, Kid. I know what it's like to be down on your luck. You just pass it on to somebody else who needs it."

"I'll sure try. Believe me, I'll sure try."

He watched the big truck turn the corner and move out of sight. The wind was still blowing, and he buttoned his coat against it. After a while he picked up his bag and walked toward the morning.

THERE IS A KIND OF RECKLESSNESS in joy, a glorious abandon, a lavish extravagance in the profusion of abundance, the awareness of good measure, pressed down, shaken together, and running over. It is evident in the beginning when the morning stars sang together, and all the sons of God shouted for joy. It is heard in the fullness of time when the angel brought good tidings of great joy, and the heavenly host sang glory to God in the highest and on earth peace, good will toward men. It is shown forth in the voice of a great multitude like the sound of many waters rejoicing that the Lord God omnipotent reigneth. It is a man who finds a hidden treasure in a field and sells all that he has to buy that field. It is a woman who finds a coin and calls together her friends and neighbors that they may share her joy. It is a father who receives his son and kills the fatted calf that they all may eat and be merry. In every instance it is the response of exultation to the well nigh incredible turn of circumstance in which the wildest dreams have been transcended in a glad reality.

JOHN MASON discovered that. The day had begun like any other day. How was it possible to know that, before the day was out, the patterns of his life would be changed? He had long since learned that there are those events which cast their shadows before them so that when they occur there has already been warning, an awareness of what is about to happen. But he had also learned that there are those events which come unexpectedly, which happen without prior intimation, which emerge from a complex web of circumstance already spun of which there was no knowledge. At times it gave him an eerie feeling to realize that at that very moment it was possible that conversations were being held which would alter his life, plans were being laid that would affect him for good or for ill. He knew there was nothing to be gained by dwelling on this notion, but he also knew that every man's life is intricately bound up in the lives of his fellows, affecting them and being affected by them. How true it was that "no man is an island, entire of itself."

"Did you bring in the afternoon paper, John?"

"No. I looked out on the porch a little while ago and didn't see it. It certainly should have come by now. I hope it hasn't blown all over the yard in this wind."

He turned on the porch light and opened the door. The days were really getting shorter and the wind had a definite bite. The paper wasn't on the porch. Maybe it had fallen in the flowerbed. He tried to peer into the shadows cast by the porch light. As his eyes began to adjust to the darkness he realized someone was standing on the walk.

"Yes?" he called.

"Papa . . . it's . . . it's me."

How long does it take to run down seven steps and across the walk to your son? How tightly do you hold him in your arms as the words will not come for joy? How gently do you draw away that you may see and know and know again that he is your son?

"William." His voice trembled. "William, you're here. You're here!"

"Yes, Papa. I . . . Papa, I'm . . . I'm sorry . . ."

"Come in the house, Son. Here, let me have your bag."

Where are the thousand and one questions which had formed and changed and formed again through the years? Where are the multiplied answers that somehow never plumbed the depths from which the questions came? How do you come to know that there is neither question nor answer, that question and answer are both transformed in the overwhelming experience which shatters the past and fills the present with an indescribable ecstasy?

"Martha! Martha! It's William! It's William! He's come home, Martha! He's home."

How deep is the well of tears broken open in the yearning of the heart as you hold your child in your arms again? How kind is the balm of fulfillment after the myriad wounds of shattered hope and bitter disappointment? How vast is the consciousness of joy that "this my son was dead, and is alive again; he was lost, and is found."

"Don't cry, Mama."

"I'm not crying, William. Not really." She buried his head on her shoulder, and swayed gently to and fro. After a while she put her hands on his shoulders and turned him toward the light. "Let me look at you, William. Why, you're just skin and bones! I bet you haven't had a decent meal in a month. John, take his bag up to his room, and you all get washed up for supper. I've got a roast in the oven and by the time you get ready, I'll have it on the table."

> When the LORD turned again the captivity of Zion, we were like them that dream.
>
> Then was our mouth filled with laughter, and our tongue with singing: then said they among the heathen, the LORD hath done great things for them.
>
> The LORD hath done great things for us; whereof we are glad.

Turn again our captivity, O LORD, as the streams in the south.

They that sow in tears shall reap in joy.

He that goeth forth and weepeth, bearing precious seed, shall doubtless come again with rejoicing, bringing his sheaves with him.

Dr. Watson closed the Bible and laid it down on the end-table. They sat in silence for a little while.

Finally, John Mason spoke. "You know, it's strange how things come back to you. I can remember my father reading that Psalm years ago. I don't think it really had much meaning for me, then. I suppose you have to live through these things before you can actually understand—and even then, you're not sure you do."

"Yes. I think that even the man who wrote the Psalm felt like that, too. As he thought back on what had happened, it seemed like a dream to him. The kind of thing that's just too good to be true."

"I've been thinking about something you said in a sermon recently. That we should 'rejoice always.' That's sort of hard for me to understand. In the Psalm the joy came after the sorrow, it wasn't always there."

"I see what you mean. I think in Philippians Paul was saying that we can rejoice always because of what God has done for us in Jesus Christ, that no matter what happens, we know the Lord is at hand."

"Yes, I see. Sometimes it is harder to do it than at others."

"That's certainly true. I'm going to have to go now. Shall we pray together before I leave?"

"Please do." As John bowed his head, he held Martha's hand in his.

"Almighty God, there are many things for which we give thee thanks, but especially right now we thank thee for William's safe return. We ask thy special guidance for him in the days ahead as he continues to sort out his life and find the way thou wouldst have him to go. Be with John and Martha and me as together we join our hearts in praise to thee. For Jesus' sake. Amen."

"I'm sorry William wasn't here to see you. I rather thought

he'd be back by now. As I said, he went over to Frank and Mary's for supper and didn't intend to be long."

"I'll get to see him later. They must have a million things to talk about. Tell him 'hello' for me."

"Sure will. And thank you for coming by, Howard. And for all the help you've been these past few years."

"WELL, WHAT DO YOU THINK?"

"I don't know, Frank. I really don't know. He's not at all like I thought he'd be. Much quieter and more reserved."

"He's sure changed a lot. He's a lot thinner, but the real difference is in the way he acts. I wonder what all has happened to him."

"Guess we'll never know it all. Well, it's getting late. We'd better turn in."

"All right. By the way, that was a first rate supper. I appreciate your having him over."

"It was fun. I was glad to get to know him after all I'd heard about him. I sometimes wondered if he were real, if he actually existed, hearing all the stories about him."

"He's real, all right. But sometimes I wonder if any of us ever really have known him."

He turned off the lamps and picked up the evening paper.

"Do you want to see the new magazine?"

"No, I'm sleepy. I think I'll just glance at the paper for a few minutes and let it go at that."

How did you understand the strange conflicting feelings that seemed to well up within you? He couldn't believe his ears when the phone rang and Papa told him the news. He'd told them he'd come right over, but even as he drove across town it was hard to realize that he was actually back. He knew there had been a time when he would have resented his coming, but that time was past now. Even so, there were still some things that didn't fit, somehow. He'd wondered what he'd say when he walked through the door. What did you say when the years had passed and the gulf had grown wide? You couldn't be casual, as though it were only yesterday. But you didn't know what he'd be like now, or how you felt about him or his coming back. You were glad he was back, of course, but there was much more than that. It'd be easy to say too much, and then wish you hadn't said it.

"Hello, William."

"Hello, Frank."

They stood looking at each other, each trying to search out the clues that would indicate the way things would go, had to go. After a while the silence becomes awkward.

"You've lost a lot of weight."

"Yeah."

"It's . . . It's been a long time . . ."

"Yeah."

"Here, Frank, sit down and take off your coat. I've just made a fresh pot of coffee, and I'll get you a cup."

"None for me, thanks, Mama. I'm getting too old to drink coffee this time of night." He'd tried to laugh, but it hadn't sounded very funny.

"Papa'll be back in a minute. He's just gone to put the car in the garage."

After a while the words came a bit easier. But somehow you were always conscious of the gaps, and wondered what to say, what to ask, what not to ask.

"You're going to be here a while, William?"

"Of course he is."

"I don't know, Frank. Sort of depends, I guess."

"Well, look . . . uh, how about coming over to our house for supper tomorrow night. I want you to meet Mary and the kids."

"OK. Why sure, if Mary won't mind."

"Good. I'll pick you up about five-thirty on my way home from the office, if that's OK."

After a while he'd left, saying that he knew William was tired and wanted to get to bed. Mary was waiting up for him when he drove in.

"I really don't know what there is to tell. He hitchhiked in and obviously hasn't been eating too regular. He's thin as a rail. I invited him over for supper tomorrow night, hope it's all right with you."

"Of course it is. I do want to meet him."

He knew she would ask the question which had to be asked, but who would have an answer?

"What happens now, Frank?"

"I honestly don't know. But I can tell you this, his coming has sure meant the world to Mama and Papa. I can't remember when I've seen them look like they did tonight." He hung up his coat and sank into the big chair. "I just hope he won't hurt them again. I surely do hope that."

Peace . . . which passes all understanding
PHILIPPIANS 4:7

11
Peace

"Can you come in for a cup of coffee?"

"I really shouldn't, Mary, but it's mighty tempting."

"It'll only take a minute. I haven't had a chance to talk to you recently, and I've missed you."

"All right, but don't let me stay past four-fifteen. George is coming home early today, and we're going to put up the storm windows." Was there a kind of urgency in her voice? Grace wasn't sure. Maybe she was just reading something into it that wasn't really there.

"Where are the children?"

"They're spending the afternoon with their grandmother. Works out real well that her Circle meets at a different time from ours. Frank will pick them up on his way home."

Grace noticed that she said "ours." She could remember that day not many months ago when they had met for lunch. And some people say miracles don't happen any more, she thought. Guess it depends on what you call a miracle. "Can I help?"

"Just get out the cups and I'll have the water hot in a minute."

They sat at the kitchen table. It was Mary who broke the silence. "Grace, I'm worried about Frank. It's probably just my imagination, but he doesn't seem the same since William came home. And I just don't want anything to interfere with what's been happening to us these past few months. It's like a barrier has suddenly grown up between us again. I can't explain it. But he's different. It's not anything he's done. It's just that he's more tense, or maybe more preoccupied. It's hard to put my finger on anything specific, and that's part of the trouble. And I don't have anything against William. I'm glad he's back. It's just that . . . well . . . Oh, I don't know . . ."

Grace nodded. How well she knew the kind of anxious feeling

that seems to cloud the horizon when you've just begun to relax a little and actually believe that you are over the hump. Would she ever forget those early days when George would come home from a crisis at the office and you could just feel the tension stretching within him? It wasn't that you didn't know that such times must inevitably arise. You just wondered whether you were ready, whether he was ready, whether there had been enough opportunity for stability so that he would not fall back into the old rut. You realized it wouldn't do any good to become resentful of the people in the office, yet there was a kind of fierce protectiveness that welled up within you, and you found yourself vowing that you wouldn't allow anyone or anything to stand in the way of your newfound life. But what could you do? Yes, she knew, how well she knew.

"Maybe if William would just say what he intends to do, Frank would unwind a little. I guess he really doesn't know yet, but it sort of leaves us all at loose ends."

Grace bit her lip. She found herself wanting to say that she was sure Frank would work it out all right and that Mary needn't worry. But she knew there was no way she could really be sure of this, just as she hadn't been able to be absolutely sure that George wouldn't drink again if the pressures became too great. It was different now, but not at the beginning.

"I understand. You figure out all kinds of solutions, but you can't really be sure that any of them will actually work."

"That's right. It's the uncertainty that's wearing me out. And I know I'm not any help to Frank when I'm on edge like this."

They sat in silence for a while. The clock struck the hour.

"Grace, I'm not going to be beaten by this. But it's not easy. I got to thinking about it while Madeline was leading the devotional at Circle this afternoon. I didn't catch the reference of that verse she kept repeating, but I kept thinking it was a lot easier to say than do."

Grace nodded. "I think it was the third chapter of Colossians, the fifteenth verse."

"I want to let the peace of God rule in my heart, and I sort of thought it did until all this happened. Madeline seemed to think it was just that simple—just make up your mind that you are going to let your heart be at peace and it will happen."

"Yes, I thought of that, too. It's one thing to talk about, something else again, to do."

"You know, it's strange. I really believed—maybe hoped is a better word—that once Frank and I began to work things out, we'd just keep on and on with no interruptions. I guess I just wasn't ready for a setback. But now that I think about it, it's not reasonable to expect that life will run smoothly."

"Even when you wish so very much that it could."

"Oh, yes! Yes! I do wish that. But I know that's just not the way things are. Look, it's four-fifteen, and you've got to go, I feel better, now. You're good to listen. I'll call you in a day or two."

"Thanks for the coffee. It'll probably help me be a better storm window putter-upper. Even if it doesn't, I enjoyed it."

Mary stood at the door and waved as Grace drove away. She wished there were words to express how grateful she was for her friendship. Even as she thought about it, she knew that Grace understood that there weren't any words, and that they had reached the place where such words really weren't needed. Nevertheless, she'd like to tell her. Thank you, God, for Grace.

She glanced at the clock as she closed the door. Not quite four-thirty. It would be nearly an hour before Frank came home with the children. She found herself thinking about the devotional again. Madeline had said over and over, "Let the peace of God rule in your hearts." She put on her apron and began to get things ready for supper. The potatoes needed to be in the oven by five. How do you let the peace of God rule in your heart? After a while she propped the Bible open on the cabinet so she could read the verses Madeline had quoted. Grace said they were from Colossians 3. Yes, there it is in verse 15: "And let the peace of Christ rule in your hearts, to which indeed you were called in the one body. And be thankful." Madeline had said, "peace of God," but it apparently was the same thing. She began to read with verse 12 at the beginning of the paragraph.

> Put on then, as God's chosen ones, holy and beloved, compassion, kindness, lowliness, meekness, and patience, forbearing one another and, if one has a complaint against another, forgiving each other; as the Lord has forgiven

you, so you also must forgive. And above all these put on love, which binds everything together in perfect harmony. And let the peace of Christ rule in your hearts, to which indeed you were called in the one body. And be thankful. Let the word of Christ dwell in you richly, as you teach and admonish one another in all wisdom, and as you sing psalms and hymns and spiritual songs with thankfulness in your hearts to God. And whatever you do, in word or deed, do everything in the name of the Lord Jesus, giving thanks to God the Father through him.

There was more to it than Madeline had indicated in the devotional. She wondered how to "put on compassion, kindness, lowliness, meekness, and patience." She knew she'd like to have all those things, even felt that in a sense she could honestly say they were true of her, at least at times. Strange how these things seemed more possible at some times than at others, and peace most of all. When it was gone, the others were gone, too. Or was it the other way around? She'd have to think about it later.

PEACE IS ELUSIVE. In one sense we use the word "peace" to describe a condition that is free from conflict or hostility. Even in this usage, however, there may be subtle variations which tend to qualify the condition. Thus, it is possible to speak of an "uneasy peace," and in so doing to recognize that, although on the surface there is no evidence of unrest, the overt calm may be shattered at any time. The term peace is also used to describe a personal attitude marked by calm and composure. Paradoxically enough, the attitude of peace may be encountered in the presence of conditions which seem to belie its possibility. From still another point of view, we speak of the peace which exists because of an inability or an unwillingness to take into account all the factors inherent in a given situation. Such a peace can rightfully be called unrealistic. At a still deeper level, it is evident that while peace involves the whole person and is unitary and pervasive, this does not necessarily imply that the absence of disturbance or distress is essential to its existence.

IT WAS HARD for Frank to realize that. It was only recently that he'd been able to think about it at all. He could remember how they used to tease him for always trying to smooth things over. But he honestly didn't like for people to be at odds with him, or with each other for that matter. Once, when he was younger, they'd called him a "peacemaker," and he'd quoted the verse in the Sermon on the Mount, "Blessed are the peacemakers, for they shall be called the children of God." But they'd laughed at him, and that was worse. He still wondered what was wrong with peace, or with being a peacemaker. He knew he liked peace, and he wished that everybody could somehow live at peace with everybody else, or at least with him.

He could still remember a man who had spoken at a high school assembly program on "Peace of Mind." That day he knew he wanted peace of mind more than anything else in all the world. It was kind of ironic that the more he tried to get it, the more he seemed to miss it. It just wasn't possible to please everybody or to get everybody to like you, no matter how hard you tried. But how could you have peace of mind when there were those who didn't always like what you did or were disappointed in you when you didn't meet their expectations?

It was only recently that he wasn't so easily upset when things didn't go right. Almost ruefully he had come to realize that what he'd thought was "peacemaking" had actually been a frantic effort to placate other persons, to "sweep things under the rug" so to speak, in an attempt to hide from sight the unpleasantness encountered in the everyday course of living.

He recalled vividly the night he and Mary were talking about the office, and it had dawned on him that he'd been bringing his resentments home and taking them out on her and the children. He'd tried to apologize, but somehow she already knew, had already forgiven him.

FRANK turned off Central Avenue onto Elm. He'd told Mary he'd pick up the children on his way home. The houses along the street reminded him of the hundreds of times he'd come this way through the years. There was the place where Mr. Ashley had made them curve the sidewalk to go around the tree. So many of the big trees had died. The one where he and William had had a bag swing was gone.

William. Why had William's coming home upset him? Things had been going so well and there was no reason at all why they shouldn't keep on. Of course he was glad William was back. He turned into the driveway and honked the horn.

"Do we have to go right this minute?"

"Yes, Bill. Mama will have supper ready by the time we get there, and we'll have to hurry. Go find Betty, and be sure she has her sweater."

"But, Dad, can't we stay just a little longer? Come on around in back. Uncle William has been playing ball with me, and he's keen. He can throw it as high as the house. Come see!"

"Bill, don't argue with me. I've already told you that we have to go right now. Now mind me and go get Betty."

"Oh, all right."

He drummed his fingers on the steering wheel as Bill ran back around the house. Sooner or later William was simply going to have to make up his mind about what he intended to do. He couldn't stay here and live off the folks indefinitely. But Papa would never tell him that. Trouble with Papa was that he was just too generous for his own good. Or for William's good either, when you came right down to it. He turned on the radio to hear the five-thirty sportscast.

"Hi, Frank."

"Uh, oh, hello, Papa." He hadn't heard him come out of the house.

"Mama's looking for Betty's sweater and will have them out here in just a minute. Haven't seen you for several days."

"No. Well, you know how it is. We've been pretty rushed this fall."

"You haven't had a chance to talk to William recently, I guess."

"No, I haven't, Papa. What's he going to do?"

"Well, I'm not real sure. He's thinking about trying to get back into school the second semester, but he may have to start all over again. He doesn't know definitely."

"Papa, when is he going to know definitely? I mean, time's passing, and he ought to be making up his mind. I know it's none of my business, but it just doesn't seem right for him to sit around and do nothing all the time."

"Yes, I'm sure you're right. But it's not easy for him, Frank. It'll take a while for him to get things sorted out in his mind and I want him to have all the time he needs."

"Why, sure, Papa. But it won't do any good to let him just drift along."

"That's true, Frank, but it doesn't seem to me that what he's doing right now is drifting. I think he's really trying to find himself and I want to help him all I can. I guess it's sort of hard for you to see, not being here with him from day to day."

"I don't know, Papa. I really don't. You know I've always sort of felt that you were too easy on William, but . . ."

"We're coming, Dad." Bill ran down the porch steps and across the yard. "Hurry, Betty!"

"Think about it, Frank. He needs you, too."

"I don't know, maybe I never was any good for him—or he for me."

"Get in Betty. OK, Dad, we're ready now."

"I hope you and Mary will come over soon, Frank. We miss seeing you."

"We will, Papa. Bill, did you and Betty remember your manners?"

"Had a nice time, Pawpaw. Tell Nana we had a nice time."

"Glad you did, Bill. You and Betty come back real soon."

PEACE IS ELUSIVE. There is about peace that strange and disturbing dimension which seems to make it disappear just as it is attained, which causes it to fall apart just when it is clutched most tightly, which creates the necessity to risk its loss in order to find it again. Only slowly was William learning that. It was already dark as he walked along Elm Street. His footsteps rustled in the leaves. He remembered the place where the tree-roots had raised the sidewalk. Funny how things came back to you. He'd hit it too hard while riding his bicycle one day and had blown out the front tire. The wheel had lurched crazily, and he'd fallen against the steps of Dr. Harris' house. His nose had bled a lot, and Dr. Harris had shown him how to put a wad of paper under his upper lip. They'd all said what a good place to get hurt, right in the doctor's front yard. He smiled to himself. Had he really been worried about those things? They seemed so trivial now. He turned up the steps and rang the doorbell.

"Come in, William. I heard you were home. Good to see you. Won't you sit down? Here, let me take your jacket."

The fire felt good after the chill of the night. He warmed his hands for a minute while Dr. Harris poked the logs.

"Mrs. Harris has gone to her book club meeting, but she said she left some cookies on the counter. Would you rather have coffee or hot chocolate?"

"Coffee is fine. I appreciate your letting me come over."

He was back in a minute with the tray.

"Help yourself to cream and sugar if you want them. I'll just have mine black."

He watched William as he picked up the cup. Has it really been eleven years since I had him in my Sunday school class? He's changed a lot in one way. He's thinner and quieter. In another way, he's just like he was then, coming by to get a handful of Marie's cookies. He waited.

"Doc, I'd like to talk to you about studying medicine. I have some questions about it—I'm already twenty-eight and I've wasted an awful lot of time. But I think it's the kind of thing I could do, and would like to do. Do you think it's too late for me to start?"

"Well, William, I guess that really depends on you. You'll be older than most of the other students. You'll be nearly forty when you finally get out on your own, and that's no spring chicken."

"I haven't said anything about this to Papa. I'm not sure enough yet to bring it up. I've caused them enough trouble and worry as it is without making them sweat through my decisions about what to do. For once in my life I'd like to do something right and let Mama and Papa be proud of me."

Dr. Harris scraped his pipe. How do you tell him that the Masons want to know about the struggle, that it is harder not to be a part of what is going on? How do you say that studying medicine is hard, that you need more incentive than wanting your family to be proud of you? How can you help this lad to find himself after so many false starts and get on the track that will lead to genuine fulfillment?

"Well, William, that's a tough one. Yet, I think I know your father well enough to predict that he'll be for you, whatever you decide, and will help you in every way he can."

"That's just it, Doc. I don't deserve to have him finance my education for eight or ten years. He and Mama have a right to a little peace and quiet for a change. If I do this, I've got to find a way to do it on my own."

"Um-hum. See what you mean." He moved the match back and forth across the bowl of his pipe, making sure the tobacco was lighted all around, then slowly blew it out and tossed it into the fire. He wondered how William would define peace in relation to his parents. As he thought back across the years, he was certain that his own definition had changed since the time he was just beginning his medical education.

"Doc, I . . . I don't know just how to say this, but . . . sometimes I wonder if it was right for me to come back. I'm not even too sure why I came back. Maybe they'd have been better off if I'd just stayed away . . ."

"Hmmmm."

"It's a funny thing. All the way across the country I kept thinking that if I could ever get home again, everything would be all right, somehow. I guess I knew that really wouldn't solve anything, but the thought was there. And then when I got to town I was almost afraid to . . . to . . . I stood out there a long time, and then Papa came out . . . For just a little while it was wonderful . . . Frank came over, and we were all there . . . When I was in the Army I read Thomas Wolfe's *You Can't Go Home Again*. Well, I believed it. And then, when I got home that night, I thought he was wrong, but I'm beginning to believe he was right again."

He got up and walked to the fireplace. "I guess this doesn't make much sense to you. I'm not sure it makes much to me, but I know this, I can't stay here. I've got to make up my mind one way or the other."

Dr. Wilson searched through his pockets for a match. How

painful it is to grow up, especially when you've lost a lot of time like William has! To be able to face up to reality, to know deep within yourself that you have to assume the responsibility for your own actions is hard. He struck the match and held it over his pipe. Trouble is, you have to fight on so many fronts all at once. How is it possible for William to see that assuming the responsibility for his own actions does not mean that he has to shut out his parents from participating with him in his deliberations, his decisions, his life? How can he know that peace for them can never be simply the absence of struggle? How can he knew that he will never find peace, himself, if he tries to avoid the struggle?

"Do you know of any scholarships I might try for? My high school grades weren't too bad, and I'd be willing to work."

"Well, William, let me put it this way. If you go to the State University you can get by on mighty little. I doubt that you'll have much chance for a scholarship for awhile, but if you keep up your grades your chances will get better. I hope you'll let your father help—I know he'd want to, and I think he has a right to. And if you'll let me, I'd like to help, too. I've got a little money ahead, and you're welcome to borrow what you need and pay me back when you get on your feet."

"Gosh, Doc, I don't know what to say. I didn't intend for you to do that. That's . . . that's not why I came over tonight."

"I know it isn't, William. Just put it down as something that would give me a lot of pleasure. I'm betting on you to come through."

It was nearly an hour later that he was walking back along Elm Street. The wind was rising and the leaves blew along before him. He could feel it pushing him and he shoved his hands into his jacket pockets. All at once he found himself wanting to run with the wind. There was a lightness in his step as the leaves swirled around him. Hurry! Hurry! Hurry! You've got to catch up! You can't stop for a minute! Run! Run! He leaped up the porch steps three at a time and stopped at the door to catch his breath. He was standing there when his father opened the door.

"Why, William, is anything wrong? You startled me running up on the porch like that."

"No, Papa. No, nothing's wrong."

He opened the screen door and took off his jacket as he went into the house. How could he describe the way he felt? How could he explain to Papa that it was wonderful to be running toward something at last, when he'd been running away from something for so long? How could he put into words the change that had taken place in him, that was taking place in him, that would continue in the days and weeks ahead?

"Papa, can I talk to you a little?"

"Why, of course, Son. Mama's in the living room but we can go back to the breakfast room if you wish."

"No, Mama's a part of it, too." All at once he wished that he could start another way, that he could go out and come in again, that there was some way they could know he didn't want this to seem like a dramatic moment, that . . . "Papa . . . Papa, I'm going to leave . . ." Why did it have to sound so somber? He could feel his mother's eyes as she watched him. "But, it's not like before. I know where I'm going this time. At least I know where I want to go, and I believe I can make it."

"William . . ." How could you tell him that he would always be welcome here, that the door would always be open, but that you understood his leaving?

"Papa, it's hard to say because the words sound just the opposite, but for the first time since I got back, I really feel at home. The strange thing is, I began to feel that way when I knew I was going to leave. It's the craziest feeling, but there it is . . ."

John Mason nodded. How many years had it been since he'd come to know that the only way you could keep your child was to give him up? He wanted to go over and put his arm around Martha, but knew he should not, not right now. He would do that later after William had gone up to his room.

"Will you go soon?"

"I'm not sure, Papa. I'm going to enter the State University, and I want to go over to check with the dean to see whether any of my credits are still good. I'll have my hands full between now and midterm, reading and trying to get the cobwebs out of my brain."

THE LATE AFTERNOON sun streamed through the stained-glass windows and etched a distorted pattern against the curved backs of the pews. Howard Watson had slipped in unnoticed and sat in the gathering shadow toward the back of the church. The great swell of the organ rolled out across the empty space and crashed against the walls and ceiling. Slowly the echo died away, and then, high in the treble, the melody sang again the song of joy and trust. He found himself thinking of the still, small voice after the tumult of the wind and the fury of the earthquake. "Be still, and know that I am God." He needed to hear that. Here in the quiet of the sanctuary, how many times had he found the peace that passeth understanding, the renewal that enabled him to pick up again the burdens that must be borne? "Thou dost keep him in perfect peace, whose mind is stayed on thee, because he trusts in thee." He folded his arms across the back of the pew in front of him and bowed his head.

Suddenly, from the street he heard the shrill scream of tires as the tortured rubber bit into the unwilling pavement. Instinctively, he tensed his muscles to hear the crash which had to follow. Two seconds passed, then another, and another. Slowly, he relaxed. It did not come. Thank God. His head was still resting on his arms, but the mood was broken. Is there no place of refuge from the violent rush and noisy strife? He sat up and opened his eyes. The sun had almost set, and the glow through the windows was soft in the deepening shadows. He could see the circle of light on the console of the organ. Outside all was quiet again.

Dear Lord, forgive me for resenting intrusions which upset the calm serenity of this holy place. I think I can understand why Simon Peter wanted to stay on top of the Mount of Transfiguration. When I think of the misery and suffering in the world, I long to have some place where I can go and hide. O God, I need a place to go, but not to hide. Wilt thou restore my soul . . .

He sat quite still and after awhile was conscious of following the words of the hymn as the organ sang the melody.

> Dear Lord and Father of mankind,
>   Forgive our foolish ways;
> Reclothe us in our rightful mind,
>   In purer lives Thy service find,
>   In deeper reverence, praise.

> Breathe through the heats of our desire
>> Thy coolness and Thy balm;
> Let sense be dumb, let flesh retire;
>> Speak through the earthquake, wind, and fire,
>> O still, small voice of calm![1]

Yes, that was it. That was what he really wanted. "Thou dost keep him in perfect peace, whose mind is stayed on thee, because he trusts in thee." After a while he got up and walked toward the front of the church.

"You're practicing late tonight, Roger."

"Oh, hello, Dr. Watson. I was just about to stop. Didn't hear you come in."

"I enjoy hearing you play. Does me good just to sit and listen. I didn't recognize that last piece you were playing. Is it new?"

"Well, fairly new. It wasn't in the old hymnbook. I don't believe we've sung it since I've been here. It's called 'They Cast Their Nets in Galilee.' Here, would you like to follow the words as I play it?"

He took the hymnbook and began to read with the music.

> They cast their nets in Galilee
>> Just off the hills of brown;
> Such happy, simple fisherfolk,
>> Before the Lord came down.

> Contented, peaceful fishermen,
>> Before they ever knew
> The peace of God that filled their hearts
>> Brimful, and broke them too.

> Young John who trimmed the flapping sail,
>> Homeless, in Patmos died.
> Peter, who hauled the teeming net,
>> Head down was crucified.

> The peace of God, it is no peace,
>> But strife closed in the sod.
> Yet, brothers, pray for just one thing—
>> The marvelous peace of God.[2]

Slowly he closed the book. "No, we haven't sung that one. At least I've never heard it before. But I think we should. Funny, your playing that one right now. I was sort of singing along with you a little bit ago on 'Dear Lord and Father of Mankind.' This says something a little different, I think."

"I was just playing through that section of the hymnbook, and this one came along. I agree that it is something we need to hear. If you wish, I'll get the choir to practice it."

"That'll be good. I'll let you know when we'll use it." He watched Roger fold the music and close the console. "Just leave the hall light on. I'll turn it off when I come."

"Good night, Dr. Watson."

"Good night, Roger."

He heard the door close. It was quite dark now, and everything was quiet. He thought of the hymn. It is right, of course. The peace of God certainly doesn't always look like peace. He'd often wondered what the disciples must have thought that night when Jesus told them he was giving them "his peace." The words were so familiar. "Peace I leave with you, my peace I give unto you: not as the world giveth, give I unto you." How strange it must have sounded! They knew that outside there were those who sought his life to destroy it and would seek theirs, also. Peace? What kind of peace was this? Yet, they must have sensed within him that deep, inner peace which enabled him to stand in the place of trial with a calm dignity, which enabled him to go to the cross and pray for those who put him to death. "Not as the world giveth, give I unto you." That was certainly true. Surely they were hesitant to hear it. They must have wanted an end to tribulation, to persecution, to bitterness, to disappointment. How could there be peace in the presence of all these distresses?

He pressed the switch as he went out the door. For a moment he looked back into the darkened sanctuary. He could hear the rush of traffic and for a fleeting instant felt an almost overwhelming desire to go back inside and close the door after him. He smiled as he chided himself. You'd probably do it too, he thought, if you thought you'd really find peace in there! Yes, he answered himself, yes, that's all too true. He missed Sarah and the children. Well, they'd be home tomorrow. He decided to make his hospital calls and pick up a bite to eat later on. It would be easy to run, to hide, to avoid all trouble, all distress. No that wasn't right, it really wouldn't be easy at all. It only seemed so. How long ago had he learned that peace, real peace, comes not in the absence of struggle but in its presence? The peace is within, not without. That's what Jesus was saying to the disciples on that dreadful night so long ago. How hard it was for those disciples, for disciples in every age, to hear. "I have said this to you, that in me you may have peace. In the world you have tribulation; but be of good cheer, I have overcome the world."

"THAT YOU, MARIE?" Dr. Harris looked up from his book.

"Um-hum. I believe you'd better come pull up the back porch awning. The wind is getting higher."

"All right. How was the book club?"

"Well, I hardly know how to answer. Gladys Hodges had the program and she did an excellent job. But, I declare, it was frightening. She reviewed a book on the possibility of nuclear war. It was a kind of science fiction really, but the author had based it on actual research, so you knew what he said was true. It really makes you stop and think. But I suppose that's what he intended. If so, he accomplished his purpose with me. The thing that was so disturbing about it, apart from the obvious horror of nuclear war, was his feeling that most of the so-called "peace movements" were really the most dangerous pieces in the puzzle. He wasn't talking about the United Nations, but about the "Ban the Bomb" type groups. I'm not sure I agree with him. I imagine there must be an awful lot of crackpots in any such group, but how do you really know? How do you separate the sheep from the goats? How do you know that the way we're going will actually lead to peace? If any of these folks are right, we may really be throwing peace away. When I come away from something like this, I just don't know what to think. Sometimes I think it would be better just to quit thinking altogether!"

He smiled as he tapped his pipe against the palm of his hand.

"I've got a first-class mental image of your ever doing that!"

"I guess you're right." She laughed ruefully. "But something like tonight surely does tempt me. Anyhow, I don't have to think about it tonight. Who came over? I see two coffee cups in the sink."

"William Mason. He called just after you left and asked if he could come talk to me. Wants to study medicine. You know, I think he'll make a great doctor."

She washed the cups and put them on the draining rack.

"You were always fond of William. What happened to him while he was away?"

"We really didn't talk much about that. But he is different. He's grown up now, or certainly well on the way. Oh, he'll have some hard knocks, but I think he'll weather them."

PEACE IS ELUSIVE. Yet it has that strangely paradoxical aspect which makes it endure in the midst of every vicissitude, once it has truly been found. It cannot be explained; there is no rationale, no reason, yet there it stands. It involves the assurance that "in everything God works for good," and that nothing "will be able to separate us from the love of God in Christ Jesus our Lord." It is convinced that "this slight momentary affliction is preparing for us an eternal weight of glory beyond all comparison," and that "God will supply every need . . . according to his riches in glory in Christ Jesus." Peace is elusive. But once it is truly found it passes all understanding, for it draws its substance from the power of God whose kingdom is forever.

In everything . . . with thanksgiving
PHILIPPIANS 4:6

12
Gratitude

"I pledge allegiance to the flag of the United States of America and to the republic for which it stands, one nation, under God, indivisible, with liberty and justice for all."

"And now, the first verse of 'America.' "

Frank listened as the uncertain voices of the children joined with those of the members of the Civic Club. ". . . from e-ev-ery-y moun-tain-side le-et free-dom ring."

"And now, let us all bow our heads while Steve Bolton, chairman of the Club Service Projects Committee, gives the invocation."

Frank bowed his head. Concentrate on the prayer. Time enough after he's finished to be sure all the children have a place to sit. ". . . for these children, and the Home in which they live." Hope they don't feel like they are on display. Everyone said the children got a big bang out of coming to the Club each Thanksgiving. Nothing to do about it now. ". . . and help us all to show our gratitude at this season of the year by being more patient and understanding with each other . . ." That's enough, now, Steve. We've got a full program. They are sort of on display when you come right down to it. But when you put money into shoes year after year it helps to see the actual children. Makes a lot of the members contribute more than they would otherwise. ". . . to the nourishment of our bodies and us in thy service . . ." Well, that would be the end. It was a big responsibility having all these children up here, and he wanted everything to go off well. He realized he was thinking more about the children than the members of the Club. Hope they will have a good time. "Amen."

"Here's one over here. And there are two vacant at that far table." He'd decided to arrange it so that the children were scattered out among the members. He hoped the men would talk to them, make them feel at home. But he'd done all he could to get them started, and he'd have to leave it at that.

"Better come sit down, Frank. Your dinner's getting cold."

"Be there in just a minute, Craig. You fellows go ahead and don't wait on me."

It probably wasn't necessary to make the rounds of every table, but he thought he'd do it just in case. Everything seemed to be going smoothly. When he finally got back to his table they were almost through eating.

"Frank, come meet these fellows. This is Jackie Miller and that's Rob Branscomb. This is Mr. Mason."

"Hi, fellows. I remember Jackie from last year. Glad to get to know you, Rob. You're going to be on the program today, aren't you, Jackie?"

"Yes, sir. Hope I don't forget my piece."

"Aw, he won't forget it, Mr. Mason. He's just about the best talker in the Home. We had a contest to see who would say the piece, and he won it hands down."

Frank could see the color rise in Jackie's cheeks and ears.

"I know he'll do just fine. But I guess it's sort of different, saying it there and saying it here, eh, Jackie?"

"I'll say it is! You all keep your fingers crossed."

Rob scraped the last vestige of pie off his plate. "Jackie, if you're not going to eat your pie, I'll take it."

Frank watched him pass it across the table. He wished he could find a word that would set Jackie's fears at rest. He could remember how knotted his stomach used to get when he had to say a piece at school.

"And now, if you all have finished, I'll ask the young people who are going to be on the program to come to the head table."

Frank held up his crossed fingers as Jackie pushed back his chair. "Knock 'em dead, Kid."

"This is a great bunch of kids, Frank. I like your idea of having them sit around with the members instead of at a special head table."

"Thanks, Craig. It makes sense to me. You don't get to see them all as well, but you do have a chance to get to know one or two much better."

His mind was on the little group gathering at the speakers' table. In all honesty, he had mixed feelings about the program. Sure, it was traditional, but maybe that wasn't enough reason to keep on running it just this way.

". . . a trio to sing 'To Grandmother's House.' "

Don was a good presiding officer; had the knack of putting the kids at ease. Frank glanced around the room. The members all seemed to be interested in what was going on—much more attentive than they ordinarily were. "Over the river and through the woods . . ." They made up in quantity what they might lack in quality. He was probably being much too concerned about them. ". . . horse knows the way to carry the sleigh . . ." But he didn't want it to be a kind of command performance. Probably no way you could ever say to these kids that we are real glad to have you all come to the meeting every Thanksgiving, that it isn't something you have to do as a kind of payment for the shoes. ". . . hurrah for the pumpkin pie!" He joined in the applause. They were nice kids. Sort of hard for them to know what to do with themselves as the applause continued. It was Don who rescued them.

"All right. That was just fine. Thank you."

They grinned at each other as they sat down. It was a relief to have it over with, but a nice feeling to know that it had gone well. One leaned over and whispered something and they all giggled. Don rapped with his gavel.

"And now, Jackie Miller will speak to us on 'The Real Thanksgiving.' "

Frank found himself crossing his fingers again. He could feel a tightness in his throat as the long rehearsed words came over the loudspeaker. Go to it, kid. ". . . and for this wonderful dinner . . ." Frank looked at Jackie's plate. He'd hardly touched his turkey and dressing. You can be thankful without being able to enjoy it, I guess—thankful that it had been done, and yet— " . . . your thoughtfulness year by year in buying shoes for all of us . . ." How else could you do it besides having them come down to the Thanksgiving meeting? What better way to give them an opportunity to say thank you, and to let the members of the Club see them as real people? I'm probably just making a mountain out of a molehill.

". . . for our land of freedom and opportunity and the part which you and others like you . . ." Would Jackie have ever thought of that if one of the matrons at the Home hadn't suggested that he put it in the speech? Well, even so, what harm does it do to remind him of the heritage of freedom in our nation? Everyone says that most kids grow up with no appreciation of the benefits they enjoy. ". . . of God who brings seedtime and harvest and under whose . . ." Well, the speech does one good thing—it reminds us that there is something more to Thanksgiving than turkey and a football game. The kid's doing OK. ". . . when all nations, everywhere, can join in glad thanksgiving to him . . ." No need to worry about Jackie—well, not about his ability to make a speech. But what about the situation that put him into a forced attitude of thanks? To what extent must thanksgiving be spontaneous to be real? Would Bill and Betty ever remember to mind their manners unless they were prompted? ". . . behalf of everyone of us I say a hearty and sincere 'thank you!' "

The applause was deafening. Frank found himself standing up with the others. Don was shaking hands with Jackie. Everything had gone well.

"Nice program, Frank. One of the best I can remember."

"Thanks, Don. I was certainly proud of them."

THE IDEA OF THANKSGIVING has about it a universal quality which makes it recognizable and familiar in every culture and in every age. Nevertheless, it is evident that many varieties of attitude and feeling may be subsumed under the outward form of giving thanks. The most abject distortion involves an overt act of thanksgiving for the purpose of placating a benefactor or gaining additional rewards. A more subtle deviation occurs when thanksgiving is regarded as a duty which should be performed quite apart from any expectation of additional benefits or the necessity to assure the good graces of the one thanked. In a similar vein, thanksgiving may become a kind of traditional ritual which can in no sense be described as a duty, but is certainly regarded as appropriate and proper. From still another point of view, the giving of thanks may become an overt act of hostility, a means of expressing resentment at being placed in another's debt, done with such an icily civil manner that no opportunity is allowed for dealing realistically with the true feelings involved. In all of these instances, as well as in the multiple variations of each, it is clear that, to a greater or lesser extent, genuine gratitude is obscured or nonexistent.

WHEN FRANK thought about it, he found it easier to say what thanksgiving was not than to say what it was. At the same time, he was not sure that any hard and fast line could be drawn on one side of which an act could legitimately be designated as genuine thanksgiving with everything on the other side labeled spurious. He supposed that thanksgiving was such a personal thing that no one could really judge the acts and motives of another. How could you tell about Jackie, for example? In his own way he certainly must have been grateful for the shoes, but the words he'd used in the speech were probably not the way he would have expressed his feeling. He doubted that Jackie had the understanding or perception to experience genuine gratitude and thanksgiving for the land in which he lived. But this, of course, was through no fault of his own since it could come only with the passage of the years. The obvious thing for which he could be thankful was that the speech was over and that it was well received. On the way out he'd heard him say, "Thank goodness that's over!" That much was real.

Craig had stopped him as they were leaving the meeting. There had been a time when he probably would have listened for some hint, some indication that Craig was pleased with him. Strange how his mind was on something else now.

"Frank, that was great. I think the kids had a first-rate time, and I know the men got a lot out of it. That Miller kid is a whiz. How'd you manage to come up with him?"

How do you respond when someone thanks you, praises you for a job well done? Do you say, "Aw, it was nothing, really"? Do you say, "Yes, I thought it went well"? Do you say, "Don't mention it"? What if you are not completely responsible for the thing for which you are thanked? Should you explain that you really do not deserve all the thanks? How do you answer honestly without appearing to seek more praise for being humble?

"The kids at the Home had a contest to see who would make the speech, and Jackie won. I can see why."

"Yeah. Say, Frank, I've been meaning to tell you—but you know how all of us tend to put things off—you're sure doing a great job on this program thing, really top-notch. Vince and I were remarking on it the other day, spraining our arms patting ourselves on the back for being the ones who talked you into doing it."

"Thanks, Craig. To tell you the truth, I had many misgivings about it. But actually, as we've gone along, it's been most interesting; I've really enjoyed it."

"Well, as I say, I believe in bouquets while you can still smell them, and you rate a big one. See you next week."

Frank glanced at his watch. Late. Nearly two.

What is the difference between what Craig said and what Jackie put in the speech? You might say that one was spontaneous and the other prepared, but does that mean that the feeling is necessarily different? He found himself wondering why he was more concerned with what was happening to Jackie than to Craig. Was it possible that what Craig said represented just as many mixed motives as Jackie's speech had? He laughed at himself. If you are going to start asking that kind of question about every remark, you're really splitting hairs! Can't you just be grateful, period? He picked up his hat and went through the revolving door.

"WE'RE HERE, PAWPAW! We're here!"

"Good. Let me help you with your coat. Hello, Frank, Mary. Good to see you. And there's my Betty girl. You got a big hug for Pawpaw?"

"Hi, Papa. It's turned biting cold. Looks like we'll have snow before night. Were you all at the Union Service? We looked for you, but never did see you."

"We had to sit in the balcony. I believe that was one of the biggest crowds I've seen in the past several years. Martha had a million things to do and we nearly didn't make it. And to tell you the truth, it's sort of hard to get yourself ready for church by ten o'clock. The old clock is just naturally set for eleven. Come in and get warm by the fire."

"Mama says we'll have turkey, Pawpaw. Has Nana fixed a turkey?"

"She sure has, Bill."

"Come on, Betty. Let's go out to the kitchen to help Nana and smell the turkey."

Mary laughed. "Wait, I'll go with you. Dad and Pawpaw can sit here and talk while we get the things on the table."

Frank stood with his back to the fire. "Any word from William?"

"Yes, he called this morning. He had hoped that he could be here today, but he has a line on a job, and the man is going to see him this afternoon. I can't imagine anybody working on Thanksgiving, but William thought he'd better not ask him to put it off."

"Papa, I've thought a lot about what you said. We may not ever see eye to eye on William, but I feel different about him now."

John nodded. How does an older brother really welcome the prodigal home again?

"The turkey's on! Hurry, Pawpaw, the turkey's on!"

"We'll be right there. Thank you, Frank. I know it hasn't been easy. This is a good Thanksgiving. Let's go in."

How many memories came back with the familiar sights and smells? The turkey, the salted nuts in little crinkled paper cups, the pumpkin centerpiece with grapes and apples and colored corn, the deep red of the cranberry jelly—yes, this is a good Thanksgiving. How could the years have passed without their being here? Frank thought of the unlikely reasons. Out of town last Thanksgiving. Bill was sick the year before that—or was it Betty? And something had happened the year before that. Had it really been four years? Thing about it was that this year there was a real thankfulness.

"When do we do the Psalm, Nana?"

"I think this is the right time, Bill. Frank, I told Bill how you and William always said Psalm 100 at the Thanksgiving table, and he wants us to do it today."

"Betty, too!"

"Why sure, Betty, you, too. Bill, you start, and we'll all join in."

> Make a joyful noise unto the LORD, all ye lands.
> Serve the LORD with gladness: come before his presence with singing.
> Know ye that the LORD he is God: it is he that hath made us, and not we ourselves; we are his people, and the sheep of his pasture.
> Enter into his gates with thanksgiving, and into his courts with praise: be thankful unto him, and bless his name.
> For the LORD is good; his mercy is everlasting; and his truth endureth to all generations.

How long has it been? Frank found himself saying the familiar words, hesitating now and again as in memory he reached across the years to another generation, another life, another world. The Lord is good. Strange that this is so difficult to see. Did he really see it, even now? Did William? They had said the words so easily. How could they begin to know what they meant? "That was very good, Bill. I didn't know you knew it."

"Nana taught it to me when Betty and I were over here. Some of it I still don't know too good."

Frank found himself wondering whether any of them really knew it in its deepest sense. But there was no way to say that to Bill. Or to himself, for that matter. "I thought you did fine, Son."

"Betty, too."

"Yes, Betty. You did just fine, too. Let's all bow our heads now while Pawpaw asks the blessing, or Nana's dinner will be stone cold."

They bowed their heads and joined hands.

"Dear God, we are thankful for this day, and for all thy mercies. For Betty and Bill, for Frank and Mary, and for bringing William home again. We ask thy help for those who find it hard to be thankful today and pray for the time when all thy people may truly enter into thy gates with thanksgiving and into thy courts with praise. For Jesus' sake. Amen."

WE HAVE SEEN that there are many subtle dangers in thanksgiving, that it is exceedingly difficult to give thanks apart from mixed motivations and feelings. There is in the very act of thanksgiving an acknowledgment of dependence, an admission of personal indebtedness, a consciousness of being the recipient of some favor or act of kindness. It is in this sense that to give is more blessed than to receive, for in giving there is an inner feeling of satisfaction, an awareness of personal resource and ability. It is pleasant to give, to have the abundance from which the gift is drawn, to experience the well-being which comes in providing some means for alleviating suffering, meeting a need, fulfilling some desire or wish. Precisely because it is personally satisfying to give, it is exceedingly difficult to give in such a way as to assure that the one receiving the gift is able to maintain his own integrity. Yet, however hard it is to give, it is infinitely harder to receive. Even when the gift is given in the most gracious manner with no expectation of return or reward, the very act of receiving carries with it the possibility of distortion. The words, "How can I ever thank you enough" or "how can I ever repay you" are expressions not only of genuine gratitude, but often of an inner resistance against being obligated to another. It is in this sense that genuine thanksgiving is the mark of maturity. It signifies that the individual has moved from a careless taking everything for granted with no thought of personal responsibility, through an egotistical resistance to accepting help in a vain endeavor to be self-sufficient, to a consciousness of genuine involvement in the give and take of life and an awareness that it is not possible to live alone. It demonstrates an understanding that to receive that which is graciously offered is the most meaningful and enduring act of thanksgiving.

EVEN AS he thought about it, William wasn't completely certain. It still seemed to him that this kind of receiving somehow suggested the old attitude of "the world owes me a living" and "I'll take everything that's coming to me with no thought of anyone else." Is it wrong to want to stand on your own two feet for a change? No, he was sure that wasn't the way to put it. To stand on your own feet was to assume responsibility, but to think that you could stand alone was presumptuous.

He pushed the tray along the cafeteria line. It had been nice to talk to Papa this morning. They were all probably sitting down around Mama's table right now. "O give thanks unto the LORD; for he is good: for his mercy endureth forever." Was that the Psalm they used to say? It didn't sound like it, but it kept running through his head. The minister had used it as the call to worship this morning.

"Pumpkin, please." It looked like pretty good pie. Of course, it wouldn't be just like Mama's. He made his way to an empty table. Remarkable how many people eat here on Thanksgiving. You'd think they'd be at home. He unrolled the silverware and put the napkin in his lap. There was a little triangular card with brief prayers of thanks for Protestant, Catholic, and Jew. Strange that there have to be three, but God probably understands why we need them. He would have bowed his head, but it made him feel self-conscious. Thank you, God, that this is this year and not last. I'd like to be at home with the family, but I'm glad I'm not where I was last Thanksgiving.

He looked around as he ate in silence. It'd be hard to tell what all these people felt. There were quite a few families. The mothers probably are glad to be away from washing the dishes for one meal. What about those who are eating alone, like me? Are they glad they are here? Do they wish they were somewhere else? Is anyone ever really where he wants to be? And if in some joyful moment he could say, "I'm right where I want to be," how long would the feeling last? How soon did the moment crumble, even when it is clutched tightly, precisely because it is clutched tightly?

He finished the last bit of roll, and reached for his pie. You have an awful lot of time to think when you are by yourself—when you are eating by yourself. It's wonderful to have something good to think about for a change. This is a good Thanksgiving. It'd be even better if he could just get the job. One-fifteen. He still had over an hour. It had been a long time since he'd gone to church on Thanksgiving. Probably the reason they had to have union services—since so many didn't go, it'd take several congregations to make a fair showing. Pretty good crowd in the Chapel this morning. And the sermon certainly gave a new twist to the usual thanks-giving theme. "What shall I render unto the LORD for all his benefits toward me?" He reached into his pocket and took out the folded bulletin. " 'A Question for Thanksgiving.' The Reverend James F. Lambert, Higgins Memorial Baptist Church." Just a young man, but he really has something to say. Never really thought of it just the way he put it. "What shall I render? I will take . . ." The way you really give thanks to God is to take what he has to offer. And yet, when you stop to think about it, well . . . "I will take the cup of salvation and call upon the name of the LORD." Maybe so. Psalm 116. I'll have to look it up.

One thirty-five. He folded the bulletin and put it back into his pocket. Maybe that's what Dr. Harris was trying to say the other night. But this is different. I've already taken far more from Papa than I deserve. I've got no right to let him just keep on putting out money on me. I'd like to be able to pay him back, make it up to him in some way, let him know I'm really grateful. But how? How do you make up for the lost years? How do you let him know that you appreciate everything he's done? How do you find the thing that really expresses your sincere desire to restore in some measure that which has been given to you?

The words of the text ran through his mind. "What shall I render? . . . I will take . . ." But wasn't taking selfish? It certainly could be, that he knew quite well. But the preacher had said that to give another person the opportunity to give was the ultimate mark of devotion. William shook his head. This kind of thing would have to be qualified a lot before he could really believe it. Ten minutes 'til two. He pushed back his chair and walked toward the door.

THERE IS A KIND of natural qual-ity about thanksgiving in the presence of good fortune or unexpected benefits. It is true, of course, that such response may be tinged with the uneasy feeling that some force or power must be praised in order to insure the continuation of the pleasant circumstance. But beyond this, there is the genuine sense of gratitude which may be expressed to chance as in the phrase "to thank one's lucky stars," or which has as its object a more personal entity, as in the phrase, "Thank God." It is this natural quality which makes the act of thanksgiving universal, however varied its form or object. It represents the welling up of that open acknowledgment of good which demands expression in a word or act of thanksgiving.

The underlying dimension of this universal response is the positive nature of the event which calls it into being. Thus thanksgiving tends to be identified with good fortune, with fulfillment, with completion. But it is not so easy to recognize the relationship between thanksgiving and apparent misfortune. Such thanksgiving presupposes the kind of faith which is rooted in the firm conviction that in everything God is working out his purpose, that there is genuine meaning beneath and beyond what meets the eye. This aspect of thanksgiving comes only slowly and may, in fact, emerge only in retrospect. It can be defined in words and phrases, but in actual experience its reality tends to be elusive.

HOWARD WATSON knew that. He took off his coat as he walked into the lobby of the hospital. After all these years it was still hard to get used to the fact that people got sick on holidays. Somehow you just associated Easter and Thanksgiving and Christmas and all the rest with festivities and gladness. He checked the patient file. You could say that these folks should be thankful that we live in a day when there are doctors and nurses and hospitals— pretty far cry from a generation ago. Guess we're never satisfied. Of course, in a way, we ought never to be. Like here in the hospital— if we'd been satisfied we'd never have voted the bond issue for the new wing. Goodness knows we need it.

He pushed open the door. "Hello, Mrs. Thompson."

"Come in, Dr. Watson. You just missed the children. They came down for Thanksgiving and left a few minutes ago. Please sit down."

"I'm sorry I didn't get to see them. Are they all well?"

"Susan had a pretty bad cold so they made her stand in the hall and wave. But all the rest of them were just fine."

What a remarkable person! The weeks had dragged on, but her spirit had never broken. She didn't talk about going home any more. He supposed she knew she would never be able to.

"Did they have a good attendance at the Union Service?"

"Sure did. The balcony was full, and they had to bring in chairs. I brought you one of the bulletins; thought you might like to see it."

"I had hoped they would broadcast it, but never could get it on my radio. Who preached?"

"The minister of the Asbury Methodist Church, Joseph Sanderson. I suspect you haven't met him yet, he only came this year."

Not everyone was able to continue an interest in life when it was no longer possible to participate in the events of the day. He knew he shouldn't stay too long here, there were so many in the hospital for whom life had lost its meaning.

"Read the Scripture that was used in the Union Service. That way I can sort of be a part of it."

"It was from the fourth chapter of Philippians, the first seven verses:

> Therefore, my brethren, whom I love and long for, my joy and crown, stand firm thus in the Lord, my beloved. I entreat Euodia and I entreat Syntyche to agree in the Lord. And I ask you also, true yokefellow, help these women, for they have labored side by side with me in the gospel together with Clement and the rest of my fellow workers, whose names are in the book of life.
>
> Rejoice in the Lord always; again I will say, Rejoice. Let all men know your forbearance. The Lord is at hand. Have no anxiety about anything, but in everything by prayer and supplication with thanksgiving let your requests be made known to God. And the peace of God, which passes all understanding, will keep your hearts and your minds in Christ Jesus."

He closed the Bible. "His subject was 'In everything . . . with thanksgiving.' He showed us how true thanksgiving comes when we learn to be grateful for the things that don't seem too good at the time. He pointed out that it is easy enough to give thanks for the good things, but that this is only the first step."

She nodded. "I wish I'd heard it. That's something I need to learn."

He started to say that it seemed to him she knew it better than most people, but changed his mind. "The kind of thing that is easy to say, but hard to do."

"For me, it is. But I am thankful, Dr. Watson. I've had a good life, and . . . I can't honestly say I'm thankful for being in the hospital, although I am grateful that we have it. But you know, to be truthful, some things have happened to me here that might not ever have happened if I hadn't had to come. I think I can be thankful for that. Maybe that's enough."

He took her hand. "Maybe so. Kind of thing it's not easy to measure, particularly when there are parts that you'd just really rather not have. Let's pray together before I go."

She closed her eyes, and for awhile there was silence.

"Dear God, we are reminded today to be thankful. Forgive us that we need reminding. Bless Mrs. Thompson and me as we give thanks for those things which are clearly good and for which thanksgiving is no problem. Open our eyes that we may see thy care of us even in those things we would not choose, that in everything we may come to thee with thanksgiving. In Jesus' name. Amen."

"HEY, MARY. There's somebody coming up the front walk. Looks like Grace and George. Can you get the door?"

"Hello. Come on in. We looked for you at the Union Service this morning, but never did see you."

"We were . . . Mary, you haven't been listening to the radio?"

"Why, no. We were over at the Mason's for dinner, and since we've been home Frank has been watching the football game on television. What is it, Grace? Grace, what is it?"

"Mary, I . . . I don't know. Maybe there's some mistake. Maybe we heard it wrong . . . I . . ."

"Grace, you're frightening me . . ."

"Mary, . . . I don't know what to say . . . We've been out for a little ride, and just as we were turning into the driveway the news came on, and . . . Mary, there's been an accident, and they said the person had been identified as William Mason. But there must be some mistake, it must not be William since they never do announce it on the radio until the family has been notified. I . . . We shouldn't have come, but we just ran right over here . . . You haven't heard anything about it?"

"Oh, no! I'm sure it couldn't be—it just couldn't! Mr. Mason talked to William just this morning and he was going to see a man about a job at two-thirty."

"Why are you all standing out there in the hall? Come on back and watch the game, George."

How do you answer when all at once there may be a vast expanse between what he expects to hear and what you have to say? Do you say, "Frank, come here. Come here quick"? But you don't know for sure. And yet how can you act as though there is nothing different? Maybe there is nothing different. Why do you start when the phone rings? Why do you want to cry out for him not to answer it when you know that not answering it will not change anything? How long can you stand motionless in the hall, paralyzed by the kind of fear that is more than fear while the pieces slowly fall into place and the world falls apart? Is there no way to move, to scream, to tear through the fabric of circumstance, to escape, to turn back the clock, to wake up?

She was still standing there with George and Grace when Frank came to the door. She wanted to run to him. She wanted to cry out that he not say what she knew he must say.

"That was Papa. William . . . William . . . is dead . . ."

When at last you can talk, the words are unreal and there is no meaning in what you say.

"Frank. Oh, no. Frank, are you sure? There must be some mistake."

Grace moved toward her. "Let's go sit down for a minute, Mary."

George threw their coats on the hall chair. "What did your father say, Frank? We heard a news bulletin on the car radio just now, but there were no details. How on earth did it happen?"

"I'm not sure I got it straight, or that he did, either. Best I could make out, some boys in an old car were in town for the game and had been drinking. They turned a corner too fast and jumped up on the curb and hit him as he was walking down the sidewalk." It isn't so. It can't be. We'll have to go over to Papa's right now. Tell Mary to get the children. No, we ought not to take the children now. We can leave them with Grace and George. But there's no telling how long we will be. Won't somebody shut off that television set? How can they play football and get excited over a forward pass? Don't they know? He twisted the dial savagely.

"Let us keep Bill and Betty, Mary. You don't know how long you will be, so just plan on their spending the night. There's no school tomorrow, so we can just play it by ear."

No school tomorrow. Why wouldn't there be any school tomorrow? What was so special about tomorrow? After awhile you remember that today is Thanksgiving Day.

Most of the leaves were gone now. The branches of the trees along Elm Street were etched against the stark November sky. It was nearly dusk. How quickly the sun drops from the sky, how soon the shadows lengthen and the evening comes!

It isn't so. It can't be. How could it be? Hadn't Papa said just today that this was a good Thanksgiving? O, God. He tried to swallow, but there was a lump in his throat and he felt as if he was choking.

"I just can't believe it, Frank. It's just so unreal, somehow. It's just that William was gone so long, and now he's just come back."

He wanted to answer but there was no way to speak. He nodded his head and clinched his teeth. There were already two cars in front of the house as he turned into the driveway. All at once he dreaded going in. What could he say to Papa? To Mama? He wanted to cry.

"Oh, Frank, I'm glad you're here. Your mother is lying down in the bedroom and your Father's in the kitchen with Dr. Watson. Come in here, Mary, and let me take your coat."

"Thank you. Thank you for coming over." He supposed he sort of knew that Mrs. Calhoun would be there, but it was comforting to see her. She could tend to things, answer the door. He walked toward the kitchen.

"Papa."

For an instant he stood in the doorway. It was the first time Frank ever realized that he was growing old. The lines seemed deeper in his face, and somehow his shoulders sagged as though under a great burden. Frank put his arms around him.

"Frank." The tears rolled down his cheeks. "He'd just come home, Frank. He'd just come home."

How long had it been since they left after dinner? Was that just today? Was that just two hours ago? How long since they sat in church this morning? Was it possible that anyone could say that in everything you should be thankful? What about that, Dr. Watson? Do you want us to be thankful that William is dead? Do you think that we should make a joyful noise unto the Lord for this? Do you believe that I ought to rejoice to see Papa crushed and beaten? Do you expect me to give thanks that a bunch of drunks killed William just as he was beginning to find himself? He clinched his teeth and closed his eyes. In a minute the surging rage began to ebb. "How did it happen, Papa? How did it happen?"

13
The Goal

> Our help is in the name of the LORD, who made heaven
> and earth.
> Like as a father pitieth his children, so the LORD pitieth
> them that fear him.
> For he knoweth our frame; he remembereth that we are
> dust.

Mary listened to the familiar words. It wasn't the same as
when her mother had died. She'd really never known William. And
yet, there was still that kind of feeling which can never be put into
words. Can death ever be taken lightly? Of course not, but that's
not the point. Some deaths just affect you more than others. It's not
that you don't grieve. But it's different.

She reached over and took Frank's hand. He started to turn
and look at her, but closed his eyes instead. What did it mean to
say "the Lord pitieth them that fear him"? Seemed as though she
never thought of it except at one of those times when you couldn't
ask. Did the Lord pity Frank? And if he did, why couldn't he have
let William live just a little longer? Frank needed for William to
live. There were too many feelings pent up from all the years that
were past, feelings which now might stay locked inside, feelings
which could drive him in tortured ways. Once or twice in the past
two days she had sensed the power of those feelings. How many
words need to be said after all the years, how much forgiveness to
be asked and given? Where now is the opportunity to set affairs in
order, to live peaceably with your brother, when your brother is
dead?

It was not the same feeling at all, not at all. When her mother
died there had been bewilderment, a kind of unreality, an agonizing
loneliness. But now there was a sense of helplessness, as though
Frank was slowly slipping away from her and she was powerless to

hold him. O God, why now? Why? Just as he had begun to find himself, why now? All he needed was one minute to say, "I'm sorry, William, will you forgive me? Can you forgive me? Why didn't I ask you before now? Forgive me, William. Forgive me, God." Too late.

> The LORD is my shepherd; I shall not want.
> He maketh me to lie down in green pastures: he leadeth me beside the still waters.
> He restoreth my soul: he leadeth me in the paths of righteousness for his name's sake.
> Yea, though I walk through the valley of the shadow of death, I will fear no evil: for thou art with me; thy rod and thy staff they comfort me.
> Thou preparest a table before me in the presence of mine enemies: thou anointest my head with oil; my cup runneth over.
> Surely goodness and mercy shall follow me all the days of my life: and I will dwell in the house of the LORD for ever.

Is it ever possible to be ready for death? John Mason wasn't sure. He knew he wasn't ready for William to die. Even less ready than perhaps he would have been two months ago when he hadn't seen him for so long. The long day had finally ended. There is a kind of numbness that fends off the sharp stab of pain, but from time to time the defenses crumble and the searing point of reality gouges deep into the heart. In a kind of incredible way, you talk and have a cup of coffee and shake hands with those who come and decide on details that must be settled and listen to the hum of voices in the next room and glance at the clock since it must be later than seven forty-two and your watch must have stopped but it hadn't, and just as you turn around you know that William is dead. William is dead. William is not alive any more.

He had the feeling that he probably ought not to be thinking of these things now. How many had reassured him with words of comfort and faith, and had said how glad they were for his faith and Martha's faith and how they knew he would come through this experience stronger than before? How could they be so sure?

Is it wrong to cry when your heart is breaking? He remembered something Dr. Watson had said about Christians sorrowing—not as those who have no hope, but as those who do. A real sorrow and sadness in parting which can be borne in the sure knowledge that you will meet again, but which is truly painful because you can't be with the person right now. Death is real. William is gone. And I'll not see him again in this life. And it would be dishonest to say this doesn't matter. O God, it does matter. I miss him. I'm lonely. Keep him in thy care, dear God. And keep us.

> God is our refuge and strength, a very present help in trouble.
> Therefore will not we fear, though the earth be removed, and though the mountains be carried into the midst of the sea;
> Though the waters thereof roar and be troubled, though the mountains shake with the swelling thereof.
> There is a river, the streams whereof shall make glad the city of God, the holy place of the tabernacles of the most High.
> God is in the midst of her; she shall not be moved: God shall help her, and that right early.

Martha Mason looked at the floral blanket that covered the casket. Why did people always say you should just remember that really wasn't William lying there? In one way you knew that, but what did you mean when you said it? This was the way you'd always known William. He looked just the same, or almost the same. But not the same at all. She remembered when they'd learned the Forty-sixth Psalm. You never really think that you'll hear it on such an occasion as this.

> Be still and know that I am God: I will be exalted among the heathen, I will be exalted in the earth.
> The LORD of hosts is with us; the God of Jacob is our refuge.

It had been a joke in the family that William could never be still long enough to know that Jehovah was God. O God, he's still now. It was hard to think of those days, they'd happened so long ago. "Sit still, William, while we all say the Psalm together. 'God is our refuge and strength.' " She did believe that. The time comes when you know that you can stand anything. Or think you can. Even this. It was strange sitting in this pew down close to the front of the church. Their regular place was about half way back on the other side. She didn't recall ever having sat right here before. The church seems different. Maybe it's because the communion table is gone. I guess I never noticed that they move it to make a place for the casket right in front of the pulpit.

> "Let us hear, also, the comforting words spoken by our Lord on the night in which he was betrayed as he sat at table with the Twelve:"

> Let not your heart be troubled: ye believe in God, believe also in me.

> In my Father's house are many mansions: if it were not so, I would have told you. I go to prepare a place for you.

> And if I go and prepare a place for you, I will come again, and receive you unto myself; that where I am, there ye may be also.

When did you first know that there was such a thing as death? When you were little, it just didn't ever cross your mind. Even when you had seen a dog run over or a dead sparrow in the yard you didn't really associate these things with death, at least not the way it finally came to have meaning. In the past two days, Frank had tried to remember, but his thoughts tended to run together. Maybe it was the time when, without any warning, you suddenly realized you'd never be doing the same thing again, ever, ever, ever. Somehow you'd always thought you'd do it again tomorrow, that the gang would meet and you'd play marbles again right here in the side yard, or that next Saturday you'd all go again to the old swimming hole down beyond the gravel pit. And then, one time, you knew this thing would never ever happen again just that way. Even though what you were doing would seem the same, it really wouldn't be. You knew you'd never pass this way again. It was the kind of thought that came with a fleeting suddenness and it scared you, and in a minute it was gone, and you didn't think about it anymore for a while. But once it had come it was always near, and sometimes you knew it was there. It wasn't always morbid—indeed, there were times when you were glad an experience was gone forever. He could remember Great Aunt Clarabel who always met every situation with a resigned recitation of "this, too, will pass." But that was different and Great Aunt Clarabel had probably found very little meaning in life, or so it had seemed to him.

> "Hear, also, the gracious words of Paul as he wrote to the church in Corinth:"

> He which raised up the Lord Jesus shall raise up us also by Jesus, and shall present us with you. . . .
> For which cause we faint not . . .
> For our light affliction, which is but for a moment, worketh for us a far more exceeding and eternal weight of glory;
> While we look not at the things which are seen, but at the things which are not seen: for the things which are seen are temporal; but the things which are not seen are eternal.

Wonder what it meant to say that the things which are not seen are eternal? Frank felt Mary's hand squeeze his again and wanted to turn and look at her, but could not. There had been a little time after William came back home, but not time enough. What would enough have been? Another day? Another week? Another year? If only he'd known that the time would be so short. Maybe if he'd driven William back to school they could have had a long talk in the car as they rode along. He had begun to feel differently about William. It wasn't right that the time was gone without warning. And how could you think of this as a "light affliction"? For any of them.

He'd been so overwhelmed by bitterness that he'd wanted to go immediately to the jail and beat those drunken bums to a pulp with his own hands. Irresponsible teen-age punks roaring around town all tanked up on liquor that they'd probably gotten from their families. Jail was too good for them. They ought to be made to suffer as he was suffering, as Papa and Mama were suffering. This was not "light affliction." It was the next day that he'd seen something he'd not been able to see before. They'd driven over to get William's things and had to go by the police station to sign for his personal effects. It was there that they had met the parents of the boy who was driving the car. Could he ever forget the agonized expression on the mother's face? She had stood there groping for words. What could she say? "I'm sorry my son killed your son?" What words were those? How could you help her say what could never be said? How do you measure tragedy? Which is more tragic, for your son to be dead or for your son to have killed someone else's son?

> "Hear, too, the words of faith as Paul writes to the church in Rome:"
>
> For I reckon that the sufferings of this present time are not worthy to be compared with the glory which shall be revealed in us. . . .
>
> And we know that all things work together for good to them that love God, to them who are the called according to his purpose.
>
> What shall we then say to these things? If God be for us, who can be against us . . .
>
> Who shall separate us from the love of Christ? shall tribulation, or distress, or persecution, or famine, or nakedness, or peril or sword . . .
>
> Nay, in all these things we are more than conquerors through him that loved us.
>
> For I am persuaded, that neither death, nor life, nor angels, nor principalities, nor powers, nor things present, nor things to come,
>
> Nor height, nor depth, nor any other creature, shall be able to separate us from the love of God, which is in Christ Jesus our Lord.

Frank bowed his head. Is it really possible to believe that? Just for a flashing minute it seemed possible. But the moment passed. William is dead. He won't come back this time. They won't find him if they look for him. If only . . .

DR. WATSON sat in his study. It had grown quite late. He should have started home long before now, but how do you ever decide that a sermon is finished? The time comes, of course, when the question is answered by the inexorable demands of the calendar. Tomorrow was Sunday, it was just that simple.

He'd gone by the Masons' after the funeral. That was the time of loneliness, the time of hollowness. The friends go back to their normal patterns of life, the house is quiet again, and empty.

"Thank you, Howard."

Sometimes when you heard the words you wondered whether or not they were said simply as a matter of custom. This time he knew it was not so. John Mason met him at the door and took his coat.

"Let me call Martha. Frank and Mary have gone to pick up Bill and Betty and will be here in just a little while. They're going to eat supper with us tonight."

He stood as Martha Mason came into the room.

"It was all just right. The Psalms we knew and loved, the words from the New Testament. There is a comfort which is real."

He nodded. These are the things which must be said, not simply because they are appropriate, but also because they express that deep inner conviction which sustains even in the midst of pain. There would be other things as well: the tears that cannot all at once be dried, the haunting question which can find no answer, the bitter pain which heals so slowly. Yet the healing had begun. In the saying of the words, in the hearing of the Word, in the company of those whose lives reached out to bear them up, thus did the healing come. In the days ahead the moods of grief would wax and wane.

After a while it was time to go. "Tell Frank and Mary I'm sorry to have missed them. I'll see them tomorrow."

On the way back to the church he could still feel the weight of sadness which can never be dispersed all at once. At the same time, he was sure they would not be overwhelmed by this experience even when the waves of loneliness and disappointment seemed to be more than they could bear.

He looked at the New Testament lying open on his desk. Through the years he had come to know the struggle of preaching week after week, the wrestling with the text until its deepest meanings were revealed, the involvement in the lives of his congregation until he could understand their hopes and longings, their questions and doubts. Even so, he was continually amazed at the way the meaning of the sermon could never be predicted precisely because there was no way to know the circumstance of those who heard from the perspective of events which changed their lives completely.

"I can do all things in him who strengthens me." He said the words aloud. Throughout the week as he had worked on the sermon he had attempted time and again to sense what these words would mean to those who heard them Sunday morning. "I have the strength for everything through Him who empowers me."[1] So read the Berkeley version. It seemed to him to be a much better translation of the Greek text. Paul obviously was not saying that he could do anything. At the time he wrote the letter he could not escape from his Roman guards, he could not be in Jerusalem and Rome at the same time, he could not be sure that the people of Philippi could "stand firm thus in the Lord." He could be sure, however, that he had strength for any situation, a strength which was not simply his own, but which had been given to him. "I am ready for anything through the strength of the one who lives within me." So stated Phillips. Not quite the exact translation, but perhaps still closer to the meaning. No way to know what will happen. No way to predict the future, to be sure that this plan will work out, that each day will be orderly and secure. Yet the confidence that there is strength sufficient for whatever comes.

What would these words say to John Mason? To Martha? They would be at church tomorrow. Of that he was sure. He could see them, now in their regular pew. They would not be down front as this afternoon, the communion table would be in its regular place, the casket gone. Would this word sound glib, superficial, irrelevant? A word spoken by one who jests at scars because he never felt a wound? It would sound like that only to those who did not know who wrote it. And this was crucial in developing the sermon. He turned the pages of the manuscript. Had he been able to let the experience of Paul come through so that the words were not hollow, not shallow? How better to say it than as Paul himself had said it? He read, again, the quotation from 2 Corinthians 11:

> . . . labors . . . imprisonments . . . countless beatings, and often near death. Five times I have received at the hands of the Jews the forty lashes less one. Three times I have been beaten with rods; once I was stoned. Three times I have been shipwrecked; a night and a day I have been adrift at sea; on frequent journeys, in danger from rivers . . . danger from Gentiles, danger in the city, danger in the wilderness, danger at sea, danger from false brethren; in toil and hardship, through many a sleepless night, in hunger and thirst, often without food, in cold and exposure.

That was it. When a person with that kind of experience spoke of being able to meet any situation through Christ, then it was possible to listen. He gathered the pages of the manuscript and fastened them with a paper clip. It was clear to him. What about those who would be listening? Not just John and Martha Mason. What about Grace and George? Crandall Simpson? Miss Morrison? Harold? Just because the tragedy of William's death seemed so close, so bitter, so pervasive, it was hard for a moment to remember that pain was not confined to those who mourn, nor doubt to those whose joy has turned into sorrow. He could not have known at the beginning of the week that by the time they gathered for worship the words of the text would come to the Masons in the midst of suffering. Now he knew. But the words did not change. Moreover he knew that, because he had been so closely involved in the lives of the Masons, he was keenly aware of their feelings. But he knew that there would also be those about whom he would not know because he had not stood so closely with them in the past two days, but whose feelings were nonetheless poignant. It was always so.

He turned out the light and pulled the door shut after him. It was too late to go by Frank Mason's. Anyhow, Frank and Mary were probably still at John's. He got in his car and started home.

FRANK sat looking into the glowing coals of the fire. The ashes had been almost dead when they got back, but not quite. He'd brought in a few pieces of wood while Mary put the children to bed, and by the time she came back it was burning brightly.

"Sleepy?"

"No. I'm sure I ought to be, and probably will be in the morning. But right now I'm not at all."

"It's been hard on Papa."

She nodded. She wanted to say that she was worried about him, but she couldn't find the right words. Besides, at supper he'd seemed different. It was as though the burden wasn't as heavy. She couldn't put her finger on it.

"Mary, I surely am grateful for you, and for all you've done these past two days. I don't think Mama could have made it without you. She never had a daughter. Never said anything about it, but it seemed to me she always wanted one. Well, you've been more than a daughter, done more than a daughter ever could."

She nodded again. All at once she realized that it was possible not to answer with words, that she didn't have to say that it was all right, that she was glad she could help, that it was nothing, really.

"In the church this afternoon I had the strangest feeling that William was there. I don't mean just in the way that everybody always says that you are aware of . . . well . . . I don't know exactly how to put it . . . but today it was something else. It was almost like he was saying, 'It's OK, Frank.' I really can't explain it."

They sat together for a long while. The fire crackled softly. She wasn't sure she understood just what he was saying, but she knew that as he talked they were growing closer together. Some of the tension she had felt so strongly was ebbing. O God, help Frank now—and me, too.

"I got to thinking about those boys who ran over him. They'll carry this as long as they live. It's horrible. I wish there was some way I could say to them that it's all right. I don't know how, though. I really don't. It's not all right that they killed William, that they got drunk and went roaring around town in the old stripped down jalopy. How do you say that, and still say something else at the same time? Papa wants me to drive up there with him on Monday. I sort of dread the thought, really. But I'm going, anyhow."

"I wish you didn't have to go. But even so, I want you to. I think it's right."

He could hear the clock ticking. It must be getting late, but still he wasn't sleepy. So many things crowded into his thinking. "Mary."

"Hm."

"I wish William had gotten to know you better. I wish we'd had him over more before he left."

How could you say to him that he shouldn't take himself to task for something that had happened and could never be changed? "I wish so, too. It's so easy to look back and see what you ought to have done. But I don't think that a person ever comes to the time when he can be completely satisfied that he's done everything just right, do you?"

"No, of course not. Even so, I had plenty of opportunities which I didn't take."

"I'm sure William understood." The words sounded so inadequate, so weak, so futile. And yet she had to say them, had to try to help him see that the past was past. Somehow she knew that this wasn't the way, but she couldn't think of anything else to say.

He smiled as he put his arm around her and held her head on his shoulder. "You know, Mary, it's sort of ironic to realize that this is Thanksgiving weekend. And the thing I'm most thankful for is you. It's like I'd lost you for such a long time, and now you're back again. Or maybe I'm back again, I don't know. Anyhow, I've missed you, and I'm glad you're here, glad I'm here."

She closed her eyes.

"You never know whether the way you feel is the way things really are, or not. People always say that they couldn't have done this or that without somebody, but how do they know? Maybe I could have made it through these past two days without you, but I honestly don't see how. Isn't it strange how things happen?"

She wasn't sure that strange was the right word. Maybe so, if it meant that you couldn't predict it, didn't expect it, really didn't believe it could ever happen. Only in that sense strange. Otherwise, wonderful. Thank you, God.

> I believe in God the Father Almighty, Maker of heaven and earth;
> And in Jesus Christ His only Son our Lord; who was conceived by the Holy Ghost, born of the Virgin Mary, suffered under Pontius Pilate, was crucified, dead, and buried; He descended into hell; the third day He rose again from the dead; He ascended into heaven, and sitteth on the right hand of God the Father Almighty; from thence He shall come to judge the quick and the dead.
> I believe in the Holy Ghost; the holy Catholic Church; the communion of saints; the forgiveness of sins; the resurrection of the body; and the life everlasting. Amen.

Grace bowed her head as she said the familiar words. She knew that most people in the congregation did not bow, but somehow it seemed more appropriate to her. It was not a prayer, but . . . she could hear George's voice. When he'd first started coming to church with her, he'd been somewhat embarrassed that he didn't know the Creed. She'd held the hymnbook with him and read it as they said it together. He didn't need the book now. She'd wondered, however, whether there were any others who felt uneasy when they saw most members of the congregation saying the words without the book. Once she'd thought about holding it open anyhow, but that didn't seem right, either. She raised her head as the organ sounded the chord for the *Gloria Patri.*

> Glory be to the Father, and to the Son, and to the Holy Ghost;
> As it was in the beginning, is now, and ever shall be, world without end. Amen.

George could see Frank and Mary standing with the Masons. He'd hoped to speak to them before church but there had been no opportunity. He thought of yesterday afternoon. From outward appearances everything was back to normal. You couldn't tell that the communion table had ever been moved, that they'd all been here just—what was it—just nineteen hours ago? Nineteen hours. It sounded odd to say it that way.

They sat down as the organ played quietly. There was something symbolic in their being here today with yesterday already slipping into the memory of the past. He found himself thinking that this was the way life moves, it didn't stop—there was yesterday, there is today, there will be tomorrow. Last Sunday William had been sitting with the Masons. Who could have known that yesterday they would come here for William's funeral? Could they have borne the knowledge? He thought of the many times he had tried to see into the future, had wondered what was about to happen, had longed to know what tomorrow would bring. "Give us this day our daily bread." It is enough. To know the future would be to crush under the burden.

> "Let us hear the reading of the Word of God, the fourth chapter of Philippians, beginning at the tenth verse:"
>
> I rejoice in the Lord greatly that now at length you have revived your concern for me; you were indeed concerned for me, but you had no opportunity. Not that I complain of want; for I have learned, in whatever state I am, to be content. I know how to be abased, and I know how to abound; in any and all circumstances I have learned the secret of facing plenty and hunger, abundance and want. I can do all things in him who strengthens me.
> Yet it was kind of you to share my trouble. And you Philippians yourselves know that in the beginning of the gospel, when I left Macedonia, no church entered into partnership with me in giving and receiving except you only; for even in Thessalonica you sent me help once and again . . . And my God will supply every need of yours according to his riches in glory in Christ Jesus. To our God and Father be glory for ever and ever. Amen.

Miss Morrison followed the words as they were read. She loved the Letter to the Philippians and especially the fourth chapter. Usually it seemed that it was written to her, personally. "I have learned the secret of facing plenty and hunger, abundance and want." She wondered how long it had taken Paul to reach the place where he could honestly say that. It certainly hadn't been true for him always. As he said, it was something he'd had to learn. And yet, she knew what he meant, at least in part. As she thought back across the years, it was clear to her that this was something that didn't come all at once. But it did come. To be sure, at times the conviction was stronger than at others. You wished you could hurry the process, not just in you but in those who hadn't yet learned the secret, or hadn't learned all of it. But how could you ever tell? When you looked at it one way, it was the kind of thing that could come only in the experiences of the passing years. The paradox was that, when you were young, you often thought that you could do anything, that nothing could defeat you. That was when you read the verse, "I can do all things in him who strengthens me," and really believed it meant you'd never find anything you couldn't conquer. She smiled as she thought of it. Did it ever really seem like that? She couldn't be sure now. Might simply be one of the tricks memory plays on you.

One thing was certain. It didn't take long to discover that you couldn't do everything. Indeed, there were times when you wondered if you could do anything, anything at all. Somewhere along the way you read the verse again. "I am ready for anything through the strength of the one who lives within me." The Phillips translation came closer. And you'd learned that defeat was one of the things that came, one of the things you were strong enough to meet, certainly the most painful, or so it would seem. "In any and all circumstances I have learned the secret . . ."

> "Let us pray. 'Almighty God, forasmuch as without thee we are not able to please thee, mercifully grant that thy Holy Spirit may in all things direct and rule our hearts; through Jesus Christ, our Lord. Amen.' "[2]

Howard Watson stood silent for a moment in the pulpit. For him, the prayer was never simply a formal word to be repeated before the sermon. There was always the awesome consciousness of the situation, the presumption in attempting the proclamation of the word of grace, the awareness of how earthen the vessel in which the treasure came. Yet he was sure that "it pleased God by the foolishness of preaching to save them that believe."

> There are times in the lives of all of us when we feel in control of things, when the path before us is comparatively smooth, when events and circumstances seem to run according to our expectations and desires. And yet, there are times in the lives of all of us when, seemingly through no fault of our own, the tides turn against us; when we struggle with all our might, yet seem to make no headway at all; when the light of the sun is overshadowed by the clouds of doubt and sorrow is our bitter lot. And there are times in the lives of all of us when we bring despair and disgrace upon ourselves and those we love, when we know that we have chosen wrong and followed the path of folly into the night, when we find the weight of guilt so crushing that we stumble and fall under its load. How well we know these circumstances! How clearly now could we describe the things which mark our lives this day! How deeply enmeshed we become, how hopefully we reach out to hear a word of comfort and of grace!

It always seemed to Mary Mason that Dr. Watson could sense their moods, that he understood the changing patterns which emerged in the varied experiences of life. It was as though he were able to gather the tangled strands and weave them into a tapestry of meaning. She'd wanted to come this morning, not simply for Frank's sake but also for her own. She knew that being here would certainly bring to life the sad memories of yesterday, that simply being in the church would be a reminder that William is dead. But deep within she also knew that to stay away would be to avoid the painful circumstance at far greater cost and to turn their backs on the kinds of things that would finally make for peace. William was dead. There was no way to avoid that. Whatever else she'd learned in these past few months, she knew that nothing is to be gained by hiding, that to run is only to make things worse.

When Paul says these words we hear them as a tremendous affirmation of faith. Everyone in Philippi knew firsthand they were not idle phrases. Even as he wrote his arm was shackled to a Roman guard. He was under arrest by reason of the treachery of those who would stop at nothing to silence his preaching. He was continually harassed in Rome by those who made mockery of the gospel for no other reason than to increase his distress. He had been saddened beyond measure by the illness of his friend Epaphroditus and dismayed by the enmity of Euodia and Syntyche. Yet, in all these things, he could rejoice precisely because of Christ who brought him strength for every circumstance.

John Mason watched the pattern drawn by the sun shining through the stained glass windows as it moved slowly along the base of the pulpit. As the days grew shorter and the sun receded to the south, the path of light lengthened across the church. In less than a month the direction would change. Imperceptible at first, the darkness would begin to retreat before the coming of the light. The sun had been low in the sky when they went out yesterday afternoon. The light was even less today, although at the moment it was brighter. But it would turn.

It is clear that the passage of the years is not in itself sufficient for one to learn the secret. Paul is here talking about quality of life, not quantity of life. It is possible to live long but to find that the years bring only greater bitterness and cynicism. For Paul the priceless ingredient was Jesus Christ. Hear him as he says, "But whatever gain I had, I counted as loss . . . because of the surpassing worth of knowing Christ Jesus my Lord. For his sake I have suffered the loss of all things, and count them as refuse, in order that I may gain Christ."

There was an orderliness here that must have been a part of what Paul had learned. The dependable certainty which stretches across the years. Not simply that the earth moves through its orbit with infinite precision, although this is a part of it. Rather the confidence comes in the sure knowledge that there is strength for each situation. John looked down at Bill sitting next to him in the pew. How could you tell him these things? How could he understand what Howard Watson was saying? How could he find any meaning in answers to questions which he'd never really asked? Not that he wouldn't ask them, have to ask them, sooner or later. But for the time being they were not his questions.

> There is here the remarkable contrast between cowardice and courage, between fear and faith, between sin and salvation. From the early days in the Garden, when Adam hid among the trees from the presence of the Lord God, to the anguished cry, "Depart from us!" of those who shrank from the face of Jesus, to the myriad ways we employ to escape the realities of our day, the pattern is the same. Alcohol, sex, prejudice, prestige, wealth; the list is long and the way is strewn with the wreckage of failure and remorse. Yet who would say that the pressure to run is slight, that the temptation to hide is simple? Not Paul. How well he knew the tortuous road until at length upon that very road he met his Master face to face.

Martha Mason heard the words and somehow felt the meaning through the tears that welled so close to overflowing. This was the place to be. Where else would she go? And yet there was an aching in her heart that could not be denied. She'd lost him once, and found him then, at last—and now to lose again. She touched her handkerchief to her eyes. Strange. She'd not cried yesterday, but that was then and this was now. William. William.

> Of course it did not come to Paul all at once, just as it does not come to us overnight. Hear Paul again: "Not that I have already obtained this or am already perfect; but I press on to make it my own, because Christ Jesus has made me his own. Brethren, I do not consider that I have made it my own; but one thing I do, forgetting what

> lies behind and straining forward to what lies ahead, I press on toward the goal for the prize of the upward call of God in Christ Jesus."

No, it does not come at once. Nor when it comes does it assure that the tenor of life will be even, that the path will be smooth. She knew that. Knew it well. Once she had thought that if only she could have this, accomplish that, attain the other, then at last everything would be all right. But it was different now. The real miracle was that you actually did become able to meet any situation. This didn't mean that you wanted to. It certainly didn't mean that you'd choose all the things that happened, or even most of them. That really wasn't the point. You just were ready, or were in the process of getting ready. That was probably what Paul meant when he said in one place that he didn't really claim to have arrived, and then said in another that he was able. It is something you are—and are becoming.

> But it did come. And with its coming there was the peace that passes all understanding, the basis for rejoicing, the assurance of real contentment in whatsoever state he found himself. It did not save him from persecution. It did not save him from suffering. It did not save him from death. But by reason of this strength he was able to meet persecution, suffering, and death, and to triumph at every point through him who was his strength.

Would it ever be so? Would the experience which the words described ever really come to pass? Frank knew that the very asking of the question told the story of a struggle yet to come. But there was something else, the kind of thing which even now resisted words yet had its own reality. It was hard not to run, hard not to hide, to close your eyes upon the world which could bring pain and death. And yet, and yet he, too, had learned that pain can come from running, though at the first it had not seemed so. Could be the secret lay in meeting pain and thus preventing its growth until it overwhelmed. If that was it, then strength to face the pain—or anything—was what he needed.

"My God will supply every need of yours according to his riches in glory in Christ Jesus." Every need of yours. Not every want, nor yet desire. The need may be the thing you would not choose, the devastation of what you seem to want, the shattering of that which seemed so good. There is new life, but always it must come through death. The things Paul first held dear were now all gone. Yet everything he counted loss for the sake of Christ. For him this was no pious phrase which could be said to close his eyes to suffering and to wrong. On the contrary, it stretched the boundaries of his life until he saw himself debtor to all men, until in truth he found no peace apart from the kind of struggle against great odds that finally caused his death. Yet nowhere is there heard a self-styled martyr's wail, a whining protest against the tides of life. No, "in any and all circumstances I have learned the secret of facing plenty and hunger, abundance and want."

"Must come through death." Frank mused upon the phrase. William is dead. But that's not really what Dr. Watson's saying. It's hard to know for certain what he means. Many things must die, have died, but in their place life springs anew. Yet it's not easy, not at all. Help me, O God.

> O God, the Rock of Ages, Who evermore hast been,
>   What time the tempest rages, Our dwelling place serene:
> Before Thy first creations, O Lord, the same as now,
>   To endless generations The Everlasting Thou![3]

Howard Watson looked out across the congregation as he sang. What had he said? How easy to speak a superficial phrase, a hollow word, a thing which has no meaning! How hard to form the word of grace which speaks to every man no matter what his lot!

> Our years are like the shadows On sunny hills that lie,
>   Or grasses in the meadows That blossom but to die;
> A sleep, a dream, a story By strangers quickly told,
>   An unremaining glory Of things that soon are old.

There was no way, really, to know the triumphs and defeats, the joys and sorrows, the hopes and dreams of all those there. What had they heard? How easy to listen and to be unmoved, to go into the world insensitive to its need, or stumble on in darkness unmindful of the light!

> O Thou, who dost not slumber, Whose light grows never pale,
>> Teach us aright to number Our years before they fail;
> On us Thy mercy lighten, On us Thy goodness rest,
>> And let Thy Spirit brighten The hearts Thyself hast blessed.

He closed the book. There was assurance that the word would not return void, but would accomplish the purpose for which it was sent.

He raised his arms.

> Now unto him that is able to keep you from falling, and to present you faultless before the presence of his glory with exceeding joy; to the only wise God our Saviour, be glory and majesty, dominion and power, both now and ever. Amen.

Notes

CHAPTER 1
1. Thomas Hood, "I Remember, I Remember," from *Familiar Quotations,* ed. John Bartlett (Boston: Little, Brown and Company, 1951) p. 390.

CHAPTER 2
1. Omar Khayyam, Rubáiyát, trans. Edward Fitzgerald (New York: Thomas Y. Crowell Co., 1964).

CHAPTER 4
1. From *The New Testament in Modern English* © J. B. Phillips, 1958. Used by permission of The Macmillan Company. Hereafter, the use of this translation of the Bible will be identified within the text as "Phillips."

CHAPTER 10
1. Lyrics here and following are from "The Lonesome Road" by Gene Austin and Nathaniel Shilkret. Copyright © 1927 & 1928 by Paramount Music Corporation. Copyright renewed 1954 & 1955 and assigned to Paramount Music Corporation.

CHAPTER 11
1. "Dear Lord and Father of Mankind." Words by John Greenleaf Whittier and used by permission of Houghton Mifflin Company, authorized publishers.
2. "They Cast Their Nets in Galilee." Words by William Alexander Percy. Copyright 1924. Used by permission of LeRoy P. Percy.

CHAPTER 13
1. *Berkeley Version of the New Testament,* trans. Gerrit Verkuyl (Berkeley, Calif.: James J. Gillick and Company, 1945).
2. The Collect for the Nineteenth Sunday after Trinity, *The Book of Common Prayer* (New York: The Seabury Press, 1952).
3. This verse and the following are from "O God, the Rock of Ages." Words by Edward H. Bickersteth and used by permission of the Church Society.

Index of Scripture References

OLD TESTAMENT

Genesis
4:9-10................. 64

Exodus
32:26.................. 84

Deuteronomy
30:19.................. 84

Joshua
24:15.................. 84

2 Samuel
18:33.......... 148, 156

1 Kings
18:21.................. 84

Ezra
3:12.................. 167

Psalms
23:1-6................ 216
46:1.................. 218
46:1-5................ 217
46:10................. 192
46:10-11............. 217
73:3-12.......... 39-40
73:13-14.............. 40
73:16-19.............. 40
100:1-5.............. 204
103:13-14........... 215
107:1................ 206
116:12-13........... 207
124:8.......... 21, 215
126:1-6.......... 176-77
130............... 139-40
130:7-8............. 141
137:1-3.............. 59
137:4-9.......... 59-60
139:7-10............ 172
139:9-10............ 173
139:23-24....... 173-74

Isaiah
26:3.................. 192

Hosea
4:1-2................. 71
4:3..................... 72
11:1-4.......... 156-57
11:8-9.............. 157

NEW TESTAMENT

Matthew
5:9................... 185
6:11.................. 227
18:21-22............ 135
23:13-15.............. 72

Mark
9:24 ....113, 115,
119, 122

Luke
7:20.................. 123
7:22.................. 123
7:23............ 123, 127
9:20.................. 123
9:59.................. 90
13:34.......... 140, 142
13:34-35............. 135
15:24................ 176
18:41................ 106
23:34................. 90
24:21................ 141
24:25................ 141

John
5:6................... 105
6:67................... 99
14:1-3.............. 218
14:27............... 194
16:33............... 195

Romans
5:1-5................ 145
5:5.................. 140
5:8.................. 158
7:15-19.............. 39
7:24.......... 39, 107-8

8:2............. 39, 108
8:18, 31, 35, 37-39
.... 220
8:28................. 196
8:39................. 196
10:10............... 122

I Corinthians
1:21................. 229
3:1.................... 22
13:4-8................ 50

2 Corinthians
4:14, 16, 17-18....219
4:17................. 196
11:23-27........... 223

Ephesians
2:1................... 23
2:1-2................ 120
2:4-5............... 121
2:8.................. 121
4:13.................. 23
4:14.................. 23
4:15............. 23, 24

Philippians
3:7-8................ 230
3:12-14.......... 231-32
4:1.................. 222
4:1-7................ 209
4:6-7................. 57
4:10-20............. 227
4:12................. 233
4:13.......... 222, 228
4:19.......... 196, 233

Colossians
3:12-17.......... 183-84
3:15................. 183

Hebrews
11:1................. 111

1 John
3:14............. 152-53

Jude
1:24-25............. 234

Revelation
3:20.............. 98-99

Suggestions for Use by Individuals and Groups

Across the years, many persons have discussed with me the ways which may be employed to gain the greatest benefit from this book. What follows is an attempt to set forth various suggestions which may be useful to you either as an individual or as part of a group.

For individual reading, the format of the book lends itself to your becoming involved in the personal struggles being experienced by the various people. There is a narrative and reflection including sections of stream-of-consciousness material in which you have occasion to perceive what is happening inside the person while seeing the overt behavior or conversation. This gives you the opportunity to leave the text and expand your own awareness of your pilgrimage in retrospect and prospect. For example, when Miss Morrison comes to see Grace (pp. 95-98), we see her wrestling with what on earth she will say once she is there. Will she act as if nothing is wrong? Will she chide and scold? Will she speak of her own love and concern? And, at the same time, we see how Grace contemplates her response to Miss Morrison's coming. Will she put up a facade? Will she vent her anger? Will she reveal her desperation? This kind of opportunity for personal involvement occurs many times in the narrative, and you can put the book aside for a while and identify your own experiences and the ways you respond to various situations.

In addition to individual reflection, families have found the conversations between husband and wife, parent and child, brother and sister opening up perspectives on their own relationships and leading to a deeper awareness of how they may respond to one another more effectively. In your own family, you may take first one segment and then another and discuss the way in which the reactions of the persons in the narrative shed light on your situation. How do you assess the tenor of the conversations between Frank and Mary, between Grace and George, between John and Martha, between John and Frank, between Frank and William, and others, in their various situations? How would you wish to do it differently, and what clues do you find that can break down barriers rather than put them up?

Numerous study groups have found the material conducive for exploration and discussion. Recently I met with an adult class that had assigned parts wherein the members acted out the situations. In this way, they could feel their way into the persons of the book by dramatizing the interchanges, using the actual conversations as a means for identifying with the several perspectives illustrated. Following this type of role-play they found rich material for exploration; and the debates were quite lively as to the meaning of this or that behavior or attitude, both in the people of the book and the people in the class.

In this connection, a professor of drama and speech in a mid-western University told me not long ago that one of his seminars had decided that the story would make an interesting movie and that they were in process of preparing a script for such a purpose. As of this writing I have not heard whether this enterprise has been completed, but the idea is intriguing.

There are, by design, thirteen chapters so that the book lends itself to a thirteen-week quarter. Some study groups have assigned several members on a rotating basis to be prepared to present the basic issues of each chapter week by week as the opening material for group discussion. Still others have asked different individuals each week to assume responsibility for this kind of facilitation of corporate participation.

From still another perspective, the varieties of uses of Scripture have been of value to many persons. There are indices for ways in which personal and family devotions can be effectively approached utilizing the traditional means of grace in a contemporary setting. Again, the ways by which various persons of the book make use of Scripture to interpret and identify meaning in their own lives may be useful to those who have not yet discovered the richness of this type of biblical involvement.

There are, obviously, hosts of variations on these basic themes. My hope is that you will be able to draw on these suggestions that have emerged from the experiences of persons across the years and discover the fashion that will enable you to move toward maturity. You will discover that the book is written at several levels. There is the narrative which tells the essential story. Beneath this, there is the "stream of consciousness," which deals with the inner perception of the persons. There is commentary and reflection on the persons and situations. There are subtle illusions to the biblical story of the two brothers (Luke 15), such as "thou never gavest me a kid" (p. 57), the Prodigal and the pig-sty (p. 171), the "fatted calf" (p. 176), woven into the narrative. You can find meaning at any or all of these levels, depending on where you are in your own movement toward maturity.

The story, itself, is a spiral as various persons live out for us the unified pilgrimage. We never see all the aspects of human growth and development in any one individual, but the movement is evident in the narrative as a whole. Thus, the turning of the Prodigal (Luke 15) is seen in George rather than in William; but it is the same experience in each, as in us all. The first part of the book focuses mainly on the despairs of life, but we are conscious that there are resolutions, even so. The last half sets forth the emergence of wholeness, but we are painfully aware that there are yet painful contradictions. Wherever you are in your own pilgrimage, I trust that your encounter with these people will help you to "mount up with wings as eagles, to run and not be weary, and to walk and not faint."

Wm. B. Oglesby, Jr.
Richmond, Virginia
Summer, 1979